OWEN WISTER OUT WEST
HIS JOURNALS AND LETTERS

Would I might prison in my words
And so hold by me all the year
Some portion of the Wilderness
Of freedom that I walk in here.

OWEN WISTER

Owen Wister Out West

HIS JOURNALS AND LETTERS

EDITED BY *Fanny Kemble Wister*

THE UNIVERSITY OF CHICAGO PRESS

Library Congress Catalog Number: 58–9609

THE UNIVERSITY OF CHICAGO PRESS, CHICAGO 37
The University of Toronto Press, Toronto 5, Canada

© *1958 by Frances Kemble Wister Stokes. Published 1958. Second Impression 1958.*
Composed and printed by KINGSPORT PRESS, INC., *Kingsport, Tennessee, U.S.A.*

To the Grandchildren of
Owen Wister

TABLE OF CONTENTS

List of Illustrations   *ix*

Preface   *xi*

Introduction *1*

July–August, 1885   . .   . .   *27*
WYOMING

July–September, 1887 . .   . .   *41*
BRITISH COLUMBIA, WASHINGTON,
OREGON, CALIFORNIA, WYOMING

July–September, 1888   . .   . .   *63*
WYOMING

October–November, 1889   . .   . .   *87*
WYOMING

June–September, 1891   . .   . .   *95*
WYOMING AND YELLOWSTONE PARK

October–November, 1892   . .   . .   *131*
WASHINGTON

February–March, 1893   . .   . .   *149*
TEXAS

TABLE OF CONTENTS

June–December, 1893 163
  WORLD'S FAIR, WYOMING, YELLOWSTONE,
  ARIZONA, SAN FRANCISCO, PORTLAND

May–August, 1894 199
  BOWIE, BAYARD, GRANT, BISBIE, TOMB-
  STONE, TUCSON, SAN FRANCISCO,
  CHEYENNE

May–August, 1895 225
  NEW MEXICO, ARIZONA, CALIFORNIA,
  COLORADO, CHEYENNE, FORT MEADE

Epilogue 251

A Wister Bibliography 262

Acknowledgments 265

Index 267

LIST OF ILLUSTRATIONS

Between Pages   *114–15*

Wister's Hunting Party in Camp at Jackson Hole, Wyoming, 1887

Wister's Party at the South Ford of Snake River, 1891

Wister at the Age of Forty

Citizens of Tombstone, Arizona, 1894

PREFACE

WHEN my father, Owen Wister, author of *The Virginian*, was twenty-five, he went West for the first time. He started in 1885 from Philadelphia, where he had been born, for a ranch in Wyoming, at that time still a territory. In Wyoming he sat beside the driver of a four-horse stagecoach, saw the sun rise as the bitter chill grew warm, and tasted air he felt had never been breathed before. He planned to shoot big game, fish for trout, camp in the wilderness, and see the Indians. There were a lot of expensively educated young men going West then, not seeking their fortunes or planning to settle but going for adventure. They shot elk, caught rainbow trout, and returned home. But Owen Wister, struck with wonder and delight, had the eye to see and the talent to portray the life unfolding in America. After six journeys for pleasure, he gave up the profession of the law and became a writer of Western fiction.

I like to think of my father as the man who after twenty-six years took his wife and children to Wyoming, the country which in 1885 rang out the emotion in him that he put into words. And I like to remember my father playing the piano for himself and us at Butler Place, where he had spent most of his childhood and where I spent much of mine.

When I first knew Butler Place, it was presided over by my grandmother, Mrs. Owen Jones Wister, Fanny Kemble's daughter. Mrs. Wister had a formal relationship with her four grandchildren, receiving us in the square high-ceilinged parlor with a white mantlepiece supported by Greek columns. Though it was only six miles north of the Philadelphia City Hall, Butler Place was a gracious country estate transformed from the farm onto which Fanny Kemble had moved in 1834 when she married Pierce Butler, grandson and namesake of the signer of the Constitution for South Carolina. It was she who brought from her husband's Georgia plantation the oleander, lemon, and citron trees still lining the driveway in red wooden tubs, which were cared for in my childhood by the same gardener who had worked for three generations of our family and often spoke of Mrs. Kemble. He provided the same bouquet the year-round for my grandmother's desk and later for my father's desk, a very tight vase of heliotrope and white jasmine with often a pale yellow rose in the middle. It was he who would not allow us to pick even one lemon or citron from one of his tubbed trees without asking his permission. When we came to call on my grandmother, she was always wearing a white lace cap and long, flowing white garments. She appeared to us tall, slender, and old, though we had often seen her riding sidesaddle in the Wissahickon Park dressed entirely in dove gray with a gray bowler hat. She always played the piano for us while we sat, freshly dressed, on the hard green velvet chairs, and then gave us our choice of four different kinds of tea, one of which was Russian. Over the fireplace hung a life-size painting of a well-rounded naked child with short auburn hair and ruddy cheeks. A piece of voluminous dull gold drapery partially covered the child and the idealized bathtub into which it was about to climb. This was a portrait of my grandmother at the age of three, but if she were asked who it was, she always answered, "Just a child."

In the hall hung two framed letters from George Washington to Pierce Butler, Sr., signer of the Constitution. In the dining room, which was exactly the same size as the parlor but with dark red painted walls, hung five portraits of the Kemble family, all of whom were Shakespearean actors. Two were by Sir Thomas Lawrence and one by Sir Joshua Reynolds. All the Kembles were beautiful, and we loved them. They presided magnificently over the room.

On the death of my grandmother in 1908, we moved into Butler Place. It was there that I first remember my father playing the piano and singing with gusto in his clear, ringing voice. He often played the light operas of Offenbach and sang the words in beautiful French, and he also played and sang "Ten Thousand Cattle"—for which he had written the words and music that were used in *The Virginian* when it was made into a play. But our favorite was, "Here I come, Dum de Dum, I'm a Plum, Dum de Dum, My appearance puts others on the bum." I did not know until 1957, when I found the manuscript score, that "Here I Come" was an air from a burlesque of *Don Giovanni* that my father wrote for the Tavern Club of Boston.

During my father's long, unidentified illness in 1910, Sir William Osler came to see him, but nobody ever pronounced what the illness was. We did not see much of him then except when we were taken into his bedroom to visit him and see his pet raccoon, Cindy, who lived in the open fireplace. He could pick her up and pat her, but we could not. My father had a gift for taming wild animals and was a bird-lover. The "Morning Room" at Butler Place, formerly used by my grand-mother as a writing room, was then used as a bird room; and my fa-ther's pet mockingbird, Gabriel, lived there in a cage, as well as un-distinguished finches and canaries.

We played for days on end gathering black walnuts fallen from the superb trees growing on the back lawn near the gardener's stone cot-tage. We played in the walled garden with box borders and sundial; there grew the pansies that we were not allowed to pick, nor did we ever pick the geraniums and heliotrope in a series of round beds lead-ing from the house to the stable. We galloped our ponies all around the drive circling the house and the huge stone barns, and we rode up the lawn between the double avenue of maples known as the tree *allée*, which Fanny Kemble had planted. We could make lemonade only if the lemons had fallen naturally from the tubbed trees, but we were allowed to pick the figs on the one fig tree at the south end of the greenhouse.

In 1908 my parents took us to lunch at the White House with President and Mrs. Theodore Roosevelt. My father had known him well since going to college with him. Though we were two boys and two girls from nine to four in age, we all had dark hair to our shoulders and white piqué suits and dresses. We were greeted at the door by

Major Archie Butt, the President's bodyguard, who took his pistol out of its holster and showed it to us. We slid back and forth on the polished floor of the East Room and sat down to lunch with the Roosevelt family. The table was laid with a white tablecloth, and President and Mrs. Roosevelt sat at the middle of the table opposite each other. We had lamb chops, with paper frills, and rice for lunch followed by whole shiny ripe raw apples for dessert; but I was too young to peel mine. The surprise and disappointment in the dessert was received in silence by the little Wisters. As Victorian children, we had eaten many a Charlotte Russe at better parties than this.

In 1912 we saw Theodore Roosevelt again when he was campaigning on the Bull Moose ticket. My father introduced him in the Hammerstein Opera House in Philadelphia. A slender, mannerly policeman with a white mustache came to our house to escort us to the rally. He spoke the same English that we did and surely had never pounded a beat. We drove to the Opera House in the family brougham drawn by the fat bay team, Parsifal and Siegfried, who had belonged to our grandmother. The importance of arriving at the Opera House and being led through the crowd by a policeman was electrifying. He took us to our grand-tier box near the stage and sat with us all evening. My father and Mr. Roosevelt, who were similar in size and build and only two years apart in age, wore dress suits and read from full-sized typed manuscripts. They shouted their speeches, and the huge audience roared with approval. I heard Mr. Roosevelt change his voice to treble to crack a joke. I heard him say "pussyfoot."

In 1911 my parents took us, their four oldest children, to Jackson Hole, Wyoming, for the summer. First we camped through Yellowstone Park. We had two teams of horses; one wagon was a buckboard with three rows of seats for us, and the other was a wagon for our camp outfit. There were two drivers and a cook. We camped beside the geysers, where the men made the campfire, put up our tents, and sometimes sang "Turkey in the Straw," with words of their own, while cooking supper. Everybody in the West seemed to have read *The Virginian*, and as soon as they heard my father's name would speak to him about it. The guides talked endlessly to him, asking him questions about the old West. It took about a week to get through

Yellowstone, and then we drove into Jackson Hole. When we reached the Snake River, we crossed it on Meaner's Ferry, a flat barge pulled across the turbulent deep river on a cable by Mr. Meaner. We paid, I think, fifty cents a team to Mr. Meaner, who had a white beard and lived alone in his log cabin by the river and ran the ferry by himself.

Mr. Meaner had the only vegetable garden in Jackson Hole, and during the rest of the summer we would often ride to call on him and buy his fresh peas—the only fresh vegetables we had. We stayed for three months at the JY Ranch on Phelps Lake, the first dude ranch in Jackson Hole. We four children had a log cabin to ourselves, and our parents had a cabin of their own next to us. Our wooden bunks were filled with pine boughs and covered with the gray blankets that we slept between. Every morning a bucket of hot water was brought to the cabin door by a filthy old man who, we thought, had something permanently wrong with his jaw. At the end of our stay this turned out to be a quid of tobacco that he had kept in his mouth in the same place for months.

The corral the horses spent the day in was across the outlet of the lake from our cabin. Every morning the old wrangler on the ranch rounded up the horses, turned loose overnight to graze, and drove them back over the hill into the corral. Many of the horses wore bells around their necks at night so that by hearing a bell the wrangler would know where to look for the horse. The delicious clanging of these variously toned bells as the horses galloped into the corral woke us up each day. The old wrangler filled us with awe and admiration. We hung around him as much as possible, for we knew he was the real thing. He wore high-heeled boots and leather chaps; the handkerchief around his neck was held by drawing the two ends together through a piece of ham bone. He seldom took off his ten-gallon hat. He could do fancy roping that none of us could learn and from outside the corral could rope whichever horse he chose while they were all madly galloping round and round. Often the horse he caught would be too man-shy to let him come near it. Then he would hand me the heavy bridle embossed in silver with Mexican wheelbit and ask me to bridle the horse for him. At last my destiny was fulfilled. With careful carelessness, I walked slowly into the corral.

We ate in the dining-room cabin, next to the kitchen cabin where a cockney English cook converted by the Mormons was in charge. She had a wooden trough filled by a bucket to wash the tin plates and cups in. She had a young daughter about our age at whom she would fly into terrible noisy rages, screaming at her, "I'll knock your blooming 'ead against the blooming wall." Knowing by her tone that "blooming" was a swear word, we could not comprehend it when the words to our Sunday school hymn next winter at home said "the blooming earth," which everybody sang with pious looks. Food at the ranch was often scanty, being driven 104 miles by team over the mountains from St. Anthony, Idaho. We had many canned tomatoes; and on days when a steer was shot for beef, we would have some of it for supper that night. The rest of it would hang, covered with a bloody canvas, from a tree until we and the flies had eaten it up. We ate dried, smoked, salted bear meat (like dark brown leather) from the year before; fresh elk too tough to chew, shot when the big-game season opened in September; trout caught by my father, who was a skilled dry-fly fisherman. We frequently found dead flies between the flapjacks at breakfast, and we drank condensed milk.

We all tried to learn dry-fly fishing from my father, but only the oldest of us succeeded. Mostly we rode, I bareback for miles each day. Fording Snake River, loping through the sagebrush with no trail, we went into the foothills as far as our laboring horses could climb. We were not too young to be stunned with admiration by the Tetons, and we loved the acres of wild flowers growing up their slopes—the tremulous Harebell blue and fragile, the Indian Paintbrush bright red, and the pale, elegant Columbine. We were not awed by the wilderness, feeling that the Grand Teton was our own mountain and the most wonderful mountain in the world, and the Snake River the fastest, longest river in America. We could ride all day and never get past the Tetons. When we returned to the ranch in the late afternoon, we would ride up the brief slope and suddenly Phelps Lake would appear in front of us. The mountains encircling it rose abruptly from the water, with Death Canyon at the far end. Often as we hitched our horses to the rail at the main cabin a cow pony was being lassoed in the corral. There was activity at the ranch; our parents were there. It was good to be back.

Once at the JY a so-called chicken hawk was shot by some enthusiast. We never knew who, and the hawk was thrown for dead on the woodpile where we picked him up intending to add his skin to our collection, which consisted mostly of pack rats whose skins had already turned white for the winter. When we found the hawk still alive, glaring in helpless, savage rage at us, we took him to our parents' cabin and gave him to our father. He found out that the bird's wings were not broken and said that he was not a chicken hawk but a mouse hawk, much more rare, which would never have preyed on the flock of about a dozen chickens at the ranch. My father explained that hawks were unusually strong and that he would try to nurse this one back to health by feeding him raw meat and keeping him for us in his cabin. We agreed that if the bird got well he should go free, for hawks can never be tamed. So, many times a day my father fed raw meat to the hawk, which perched resentfully on his wrist, digging the claws into his skin, watching us hostilely while eating. The bird never became friendly, and one day while we were all there he suddenly without effort soared into the air from my father's wrist and disappeared.

We stayed at Jackson Hole until the snow came in late September. The first elk had been shot. We rode far up into the foothills to watch it being skinned and saw the bullets flattened against its shoulder blade. The pack horses were laden with the carcass and led down the mountain.

At last we had to return East. We could not stand the thought of leaving. What—sleep in a real bed again and see trolley cars? How frightful! No more smell of sagebrush, no more rushing Snake River, no more Grand Teton. Why did we have to go back?

To get to St. Anthony, Idaho, we drove 104 miles on a single-track dirt road all the way, fording the Snake River and crossing the mountain pass. We spent four nights in roadhouses, the only place for travelers to sleep. The first one, the Lee Road House, was still in Jackson Hole. There the walls were papered with ancient yellow newspapers. Then came Canyon Creek, where arriving in the dark we made a treacherous descent down the steep road to a villainous-looking group of cabins and one barn beside a narrow, roaring river at the bottom of a black canyon. Here I slept behind a curtain on the landing of the stairs. The next day we reached Driggs, a town of one street. It had boardwalks for sidewalks, false fronts on some of the houses to make them look as if they were two stories high, and saloons with half-length swinging doors at the corners. All the roadhouses lacked plumbing, and at all of them we ate at long tables covered with white oil-cloth. We used to eat from enameled plates and cups, tin forks and spoons, and we sat on backless benches, talking to the other transients. When we got to Victor, we saw some real two-story houses. The last stop of our journey was St. Anthony, where we boarded the train.

In 1912 we returned to Jackson Hole. We were back with a ranch of our own, for my father had bought 160 acres, and we could not drive fast enough to get to it. When we came to the stone marking the boundary between Idaho and Wyoming, we yelled with joy. Every rock, every sage bush, every aspen tree was different and better because it grew in Wyoming. The landscape changed radically. There was no such other state. With condescension we had looked at Utah, Montana, Idaho, but here at last was Wyoming.

That year we brought our youngest brother, who was then three, and our German governess to look after him—surely the first German governess to set foot in Jackson Hole. We also brought our Negro houseman from home, who attracted the attention of Westerners who had never seen a colored man. We brought him to help us build our cabin and to cook for us. We were going to live on *our* ranch.

We also brought with us from home our pet black and white Japanese waltzing mouse in a round "butter tin" with wire handle and tight-fitting cover with holes punched in it for air. Her name was Psyche, which we knew to be "Greek Goddess of Beauty" but pronounced by us "Peeshee." I suppose our parents, who gave us permission to take her on our long journey, never knew what her name really was. Peeshee spent the summer waltzing in Jackson Hole.

We stayed at the JY while building our two-story cabin. The whole family worked, and I can remember no outside help at all. Our ranch was on a sagebrush plain not far from the JY, and we moved in before the cabin was finished.

In October, with hideous reluctance, we had to start East; the weather was cold, and there had been snow. To keep Peeshee warm on the long drive, we took turns holding her in her tin on our laps in the buckboard, but by the end of the day somehow we had all had enough of her. Then my father, who was riding, took her as it began to get dark and much colder. He put on the top of the pommel of his Mexican saddle a hot-water bag; on the top of the hot-water bag he balanced Peeshee in her tin. I cannot now imagine how he got the hot water, but Peeshee survived the trip.

Thinking back forty years to our summers in Wyoming, I see that going West in 1885 made my father. Taking us to undomesticated Jackson Hole linked us to his youth, making us in spirit next of kin to the country of his choice.

FANNY KEMBLE WISTER

Introduction

OWEN WISTER in writing *The Virginian* over fifty years ago created the prime romantic novel of the Wild West. For the first time, a cowboy was a gentleman and hero, but nobody realized then that the book was the master design on which thousands of Westerns would be modeled. Its hero was the first cowboy to capture the public's imagination, and hundreds of young girls fell in love with him. Before this, cowboys had been depicted as murderous thugs. The Virginian was utterly different from the heroes of his day; besides being handsome, he was humorous and human. He got drunk, played practical jokes, and through him Wister coined the phrase now part of our language, "When you call me that, smile!" The book was considered daringly realistic, the American novel at that time being about as realistic as the bustle. The Virginian himself is the progenitor of the cowboy as a folk figure. Because of him, little boys wear ten-gallon hats and carry toy pistols. This one novel set the tradition of the West permanently. We still have Western stories, Western movies, and Western radio and television drama in which the cowboy hero defends justice and his girl's honor and shoots it out with the villain. *The Virginian* stands among the ten best-selling novels of the past fifty years. It was written as fiction but has become history.

The author of *The Virginian* was a Philadelphian of well-to-do parents. He was educated at Harvard and also in Europe. By the time he was twenty-two he had traveled all over Europe. At the age of twenty-five, when he was planning to study law, a trip to Wyoming for his health led directly to his becoming a writer. His Journals must be thought of in relation to his whole life, the nineteenth century in which he grew up, and the inheritance and influence of creatively gifted forebears.

Now that Wister's Western Journals have been found, one can follow the firsthand experiences he wove into *The Virginian,* see how he developed as a writer, and feel his great love and awe of the West. In all there are fifteen notebooks, comprising the record of his Western journeys from 1885 to 1900.[1] He often spent six months at a time hunting in Wyoming, living in U.S. Army camps as the guest of officers, observing Indians; becoming intimately acquainted with cowpunchers, cattle thieves, saloonkeepers and prospectors; noting true incidents and reporting real conversations; making lists of words in common use that he had never heard. He ranged through the North and Southwest, from Oregon to Texas; but he loved Wyoming best of all, and *The Virginian* is set in Wyoming.

Owen Wister was born July 14, 1860, at 5103 Germantown Avenue, long since become a part of Philadelphia. The house is still standing. He was the only child of Dr. Owen Jones Wister and Sarah Butler Wister. His father's forebears had been foresters for generations to the Palatinate prince in Hillspach, a village near Heidelberg. They came to America in 1727, settled in Philadelphia, and became prosperous merchants.

Dr. Wister had joined the United States Navy as a young man and sailed round the world in 1853. He was a beloved and successful country doctor, known for his quick wit, and his jokes were often repeated by his patients to their children.

Dr. Wister's wife was half English, being the daughter of Fanny Kemble, the most famous Shakespearean actress of her day, and Pierce Butler, grandson and namesake of the Pierce Butler who signed the Constitution of the United States for South Carolina. Fanny Kemble had sailed in 1832 with her father to act in America. She was the youngest of the renowned Kemble clan. While touring the cities of the Eastern seaboard she met Pierce Butler and married him. He was handsome, rich, and fashionable. She was beautiful and fiery.

[1] For an explanation of the editing of the Journals and letters, see pp. 28–29.

She had published a play when she was twenty and continued to publish poetry and memoirs. They settled at Butler Place, then a farm six miles from Philadelphia.

Owen Wister was brought up in an intensely intellectual household. His parents knew and entertained all the distinguished people of their era. They moved into Butler Place when Sarah B. Wister inherited it from her father. Owen was twelve when Henry James first came to stay. James had been a friend of Fanny Kemble.

Owen Wister's mother, Sarah, differing in background from her friends and neighbors, was not like them. Fanny Kemble had been sought after and associated with the talented and prominent people of England and America. As a girl she had gone to visit Sir Walter Scott, and we have letters to her from Thackeray and Robert Browning. She speaks in her diary of her friendships with the composers Mendelssohn and von Weber, and she complained bitterly of the provincial life in Philadelphia. Her daughter grew up speaking Italian and French well, accustomed to travel in Europe, and playing the piano well. At Butler Place there was a "Morning Room" on the second floor facing east. It was exclusively for the use of Sarah, and there she translated the poetry of Alfred de Musset into English and wrote unsigned essays for the *Atlantic Monthly*.

Sarah Wister was the great lady of her neighborhood, and young and old admirers from far and wide came to call on her. One who became a regular visitor said sixty years later that it was for the "stimulation" of Mrs. Wister's conversation that he so frequently went to see her. It was this same man who, when very young, called on Mrs. Wister after his first trip to Europe. He had especially bought for her a trifling souvenir. When he gave it to her, she handed it back, saying so gracefully that she had no use for it that his feelings were not hurt. Even now her charm is spoken of by those who knew her.

Sarah Wister was of regal appearance and very much aware of the fact that she was a personage. She swept into the opera and symphony concerts in black velvet and white lace. The daughter of an eyewitness remembers that when her parents went to dine at Butler Place with Henry James, Mrs. Wister carved while wearing white kid gloves. She could not get along and did not try to get along with any except those in her own walk of life and intellectual bent. Her mother said of her, "S—— was as fond of her baby as I think she could be of any creature too nearly resembling a mere animal to excite her intellectual interest, which is pretty much the only interest in infants or adults that she seems to me to have."

Dr. Owen Jones Wister worked very hard. For years he rode his medical rounds on horseback; as an older man, he drove a buggy. Before starting to practice he had seen the world. He had been commissioned in the Navy in 1848 and was with the fleet that sailed into the port of Macao in 1853 and opened the port to the Occident.

Dr. Wister was not intensely social as his wife was and did not enjoy dining out and entertaining as she did. There is an anecdote about him throwing a beefsteak out the dining-room window because he did not like the way it was cooked. Another story concerns a white Persian cat belonging to Sarah Wister. She was a cat fancier and had a series of white Persians, one of which she named "Omar Khayyam." One night she stood on the porch at Butler Place calling in vain, "Omar Khayyam! Omar Khayyam!" but the cat paid no attention. Then Dr. Wister came out on the porch and called, "Here, Pussy, Pussy!" and instantly the cat returned.

There was a temperamental clash between Dr. and Mrs. Wister, according to at least one regular visitor at Butler Place. This can readily be understood; but Owen Wister always spoke with admiration of his parents.

Butler Place had been a farm when Fanny Kemble came to live there, and she disliked her unkempt, rural surroundings. However, the house was added to several times both before and after Owen Wister went there to live. In the end it had a two-story porch with pillars in front, as well as a terrace with flagstone path and English ivy on the retaining wall. Fanny Kemble had turned the large fields into a lawn on all sides of the house. She brought shrubs and bushes from the South. Oleanders, lemon trees, and orange trees, in tubs, lined the driveway. She planted black walnut trees and a double row of maples to make an avenue to the front door. There were many flower beds, as well as a walled garden with box hedges and a sundial. There was a grape arbor and a vegetable garden, pastures, a greenhouse, and an orangery, in which the tubbed plants spent the winter, built of brick with a glass front. A large stone barn formed two sides of a square with a high wall enclosing the barnyard. There were two stone tenant houses. Butler Place had become a lovely, civilized country estate.

It was from Butler Place in 1870 that Owen Wister went to boarding school for a year in Hofwyl, Switzerland, while his parents traveled in Europe and visited Fanny Kemble in England. It was not his first trip to Europe, for when he was six his parents had left him to board in another Swiss school for three months. At Hofwyl he wrote to his mother the first of many hundreds of letters. He wrote to her regularly until her death in 1908, and she kept every letter.

After the first two months at Hofwyl he wrote her a letter in grammatical French and in the inside of the sheet a letter in English to his father, saying that as his father did not speak French he would not write in French. The following year he lived in England with his mother's sister, wife of the Reverend James Leigh at Hereford, where his uncle was dean of the cathedral. He went to a nearby school, apparently as a day pupil.

Back at Butler Place again, Owen Wister went to Germantown Academy, a day school, briefly, and in 1873 he was sent to board at St. Paul's School, Concord, New Hampshire. This was modeled after the English schools, with a clergyman as headmaster. At St. Paul's, from which he graduated in 1878, there were no holidays between Christmas and June. He was accepted in the school choir the first winter and wrote his mother—printing in large capital letters the exciting news. Later while in school he often wrote musical quotations in his letters in neat, clear musical script.

His first "published" story—titled "Down in a Diving Bell"— came out in the school magazine during his first year at St. Paul's, and he became an editor of the magazine and a regular contributor. He wrote four articles on the Centennial Exhibition held in Philadelphia in 1876, remarking that it had made America aware of Europe and that only two other boys besides himself in his class had been to Europe. He wrote poetry for the school magazine but no more stories, only articles about real experiences. We find him in 1874 describing his fellow boarders in the house where he stayed during a summer at the seashore: ". . . the boarders are of such low class, with one or two exceptions, that it is impossible to distinguish between master and man without noticing which of the two waits on the other." He was already an observing boy at fourteen.

At home during the holidays he saw his grandmother, who lived then at York Farm in a small house across the road from Butler Place. After giving up the stage she had read Shakespeare in public and achieved renown while supporting herself for twenty years. A reading of her memoirs establishes her as a woman of great moral stature as well as talent. "During the time that I spent in Boston," she writes in 1875 from York Farm, "the persons I knew best and saw most frequently there were Dr. Channing, Prescott, Motley, the historians; Felton, the learned Greek professor; Agassiz, the great scientific naturalist . . . Emerson, Oliver Wendell Holmes, Lowell and Longfellow. . . . I had the honor, pleasure, and privilege of the acquaintance and friendship of all these distinguished men and was received by then with the utmost courteous kindness in their homes and families. . . ."

About her grandson she writes at the same time, "[He] is not at all a 'precocious American young man' but an uncommonly clever and gifted boy. Like most of his country's people, he is deficient, I am sorry to say, in animal spirits, and this rather unusual reasonableness prevents him from appearing, or indeed being, young for his age." The following year she says she is "writing . . . the libretto of an opera, at the request of my grandson, who is composing the music for it." He frequently played duets with her at his request.

At Harvard, where he majored in music (having decided to become a composer), Wister soon met Theodore Roosevelt, who was two years ahead of him in college. His friendship with Roosevelt grew from the first; they both belonged to the Porcellian Club and were invited to all the best parties in Boston. Wister also met and formed lifelong friendships with Major Henry Lee Higginson, founder of the Boston Symphony Orchestra; William Dean Howells, soon to become editor of the *Atlantic Monthly;* the elder Oliver Wendell Holmes, the "Autocrat of the Breakfast Table"; and the younger Oliver Wendell Holmes, later to become Chief Justice. While at Harvard he wrote for the

Hasty Pudding Club "Dido and Aeneas," both words and music. When it was given in New York, the critic for the *Herald* said that the music was in the manner of Offenbach and very pleasing, not like a college show at all. Elected to Phi Beta Kappa, Wister graduated *summa cum laude* from Harvard in 1882, the same year in which a burlesque novel of his was published. The book, entitled *The New Swiss Family Robinson*, made fun of the popular *Swiss Family Robinson* that was considered "wholesome" reading for the young at the time, and it brought a letter of praise from Mark Twain.

With the book and his degree behind him, Wister went to Paris for a year to study composition with Ernest Guiraud at the Conservatoire; but before settling in Paris for the winter he went on the grand tour with college friends, leaving his mother in England. He had written to his mother from college in the spring that they both must stay in Europe a year, that the short summer trips had not been enough.

He and his friends did all the standard things, starting through Switzerland and walking some of the mountain passes. His grandmother had given him a letter of introduction to Franz Liszt, then seventy-four years old. Fanny Kemble had toured Europe with Liszt as a chaperone while her younger sister, Adelaide, sang in joint concerts with Liszt, who was then a virtuoso pianist. Wister headed for Bayreuth, where the fourth performance in the world of Wagner's opera *Parsifal* was to take place. Wagner was going to be there and Liszt was Wagner's guest. About his experience at Bayreuth, Wister wrote to his mother:

HOTEL SACHER

VIENNA, *Aug. 29, 1882*

Dearest Mother:

Stone, Wendell and I traveled all day, leaving Lucerne at 7:30 A.M. and reaching Nurenberg at 11:30 P.M. Here we found every hotel full on account of an exhibition which is going on, but luckily we got tolerable lodgings in some mysterious place on the banks of the river. Next day at 10 we went to Bayreuth. This occasion was one of a special interest—it was King Ludwig's birthday, and also the day

of the marriage (or *1st half* of the marriage) between one of
Wagner's daughters & an Italian who she met at Palermo
last winter. So Bayreuth was doubly exciting. The Grand-
father Liszt had come, and there we saw the whole party
in Wagner's private box, when we went into the theatre,
Wagner looking rather cross (so Wendell said, who saw
him outside) but Liszt beaming on everyone, & looking
strikingly handsome it seemed to me. The performance was
literally just what I expected, & of course to me very
interesting & absorbing. The scenery quite unearthly in its
splendour, & the orchestra perfect. Part—many parts—
were tedious and undramatic, & Parts were in very bad
taste. But some of the music was very beautiful, though it
recalled *Lohengrin* somewhat. Even this I had expected,
however, for I hardly saw how Wagner could treat of the
Holy Grail without suggesting *Lohengrin.* In the last
Entract (of one hour) I walked up to Liszt & gave him the
letter, & then disappeared, but followed him into the res-
taurant where we all dined promiscuously, but not un-
comfortably. Liszt read the letter at table, & when I saw he
was disengaged I walked up & presented myself. He was
amiability incarnate, said that he would be busy with the
2nd half of the marriage tomorrow, but I must call in the
afternoon. So I went. First time he was asleep. (N.B. Result
of Wedding breakfast.) I was requested to call again in an
hour or so, which hour I spent in meeting Materna & lots
of other artists,[2] who hearing I had a Banjo ordered me to
remain in Bayreuth for a week & send for the Banjo to
Nurenberg. But of course this was out of the question.
Then I saw Liszt for nearly an hour entirely alone. But I
must stop. Write to Drexel, Harges & Co., *Paris.* I shall go
to Paris in about 10 days, but *not* to Tours from Paris. I
shall return to Germany after Stone has gone, & shall not
come to Paris again till you do—i.e., at the very end of

[2] Materna, great Wagnerian soprano at the height of her career,
obviously found Owen Wister attractive.

September, as I wish to hear as much German Opera as possible. Love to my Grandmother.

Your loving son,

O. W.

The interview with Liszt occurred in Wagner's house, and during it Wister played his composition "Merlin and Vivien." Liszt "jumped up in the middle and stood behind me muttering approval, and now and then he stopped me and put his hands over my shoulders onto the keys, struck a bar or two, and said: 'I should do that here if I were you.' And he wrote his old friend, my grandmother, Fanny Kemble, that I had *'un talent prononcé'* for music."

Wister had already published a piano piece in 1879, and several songs for voice and piano were composed by him and published within the next two years.

His mother had obviously gone to Paris to spend the winter of 1882–83 with him, and they may have been living in the same hotel, for there is a gap in his letters to her from the end of September, 1882, to December and again from January, 1883, to April. There are no more facts about his studies, but we do have the manuscript score of a trio he wrote that winter. The night before he returned to America, asked by his father to come home after one year of study, he rode around the city in a cab with Professor Guiraud, who kept repeating, *"N'abandonnes pas la musique!"*[3] By this time Owen Wister played the piano almost professionally and spoke beautiful idiomatic French. He told a member of his family forty years later that if he had really been meant to be a composer, he would have refused to come home.

Major Higginson had offered him employment in his firm in Boston, but it turned out that there was no place after all in Lee, Higginson & Co., and Wister went to work in the Union Safe Deposit Vaults, computing interest on the depositors' balances. He was very bored by the bank, but that year the Tavern Club was founded in Boston, with William Dean Howells as its first president. Wister became a member.

[3] This remark and Liszt's praise for Wister's musical talent are quoted in Wister, *Roosevelt, The Story of a Friendship* (New York: Macmillan Co., 1930).

In 1884, on the advice of Howells, he did not show to any publisher the novel he had written with his cousin Langdon Mitchell, the son of Dr. S. Weir Mitchell. Said Howells, "Were it a translation from the Russian it would not offend American modesty, but coming from an American and being about America, it was altogether too plain spoken." There was "too much knowledge of good and evil in it," and "a whole fig tree couldn't cover one of the women characters in it." This lady was entirely the creation of my father. But Howells also said there was a novelist inside Owen Wister. Mr. Howells' advice was so well taken that nobody has ever seen the manuscript.

In 1885 Owen Wister's health broke down, and at the advice of Dr. Mitchell he went to Wyoming in June to stay on a ranch of some friends. Theodore Roosevelt had preceded him to the West and had written to him about his experiences. Wister, who was nearly twenty-five, started a diary when he boarded the train in Philadelphia. It turned out to be the first of fifteen diaries—forming the substance of this book and unknown even to his family till long after his death—which recorded day by day all his many trips West. Though he did not realize it immediately, the impression made on him that summer determined his career.

On his return from Wyoming that autumn he entered Harvard Law School and graduated in 1888. Going back to Philadelphia, he moved into the Hotel Hamilton and lived there as a bachelor, spending only week ends at Butler Place with his parents or living there to keep his father company when his mother was away. He went to work for the firm of Robert Ralston and Francis Rawle at 402 Walnut Street and became a member of the Philadelphia bar in 1890. He continued his trips West in the summers.

He had wanted to be a composer and now was making the law his career. But he says of himself in *Roosevelt, The Story of a Friendship:* "And so one Autumn evening of 1891, fresh from Wyoming and its wild glories, I sat in the club dining with a man as enamoured of the West as I was. This was Walter Furness. . . . From oysters to coffee we compared experiences. Why wasn't some Kipling saving the sage-brush for American literature, before the sage-brush and all that it signified went the way of the California forty-niner, went the way of the Mississippi steam-boat, went the way of everything? Roosevelt had seen the sage-brush true, had felt its poetry; and also Remington, who illustrated his articles so well. But what was fiction doing, fiction, the only thing that has always outlived fact? Must it be perpetual tea-cups? Was Alkali Ike in the comic papers the one figure which the jejune American imagination, always at full-cock to banter or to brag, could discern in that epic which was being lived at a gallop out in the sage-brush? 'To hell with tea-cups and the great American laugh!' we two said, as we sat dining at the club. The claret had been excellent.

" 'Walter, I'm going to try it myself!' I exclaimed to Walter Furness. 'I'm going to start this minute.' "[4]

Wister went to the second-story library of the Philadelphia Club and wrote most of "Hank's Woman" that night. It was his first Western story, and H. M. Alden at *Harper's Magazine*, the first editor to whom he sent it, accepted it and a second Western sketch called "How Lin McLean Went East" in January, 1892. "What else had been written up to that time," Wister commented later in the Preface to *Lin McLean*, "was not about the West."

Though giving up music as a profession, Owen Wister had not given up interest in music. As a trained musician he could read an orchestral score, and he often put a score on the piano and played from it. He could sight-read piano music rapidly and sight-sing. Through Major Higginson, founder of the Boston Symphony Orchestra, he knew many professional musicians, with whom he could talk on their own terms. Once when Major Higginson wrote to him asking him to tell his friends about the coming first appearance in Philadelphia of Paderewski, the Polish pianist known the civilized world over except in Philadelphia, Wister tried to persuade his friends to go to the recital. He went to the railroad station to meet Paderewski, talking in French with him, and escorted him to the hotel. He invited Paderewski to have dinner with him after the concert, and Paderewski accepted. The afternoon of January 19, 1892, Paderewski played in the Academy of Music, which holds three thousand people. There were about ten rows filled. Wister clapped as hard as he could and after the

[4] Wister, *op. cit.*

concert he went backstage to speak with Paderewski and to take him out to dinner. But Paderewski was too angry—he did not go.

In the spring of 1893 Wister went West at the request of Harper and Brothers to write Western articles and Western fiction for them. After that successful venture he gave up the law. His short stories continued to appear, and in 1895 his first book of stories, *Red Men and White*, came out. He went West year after year searching for material and so became intimately familiar with the region that at first sight had cast a spell on him.

Because he wrote to his mother regularly from Philadelphia to Butler Place, it is easy to follow his life at that time. Even after giving up the unpalatable grind of the law and devoting himself to writing, he was restless and unhappy. He dined out with a large circle of friends constantly, went to the opera in New York, and somehow was always able to accept invitations to stay with Rudyard Kipling in Vermont, Frederic Remington in New Rochelle,[5] and Henry James in England. Not till 1898, when he married, do we find Owen Wister at ease with himself.

The first time Owen Wister saw his cousin, Mary Channing Wister, whom he married in 1898, she was a few weeks old. He was ten years older, and his mother sent him to call on his new relation. Daniel Wister was Owen's great-grandfather and Mary's great-great-grandfather. Born in Germantown only about a mile from Butler Place, she was the daughter of William R. Wister, a Philadelphia lawyer, and Mary R. Eustis of Boston, a descendant of William Ellery, signer of the Declaration of Independence for Rhode Island, and of William Ellery Channing, noted abolitionist, preacher, and pioneer in founding the Unitarian faith in America. By 1898 Owen Wister had played in an eight-handed piano quartet with his future bride over a period of five years. Mary Channing Wister, when she was married, had already been appointed a member of the Philadelphia Board of Education. She was known and admired throughout Philadelphia.

The Owen Wisters bought a house at 913 Pine Street, Philadelphia, where four of their six children, three boys and three girls, were born. The satisfaction and peace of mind of at last having his own house

[5] Remington was then illustrating Wister's stories.

must have been a blessing to Owen Wister. His mother still lived at Butler Place, sometimes going South in the winter and to visit in New England during the summer, and he still wrote to her at least twice a week. The couple hung the portrait of Fanny Kemble by Sully in the parlor and the two paintings by Remington, which were the illustrations for "Evolution of the Cow Puncher," in the front hall. Wister went every morning to 328 Chestnut Street, now the office of Francis Rawle, to write, and he kept his desk there for the next twenty years. His wife's steady nerves and health made all serene around her.

The felicitous, even tempo of life in his own house that first winter must have been of huge benefit to my father. He and his wife's temperaments blended and complemented each other. Although she was not the trained musician he was, she could sight-read piano music well, transpose easily, and music was part of her daily life. She was filled with the zeal and crusading spirit of her Unitarian great-grandfather. Thus Owen Wister had not only married his cousin, a girl sometimes thought shy by the older men and women who at the time of his marriage were already doing their best to spoil him and felt possessive about him, but a girl of achievements of her own. She was well started on her successful life of civic betterment and did not give it up.

In the winter of 1901/2 the Wisters went to Charleston. They had had such a delightful time there on their honeymoon four years before and made so many friends that it was the most felicitous place for Wister to work while he wove the short stories planned as *The Virginian* into the novel. He wrote to his mother about his work:

Sunday, February 9, 1902

Dearest Mother:

My book is like going up a mountain. Each time
I think I have reached the last rise another unfolds; and I
am going to write you a line at a certain hour each day (as
if I were my Grandmother), for it is perfectly awful to have
let 11 days go without sending a word to you. What
happens if I don't is, that before the notion of a long and
sustained letter I shrink after the many words I have been

turning out all day and every day. I am so sorry and ashamed to have left you all this long while in silence so let me send you little lines like a diary until my heavy task is done. What I have is satisfactory; and some I think is good, some of the dialogue ahead of any, I think, in the way of lightness and immediacy; wholly new work I don't mind, and at times greatly enjoy. It is the revision and interpolation that I do certainly hate. If you look at this sheet of paper you'll see cuts—knife cuts. Those are where I have sliced my short stories and pasted them in pieces with the interpolations between. Sometimes a page needs a change for consistency; sometimes it needs an addition for clearness and emphasis; sometimes it needs some elision; sometimes the style offends me and I re-write it according to my present standard. It is surprising how much of my old writing offends me for various reasons, and whenever I can't stand it, out it goes. This is my 40th day of work, and I think I have written 20 thousand new words. These constitute 4 entirely new chapters, the revision, simplification, elaboration and general licking into shape of "Emily" and "Where Fancy was Bred," which two old stories occur near the beginning of this now quite long book. My typewriter (a lady self-supporting, named Jervey) has pleased me by mentioning that she's sorry she did not meet the Virginian before Molly Wood did.

> *Your loving son,*
>
> *D.*[6]

When he had almost reached the top of the "mountain" several months later, he wrote to Judge Oliver Wendell Holmes:

[6] Dr. Owen J. Wister wanted his son christened Daniel, and his mother wanted him christened Owen. However, they both called him Dan, and so did his family and friends. That is why so many letters are signed "Dan" or "D."

382 CHESTNUT STREET
PHILADELPHIA, PA.
Monday, May 19, 1902

My dear Judge:

In a few days a piece of fiction—long laid out in mind, and fragments of which have from time to time been published—will appear in its complete design. I may be wrong in thinking it my best so far: I set out to draw a man of something like genius—the American genius— and to make the reader feel this by methods other than assuring him of the fact. None of your "At this point the conversation became both witty and brilliant"; but *action,* sir, action and manifestation. Well—I may be overweening in my estimate, and as you are going to receive a copy, you will know. . . .

Thank you, O Judge. And my love to Mrs. Holmes.

Yours affectionately,
Owen Wister

The Virginian met with instant success and was reprinted fifteen times in the first eight months after publication. One of the first congratulatory notes came from Theodore Roosevelt, to whom Wister answered in the following letter.

June 10, 1902

Dear Theodore:

Your note hits the right spot and is delightful—as indeed your notes would always be, even, I think, if they contained reprimand! For it would issue from a friendly source. But in speaking of "Superstition Trail," you single out the chapter I most value myself.

Goodness gracious—review the book? Why, you would be estopped anyhow, even if you were simply Roosevelt of Oyster Bay. The fellow a book is dedicated to can't really, you know. He simply can't.

Yours always,
Owen Wister

16

Owen Wister, now a middle-aged man, was famous. Hundreds of letters of praise poured in. He was in demand as a speaker, and his name was known throughout the United States.

Within a few months after publication, the mother who had not written regularly to her only child during his first winter at a New England school wrote to the middle-aged man about his novel, already a huge success and destined to achieve a lasting place in American literature. The boy had asked his mother (October 24, 1873), "Why don't you write to me? Are you so displeased with my last monthly mark that you do not wish to own me?" The woman of sixty-two who had never been west of Chicago and had her own small reputation as an author likened her son's book to the novels of Ouida, whose best-selling English thrillers of that day were much read but looked down upon. Sarah B. Wister's intellect had always dominated her heart, and neither sentiment nor maternal feeling came between her and her judgment. Her failure to understand and admire *The Virginian* can be explained by her background and generation, but the essence of Sarah B. Wister is in her letter. The original letter no longer exists, but in Owen Wister's answer it is plainly seen.

SAUNDERSTOWN, R.I.

Saturday, July 5, 1902

Dearest Mother:

Now for your judgment of *The Virginian*. You say

(1) It's piecemeal.

(2) Last chapter superfluous.

(3) Heroine is the failure.

(4) That it's of doubtful morality, as to the justification of lynching, and as to the hero's conduct.

(1) I doubt it's being piecemeal to any one ignorant of the original stories.

But this is only a guess, a personal guess. It does not pretend to the regulation construction.

It claims to be

(1) The portrait of a man

(2) The picture, the whole large picture of the era and

manners in which he existed, for a background. I think his unflagging and developing personality does unify the book quite fundamentally rendering the ordinary construction unnecessary.

I take side after side of the manners and life, omitting none, and when I'm through you have the whole, with the men standing out in the middle. The proof of the fundamental unity is that every critic (who speaks of it at all) explains it's without construction and then adds that the *interest* holds from the first page to the last. That is the proof of a very deep kind of unity. But of course I agree it has no orthodox construction.

(2) I agree the last chapter is superfluous but very wise on my part. I should write it the same way over again. After the harsh drama preceding it was desirable to have some serene closing cadences.

I think it was essential the hero should meet the Great Aunt. Indeed I know it. And it was desirable his unromantic future should be indicated in a book of this kind, and no chance left for the reader to ask which did they do? In a poem, or in a pure romance like Undine, it would have been a discordant error.

(3) I agree that the heroine is the failure. She seems to me without personality.

(4) As to the lynching, and the hero and Ouida, your facts are so wrong and your theory so fallacious that I could not attempt on a discussion. I will take up only one of the points you make about the lynching. You say the results proved the viciousness of the lynching principle since the Thieves succeeded after all in the end. Your theory is fallacious; for one result proves nothing. Your fact is wrong, for in real life the lynching was perfectly successful in Montana and ended the reign of the Thieves there! You could not know this, naturally, from the book. But knowing it now will show you your fallacy of arguing against principles from one result.

Well—never mind—I wish this book was 20 times better
than it is. I'd already like to have it back to make certain
things better. But I think it is very much of an advance
on its predecessors. And the *next* time I shall write a very
big book indeed, if I can do it as I feel it in my bones. But
never again can I light on a character so engaging. That
only happens once, even to the great ones of the earth.

Some of the lesser newspapers are falling foul of my title.
I don't feel as if I could judge. The falling foul amazes
me. The resemblance they complain of to Thackeray is
so lost sight of—to me—in the utter difference of theme and
everything, that it seems to me of infinitesimal importance.
And the bright penetrating Ledger says, "This is a book
of incident rather than of character drawing."

> *Your loving* [*son,*]
>
> [*Owen Wister*]

The novel was translated into German that first year and serialized
in a German magazine. It was translated into Spanish and Czech
early in its career as a best-seller and within recent years (1954–57)
into German again, as well as French and Arabic. It is still selling in
America.

Wister made a five-act dramatization of the book, but it was too
long and cumbersome to act. Mr. Kirk LaShell then did a dramatization but used Wister's third act as originally written. The play was
tried out in Boston in the fall of 1903 with Dustin Farnum as star and
Frank Campo as the villain, Trampas. It opened in New York that
winter and achieved a successful run. My father worked on the script,
going to Boston and making changes during the tryout. He wrote for
it the song, "Ten Thousand Cattle," both words and music, which
Frank Campo sang. He also wrote the overture to the second act, the
manuscript of which is now lost. "Ten Thousand Cattle" was printed
as sheet music and later when the copyright ran out was included in
books of cowboy songs, giving no credit to Wister.

Dustin Farnum toured all over the country with *The Virginian*,
and it became a standard in stock companies for twenty years, being

played as late as 1938 in summer stock by Henry Fonda. Dustin Farnum also acted in it when it was first made into a movie in 1914, and it has been made into a film three times since then. As the first and basic Western, it in a sense has been seen and read under hundreds of other titles ever since.

In the summer of 1909 Corporal Skirdin, then a policeman on the Philadelphia force, came to spend the day at Butler Place. The Wister children knew that he had been a friend of their father's in the West and that he had been referred to many times as the original of the Virginian. But Owen Wister said of him in the Preface of the Collected Edition, "Skirdin was a sort of reincarnation of my already imagined character of the Virginian." While on duty as a policeman in Philadelphia, Skirdin, in attempting to disperse a crowd of people who were milling about and drinking, and who insulted him, fired his revolver into the ground in self-defense. He had already broken his club. The bullet ricocheted and killed one of the hoodlums. Skirdin was tried for first-degree murder. One of the counsel for him was Francis Rawle, in whose office Owen Wister still kept a desk. He stated in his defense that Skirdin was a long-time friend of Owen Wister, dating from 1894 in Arizona, and that Skirdin was an honorable, upright man. Skirdin looked exactly like the Remington paintings of cowpunchers. He had a drooping, slender mustache, a hooked nose, and gray eyes. Mr. Rawle's defense led to his acquittal.

The summer of 1913, when the Wisters were expecting a child, ended tragically at the Saunderstown, Rhode Island, house recently built for them. There in August Mary Channing Wister died in childbirth, leaving her husband with six children. The flags of the public school system in Philadelphia were flown at half-mast for her. The city had lost its most prominent and best-loved woman.

This would have been the time for Owen Wister to go to pieces. He had been married only fifteen years and a few months. Fortunately he was surrounded by relations and many old friends who came to his side to offer affection and advice. Although he counted on them and found strength in them, he had the fortitude, perhaps enhanced by his severe upbringing, to go on with his life.

In many ways Mary Channing Wister had been the antithesis of

Sarah B. Wister. Owen Wister's wife moved unharassed through life. Her house ran smoothly; her servants adored her. She kept her husband comfortable at all times, fending off annoyance and holding boring people at bay. She had nursed him herself during the first few months of the unidentified fever he had in 1910. She had gone with him frequently to stay with the Theodore Roosevelts at the White House and also to visit them at Oyster Bay. When Mr. Roosevelt wrote to Wister, he always ended his letters by saying, "Give my love to Mrs. Wister." Although these two men had known each other since college, they never spoke of each other's wives by their first names.

All his life Owen Wister had been a favorite of many older men and women who made much of him and could have spoiled him. But even the possessiveness of this large circle with whom he was intimate before his marriage had not daunted his wife. She was oblivious of the fact that such a situation could prove difficult. Hence there was no rub, and the pattern of Wister's life after his marriage remained the same with the augmentation of his happiness. Now he was alone, faced with a burden he was not equipped to bear. The marriage that had nourished and sustained him was over. He did not marry again.

In 1914 he went to Europe with Dr. and Mrs. John K. Mitchell. It was Dr. Mitchell who had gone with him to shoot big game in Wyoming in 1885. They went to school together, and each had been best man at the other's wedding. In this first summer after the death of his wife, Wister was fleeing his loneliness. He was in Munich when the first World War began. At once he felt passionately that his country should join England and France, and in the next two years he did everything in his power to influence America toward declaring war on Germany. He corresponded with Theodore Roosevelt, who was violently crusading to get America prepared to fight.

Wister made an address at Trinity College, Durham, North Carolina, at the commencement exercises on June 9, 1915, and a longer version of it became an article in the *Saturday Evening Post* and was published as a small book called *The Pentecost of Calamity*. This reasoned but passionate plea for his country to go to war against Germany was translated into French, Dutch, Italian, and Japanese and was a huge success at home. It was *The Pentecost of Calamity* that made so many friends for Wister in French and English public life. The British, for example, asked the United States Department of State to give Wister a passport, which the United States had earlier refused to do, saying an author had no real purpose for going to see the battlefields five months after the Armistice. Thus he saw the battlefields in preparation for writing two more books of political comments about the relationship between his country and France and England. He took his children to see the battlefields two years later and took them also to Rheims Cathedral so that they would know what war meant.

After World War I Wister spent part of nearly every year in Europe until the end of his life. In England he stayed with his nearest relative, Lady Butler, the cousin whose mother, Mrs. Leigh, he stayed with in England in 1870. In London he continued to see the political friends who had asked the American government to give him a passport. He also formed friendships among contemporary English writers —Lord Dunsany, Joseph Conrad, and E. F. Benson (who often played Bach on the piano in his house on Brompton Square)—so that the time he spent in England was rewarding.

He took his children to France to see the chateaux of Touraine, which he found delightful. He had made a considerable study of the French cathedrals, which were an immense joy to him, especially Chartres Cathedral. He traveled in France, Italy, and Spain, mostly with college classmates and their wives in a party of four or five. Often they would settle in some small town particularly pleasing to them.

He became a connoisseur of French wines, visiting dozens of vineyards, talking to the owners, watching the tending of the vines, and seeing the wine being made. He felt French wines were a complement to daily life and imported many to drink at home. In his seventies, he started a book about French wine, but he never finished it.

Owen Wister's gift for friendship and acceptance of new people instead of diminishing with the years remained as one of his dominant characteristics. He belonged to several clubs and at them he met many younger men. Instead of being afraid of him and staying at a formal distance, they soon asked for his advice and poured out their sorrows to him, and called him Uncle Dan. They were blighted in love, thwarted in their careers, thrown out of college, striving to be poets, novelists, and composers. They found a listener who gave them sage counsel and affection. Wister had never been conscious of his fame; he seemed unaware of it and often uncertain of himself to the point of asking his contemporaries for their opinions about his manuscripts. Being himself an asker made him an understanding listener.

He never held forth, never took the conversational bit in his teeth, did not lord it over anyone. Perhaps it was his mother's impossibly high standard in all intellectual matters and her cerebral approach to life that made him diffident. Apparently she had never allowed him to feel that he came up to her expectation. But he was not a one-topic man. To the end of his life he took a marked interest in American and foreign politics and contemporary English and French literature. He was one of the earliest admirers of Ernest Hemingway, and young composers played their scores to him; for he gave his attention to others gladly.

The Tavern Club of Boston was one of the great lasting enthusiasms of his life. In 1884 when he was working in the cellar of the Union Safe Deposit Bank in Boston, he became an original member of the Tavern Club, which was first an informal gathering of bachelors who found it pleasant to dine together at restaurants. The *Semi Centennial History of the Tavern Club* says of the group, "They [the young men] were all interested in artistic, literary, or scientific subjects, and they soon formed a small set among themselves, apart from the other frequenters of these places." When the club was formally organized, it began to hold dinners or suppers once a month, ". . . at each of which was present some special invited guest, in whose honor the dinner was given."[7] From Philadelphia Wister went as regularly as he could afford to Boston to the monthly Tavern Club dinners and later on and for the whole of his life to all the monthly dinners and celebrations. He became president in 1929, and at the fiftieth anniversary in 1934 he was one of the original members present.

In 1916 he wrote the words and music of an operetta especially for

[7] M. A. DeWolfe Howe, *Semi Centennial History of the Tavern Club,* as stated in that volume by Dr. Bullard.

23

the Tavern Club to be acted and sung by its members. *Il Commenda-tore*, a burlesque of Mozart's *Don Giovanni*, was climaxed by the song "Here I Come, Dum de Dum" which was such a great favorite of his family. Wister kept up his music all his life and always went straight to the piano on his return home late in the afternoon, to sing and play for himself. He often sang "Ten Thousand Cattle" from *The Virginian*, the Shakespeare verses he had set to music and published, and the songs from *La Belle Helene* and *La Fille de Madam Angot*. He played four-handed piano duets many evenings with his oldest daughter.

In 1925 he again wrote an operetta for the Tavern Club. Called *Watch Your Thirst*, it satirized Prohibition through gay verses sung by characters from Greek myths. *Watch Your Thirst* was performed again at the Tavern Club in 1934 at the fiftieth anniversary. The "composer" attended all the rehearsals both in 1925 and 1934 but did not play the piano himself at the performances.

Owen Wister never talked about the West to his family. I never heard him say a single word about the fifteen years spent mostly in hunting big game and collecting material for his books. Perhaps it was because by the time we were old enough to hear about them, those years were long past. He had taken us to Jackson Hole to let us see for ourselves.

In 1951, after my father had been dead thirteen years, a letter came to me from N. Orwin Rush, at that time director of the University of Wyoming Library at Laramie. Mr. Rush said that 1952 would be the fiftieth anniversary of the publication of *The Virginian* and that he hoped to collect for the library's Owen Wister Room a copy of every edition of *The Virginian* ever published in any language. He also said that the library was going to celebrate the anniversary with a ceremony. Did we, he wondered, have any manuscripts that we would give to the Wister Room? Because we had always been told that my father destroyed his manuscripts as soon as they were typed (and we had never seen a manuscript of his), we assumed there were none. I replied to Mr. Rush that there was little we could do to add to the Wister Room.

24

A few months later a letter from the Library of Congress mentioned the anniversary year of *The Virginian* and asked the Wister family to give all Owen Wister's papers, including manuscripts and letters to the Library. Again we replied that we had few if any but would give what we could find. At about this time Mrs. George Vaux, a niece of Henry James, telephoned me and asked if we had any letters from James to my father. I said that if there were any letters, they could be easily found; for during the last years of my father's life he had employed a friend of the family (a trained librarian) to sort through all his papers and file them. Though I never knew exactly what was in the files, I had gathered from conversations with the librarian that the papers were the records of the Butler family. Barrels and boxes of papers had been moved by me but not looked at when Butler Place was given up and we had moved to Longhouse, Bryn Mawr, Pennsylvania. I did not go through them or throw away anything.

After talking to the niece of James, I called my brother, who was still living at Longhouse, and asked him to look in the files for James's letters. The files were neatly arranged in drawers and shelves of two old-fashioned wardrobes in the attic. My brother found forty letters from James to Sarah B. Wister and Owen Wister, but he also found the letters written by my father to his mother from 1870 to 1908. And so it was that the Library of Congress received the Wister papers.

I then got another letter from Mr. Rush asking whether we would give to the Wister Room my father's Western diaries. None of us had ever heard of them, and they were not in the files, as I told Mr. Rush. He wrote back, quoting from page 28 in my father's book about Theodore Roosevelt. ". . . Upon every Western expedition I had kept a full, faithful, realistic diary: details about pack horses, camps in the mountains, camps in the sage brush, nights in town, cards with cavalry officers. . . ." Where are those diaries? Mr. Rush wanted to know. It seemed hopeless to try to find them, but I determined to look. I rounded up my brothers, and we met at Longhouse. My youngest brother said that he would start with our father's desk, which had been in the second-story library that adjoined Owen Wister's bedroom and that was his study during his life at Butler Place. The very first drawer my brother opened contained the Western Journals.

The fifteen Journals had been in the drawer for sixty-five years. The cover of each is inscribed with my father's signature and a date and the names of the places he visited. Inside, the tiny, faded pencil handwriting—almost illegible except for the first sentence of each— relates the Western adventures at the heart of Owen Wister's work.

We agreed that the University of Wyoming ought to have the Journals, and, through Mr. Rush, we asked only that a copy be made for us. The legislature of the state of Wyoming appropriated money for transcribing the Journals, and the university library had it done. In the course of a year, transcripts of the Journals arrived separately but not in sequence.

When I had read them all, I saw that combined with the letters they would tell the story of my father's discovery of the frontier in his own words. In these records Owen Wister avows his romantic love of the West. In them he is seen not only observing and recording but also taking to his heart the region and the epoch. And so the vaga-bond men of the West—resourceful, young, and wild—became for Owen Wister part of the whole glorious scene, and from his pen the cowboy myth soared into the imagination of the country.

July—August, 1885

WYOMING

IN 1885 Owen Wister's health broke down (though we have no exact record of the nature of his illness), and on the advice of Dr. S. Weir Mitchell he went to Wyoming in June to stay on a ranch belonging to Major and Mrs. Frank Wolcott, who apparently were friends of his parents. When he boarded the train at Philadelphia, he began a diary that turned out to be the first of fifteen diaries recording his many trips West. The impression made on him that summer (when he turned twenty-five) determined his career.

Ten diaries as well as selections from the existing Wister correspondence have been combined to form the essential and readable narrative in Wister's own words of his discovery of the West, with a few explanatory comments at the beginning of each year's entries. The Journal labeled "Cinnabar and Return, 1892" has been omitted because it covers only eight uneventful days, mostly of train travel. "Frontier Notes, 1893" has been omitted because it contains only disconnected facts about Indian lore and nothing about Wister. "Frontier Notes, 1894"—condensed notes and scraps of dialogue—is interwoven with the 1894 Journal insofar as it completes the narrative. The Journals of 1896 and 1900, revealing little of Wister or of the West, have been omitted for their lack of interest.

Utmost care has been taken to omit only what is not interesting as either firsthand experience or firsthand observation. Many long descriptions of scenery have been deleted because they repeat passages already written. Dull facts about big game hunting and colorless details of Army post life have been omitted too; and where references and reflections on friends in the East are no longer pertinent, they have been cut from the letters. The editor conscientiously has omitted nothing concerning Wister that illuminates his character. There are no startling revelations or new discoveries about him. The Journals are never unseemly, and there is nothing to suppress. The hunting journals were written at night by the

28

campfire, and the journals of material gathered under the sponsorship of *Harper's Magazine* were written at Army camps, in local hotels, and on the train.

Kept solely for Wister's private use under such conditions over a period of years, the Journals often show signs of haste. At the request of the publisher, who felt that Wister himself would have polished his notes had he prepared them for publication, the Journals have been lightly edited to make them clear to contemporary readers. Spelling has been made uniform, current usage adhered to in some cases, and punctuation at times changed for coherence. The letters are identified by their headings, which are made consistent according to present practice; all else save a sprinkling of notes and brackets comes from the Journals.

At first on the 1885 trip Wister was accompanied by two maiden ladies twenty years his senior, Miss Masie and Miss Sophy Irwin of Philadelphia, who were friends of his mother. It is not known when or why they decided to make the hazardous expedition, but at any rate they returned home before Wister went shooting. Dr. John K. Mitchell, son of Dr. S. Weir Mitchell, joined Wister at the Wolcott camp beyond the ranch and went shooting with him.

The description of the town of Medicine Bow, Wyoming, which is the only town named in *The Virginian*, appears in the 1885 Journal much as it was to appear in the novel.

1885

July 2.   One must come to the West to realize what one may have most probably believed all one's life long—that it is a very much bigger place than the East, and the future America is just bubbling and seething in bare legs and pinafores here. I don't wonder a man never comes back [East] after he has once been here for a few years.

July 3. The country we're going through now was made before the good Lord discovered that variety is the spice of life. But it is beautiful. It reminds me of the northern part of Spain. The same vast stretches of barren green back to the skyline or to rising ground. We stopped at North Platte for breakfast. I paid twenty-five cents and ate everything I saw. Some of it was good. Just now we stopped at a station where a black pig was drinking the drops that fell from the locomotive tank, and a pile of whitened cattle bones lay nearby. Here and there, far across the level, is a little unpainted house with a shed or two and a wagon. Now either a man on horseback or a herd of cattle. We've passed a little yelping gang of collies who raced us but got beaten. The sky—there is none. It looks really like what it scientifically is—space. The air is delicious. As if it had never been in anyone's lungs before. I like this continual passing of green void, without any growing things higher than a tuft of grass.

The night has descended, and we are approaching Rock Creek. God knows what we shall find to sleep in there. Have said farewell to my various train acquaintances. Sorry to leave the train. Had begun to feel as if I grew there. A sort of Eastern air-feeding orchid.

The remains of the moon is giving just enough light to show the waving line of the prairie. Every now and then sheet lightning plays from some new quarter like a surprise. The train steamed away into the night, and here we are. We passed this morning the most ominous and forbidding chasm of rocks I ever saw in any country. Deep down below, a campfire is burning. It all looked like *Die Walküre*—this

which is much more than my most romantic dream could
have hoped.

It's a quarter of twelve. We start for a fifty-mile drive
tomorrow at 6 A.M.

July 6.   Off on stage, 6 A.M. 9:30 A.M. Stopping for
the one meal we'll get—this station is the middle of all out
of doors. Inside in the "Smart room," where canvas covers
the wood and mud of the walls, a man is playing the fiddle
to the guitar accompaniment of a red and black chap. There's
a collie, three pups, a tame young antelope, and the coffee
mill is nailed onto the side of the house. The mountains to
the N.E. are serrated and lovely. In the sleeping apartment
of this station hang the skins of various animals unknown to
me. Have seen heaps of antelope and wild dog or prairie wolf,
or coyote.

I can't possibly say how extraordinary and beautiful the
valleys we've been going through are. They're different from
all things I've seen. When you go for miles through the piled
rocks where the fire has risen straight out of the crevices, you
never see a human being—only now and then some disap-
pearing wild animal. It's like what scenery on the moon must
be. Then suddenly you come round a turn and down into a
green cut where there are horsemen and wagons and hundreds
of cattle, and then it's like Genesis. Just across this corduroy
bridge are a crowd of cowboys round a fire, with their horses
tethered.

July 7.   Been here at the ranch a day and a half.
Everything is immense, including my case of sunburn. Major

and Mrs. Wolcott are delightful hosts. House a sort of miracle for these parts—so clean, comfortable, pretty. I sleep out in a tent and take a bath every morning in Deer Creek. Yesterday got on a broncho for the first time. The animal undertook to lie down with me. But after that we got on well—I didn't get off. I like this scenery. As for game—ducks, curlews, snipe, prairie chickens, grouse, sage hens, antelope, and rattle-snakes. If I don't learn to shoot, it won't be the fault of the wild animals of these parts.

Saw the calves branded and cut yesterday—in all, seventy-nine.

Wednesday, July 8. This existence is heavenly in its monotony and sweetness. Wish I were going to do it every summer. I'm beginning to be able to feel I'm something of an animal and not a stinking brain alone. Nailed up a strip of cloth over the crack of the big dugout door to keep the flies from the meat.

Friday, July 10. Went out for the first time yester-day with my gun, and surprised myself by killing two grouse in four shots. All I need is practice, and this summer I'm going to get practice. I find riding these bronchos the easiest long-distance riding I've ever experienced. I'm afraid the creek will run dry and stop my morning baths. This country doesn't get enough water to make it a great country. They'll have to irrigate from Lake Superior or something, which they probably will if some American doesn't invent a way to pull a string and have it rain. American! There are very few of them so far in our history. Every man, woman, and cowboy I see comes from the East—and generally from New England, thank goodness. If that's the stock that is going to fill these big fields with people, our first hundred years will grow to be only the mythological beginnings in the time to come. I feel more certainly than ever that no matter how completely the East may be the headwaters from which the West has flown and is flowing, it won't be a century before the West is simply the true America, with thought, type, and life of its own kind.

July 14.   I'm a quarter of a century old today.

July 16.   Today we've had the border element. A year ago Major Wolcott had a gardener, named Branan, to whom and to whose brother he gave work in winter when they were pretty nearly stranded. This gardener at the instigation of one Beech—a damn scoundrel apparently—one day when the Major was away squatted on some land that had already been taken up and improved by Wolcott. Wolcott warned him, then showed him the papers that gave him his claim, then had the sheriff and an injunction. But Branan stuck, backed by Beech who had an eye on the $1,200 the two Branans had saved—they have $750 left now. Today they started to dig a ditch on this land, and the engineer found them at it. Wolcott went up there and found Branan at work with a cocked rifle by him. The Major said Branan might as well give up this kind of work—but Branan confessed he didn't amount to much, but if the Major would step down to his tent, they would talk business. This meant: "How much will you give me to clear out?" "Not a nickel will you ever get out of me that way," said Wolcott.

It appears that a year ago down here they had some words to the same effect, and Branan in the midst of the talk threw up his hands and rushed out saying he wasn't going to talk with him. Today the Major returned for his gun, and when I saw him riding off to the pasture with it to continue talking business to Branan, I certainly became anxious to know what would next happen. But nothing happened—Wolcott came back.

"Adelaide," said he to his wife, "I suppose when a man gets mad and uses bad language, that shows he's a low fellow?"

Silence.

"Well, my dear, I did curse that man by everything I could think of—and it's no way to get anything done, I know."

"Well, Frank, of course I think swearing is needless."

"Yes, my dear, but I couldn't help it—forty acres—and tho' it's not much among five or six thousand, it's their damn scoundrelism of the scheme that bites me—just blackmail. But I'll make it hot for 'em. There's a stone dam of mine on that land and a ditch six feet deep, and if that's not improved land I don't know what is. We get a cheap dose of this kind of thing. Some men I know have had their land jumped on in this way, and it has cost them $500 just to take their witness to the court in Denver—more than the land was worth. Now I'm justice of the peace, and I'm thinking I'll have a little court on the premises. Very cheap, my dear Adelaide, and Regas is a constable. I think I'll send him up and arrest them. Well, I don't know, but I'll think about it. But before I've done with them, they'll be ruined."

In the Old Testament Lot and Isaac and Uncle Leban and the rest had times not unlike this—only guns weren't invented.

Caught a gopher. Meant to tame him, but he got out of his box and skedaddled. Stockings—that's the broncho that sat down with me first day—opened the gates this evening and let all the horses out into the wide, wide world. I got on another broncho, which the Major had just come back on from Branan's, and chased them back home. An hour later I caught Stockings trying to open the gate again, and I whaled him with a rope and then tied the gate up. Stockings is big— about 14 hands, very thick mane and topknot—and rather handsome. He's about the most knowing-looking animal I ever laid my dear eyes on. I am convinced he could speak French if he tried.

The details of the life here are interesting. Wish I could find out all about it—and master it—theoretically. It's a life as strange as any the country has seen, and it will slowly make room for Cheyennes, Chicagos, and ultimately inland New Yorks—everything reduced to the same flat prairie-like level of utilitarian civilization. Branans and Beeches will give way to Tweeds and Jay Goulds—and the ticker will replace the rifle.

July 18. The would-be squatters have crawled.

Had a roundup yesterday and cut out the black cattle— most entertaining morning dashing about on a broncho, trying to think I was of some assistance.

July 19, Medicine Bow. Got here at 5:30 this evening, July 19, after nineteen hours of driving and a night in the mountains. We're expecting by the midnight train some trout and bass for stocking.

This place is called a town. "Town" will do very well until the language stretches itself and takes in a new word that fits. Medicine Bow, Wyoming, consists of:

1 Depot house and baggage room
1 Coal shooter
1 Water tank
1 Store
2 Eating houses
1 Billiard hall
6 Shanties
8 Gents and Ladies Walks
2 Tool houses
1 Feed stable
<u>5</u> Too late for classification
29 Buildings in all

The lady who waited on us at supper I do not believe is in a family way. I believe she has a gross stomach. I slung my teeth over the corned beef she gave me and thought I was chewing a hammock.

I have walked nearly two acres in order to carefully ascertain the exact details of this town, and I feel assured my returns are correct.

Killed today the first deer I ever shot at. Hit it plumb in the shoulder and broke its heart.

July 21. I slept from ten to twelve-thirty on the counter of the store at Medicine Bow, and then the train came in, bringing the lawyer and the fish. And after much business talk and lifting tin cans we started off across the plains at two o'clock. At three we discovered we had lost our way, but found it inside of thirty minutes. On the way home the sun killed the trout, but the bass survived. After a stunning drive up through the cañon, where there were rocks thrown together in such architectural heaps that I could have imagined a druid sitting beneath them, and where the lifeless trees stood up on the plain like monsters on their hind legs or lay sprawling like the skeletons of fearful spiders, we saw a sunset more remarkable than any yet. The mountains rose between us and the sun, but from behind them rose a saffron and gold vapor that seemed to be exhaled from some heavenly volcano. All round the sky big patches of woolly clouds made a crimson stationary background, while over the face of this, long lines and fragments of slate-colored streamers sped like messengers.

We saw eight mountain sheep—I missed them—they were too far for my light rifle. Reached here at seven, having driven for seventeen hours. Pretty tired—slept nine hours. Today killed some rabbits. Shall keep the horns of my first deer as a memento. Hope it isn't the last, however.

August 1. Mrs. Wolcott has the Puritan virtues, and she congealed early. She had a cold, intelligent eye. When she smiled, the various facial muscles that are necessary for that expression of emotion worked very perfectly and disclosed many regular and beautiful teeth. But in spite of this perfect mechanism there was no smile there. The North Pole might smile a farewell to a south-bound iceberg like this.

Dissecting our friends in society is one of the offices in which the human tongue approaches perfection. It may be called the Black Art of conversation.

As for me, I'm better (and I hope I'll keep on), but I must have been very thoroughly wrong somewhere—nerves, I fear. Sometimes the mere shape of a grasshopper makes my head vibrate. Hell, and whenever I've been bending over, I get up with the vertigo. For action in this world a too keen perceptiveness is a hindrance.

August 2. Puritanism is the protest of one stage of civilization against a later stage at which itself in its turn is bound to arrive. It is a confusion of language to speak of one spirit as ousting another or to describe progress in any way that implies more than one agent. Change in matters of thought is not wrought by the action of a thing upon another thing. There is but one thing. The common intellect of our race. Whatever dissensions arise are only the result of some portion of this great progressive organism getting ahead of the rest, or pulling contrary to the general direction of development. The chameleon simile is nearest the truth. Whatever the momentary colour may change to, the same beast is beneath all the while. When Luther was at logger-heads with Rome, he was fighting with a portion of himself that he had left behind.

August 4. At a roundup—it's very interesting, but beastly hot.

August 6, Thursday. On Tuesday we left camp on horseback for the roundup at five minutes before seven. On the way I rode over two rattlesnakes, who played a duet with their tails, allegro energetic. The darker one got away into his hole before I could stop him, but I killed the second and handsomer of the two. After I had cut his head off, it struck at me. The eye of Satan when plotting the destruction of the human race could not have been more malignant than the stare which this decapitated head gave me with its two clouded agate eyes. They had speculation in them full five minutes after the trunk was in my hands being skinned. He was four feet long, and when I put my foot on him as he was trying to get away into his hole, he felt very solid.

We reached the roundup about nine. It took place in the

big plain beyond our camping ground of the first night. There were two big bodies of cattle—many hundred—and about twelve cowboys scudding round and through them, cutting out those of the V. R. brand. The mass of animals stood still for the most part but now and then moved slowly round its own center, giving the effect of a gigantic leisurely eddy. Once or twice they broke ranks, which caused extra riding and barking and whistling from the cowboys, who flew this way and that to head them off, whirling their quirts and making sudden turns as if their ponies worked on a pivot. The sun grew very hot and shone down on the brown extent out of a cloudless sky. To the East the peaks were covered with a light blue stifling haze and looked something like the scenery in the Dolomites, which I've noticed before.

When our V. R. cattle had been cut out and bunched, the cowboys started the rest away over the hills. The whole mass began to move westward creeping over the undulations in the plain—moving steadily forward as a body and moving constantly backward and forward within its own ranks. A couple of cows would get ahead by trotting, then slow up and be overtaken by half a dozen more at different distances, while in the middle there was a constant seething to and fro. The twelve cowboys all gathered in a long line abreast behind their own cattle and drove them away in the opposite direction. Tom King, the foreman, says he likes this life and will never go East again. On Miss Irwin's inquiry whether he will not get tired of it when he grows old, he replied that cowboys never live long enough to get old. They don't, I believe. They're a queer episode in the history of this country. Purely nomadic, and leaving no posterity, for they don't marry. I'm told they're without any moral sense whatever. Perhaps they are—but I wonder how much less they have than the poor classes in New York.

Wolcott Camp. Miss Sophy asked me if I didn't think if Jack Mitchell didn't come today that she could ride down to the ranch and stay with him till he could come. I told her with some asperity, improperly, that I thought that such a step would be highly unwise and would probably displease our host. She'll listen to me and won't go. If she goes, I shall make a very strong remonstrance. It would be ridiculous of a woman forty-odd to leave her party and ride twenty miles to a ranch in order to comfort a young man of twenty-six because his joining her party is delayed necessarily for a day or two. Miss Sophy is not always very wise. But she's very delightful company for all that, and I'm going to tell her I had no right to be severe on her plan of staying at the ranch. Such a sentiment of repentance befits even a pagan.

On Tuesday we were six hours and more in the saddle and I was not tired—to my satisfaction.

July–September, 1887

BRITISH COLUMBIA, WASHINGTON
OREGON, CALIFORNIA, WYOMING

WISTER, who had entered Harvard Law School in 1885, did not go West in 1886. But in the spring of 1887 he wrote the following letter to his father.

PORCELLIAN CLUB, HARVARD COLLEGE
CAMBRIDGE, MASS.

Tuesday

My dear Father:

Are you able, and if able, are you disposed to make me a present of money in order that I may do one of two things this summer. I want to go West and ride through the Big Horn Mountains and the Yellowstone and if possible travel through the Valley of California, and that will be the most expensive thing. And I want to take a steamer to Bordeaux and travel through the South of France and Provence on foot, and that will be the cheaper thing to do, if I can find a line of steamers that run to Bordeaux, which I believe exists. That I would undertake on $400 of which I could furnish $150. My dividend on July 1, and I suppose Miss Fox will give me a birthday present.[1] Both plans are the results of invitations, and both are in order to be out of doors as much as I can this summer. I'll not add anything to what I've said by way of persuasion, for I'm sure you would like me to do this sort of thing if it can be afforded. I shall come out of Cambridge with a small balance on the last cheque you sent me and no bills unpaid, I believe. I am awfully hard worked and very tired. Somehow this year the work is harder, or else I don't know so much as I did last. Which is not because I've loafed more, but from causes unexplained. I certainly feel gloomy about the examinations. I work seven days in the week from 9 till 1, from 3 or 4 till 6:30, and from 8 till 10:30 or 11. And it's rather sustained, I can tell you.

Your affectionate Son,

Owen Wister

[1] Miss Mary Fox was Owen Wister's godmother.

Obviously Dr. Wister did give his son the money to go West again, because the second Journal starts on July 1. The "hard-working" law student went from Boston to Niagara and then to Toronto, leaving at once for Owen Sound and crossing Sault Ste Marie by steamer. From there he went to Port Arthur and Winnepeg, and from Winnepeg to Vancouver and Portland and arrived at San Francisco in the middle of July, from which he went to Wyoming.

He makes no mention at the beginning of the 1887 Journal of George Norman, a contemporary from Boston who apparently was with him from the very beginning. He says of Copley Amory, also of Boston but six years younger, that he joined "us at Qu'appelle, Canada."

Mr. Amory during an interview in the summer of 1955 recalled that the Indian guide Tigie, one of three guides on the shooting trip, was a famous hunter and tracker of big game. Tigie was engaged for the trip for them by Colonel Homer W. Wheeler, commanding officer of Fort Washakie, Wyoming, who as a young man had been in the Civil War with Mr. Amory's father. Mr. Amory also said the bear Wister shot was a grizzly—the finest shot or seen on the trip. It was Tigie, according to Mr. Amory, who found George Norman after he had been lost the whole day, shooting by himself, and brought him safely back to camp.

Taking up the 1887 Journal on July 4, Wister's reference to the date must mean the golden jubilee of Queen Victoria. His observation about what music was accepted as suitable to be played on Sunday suggests the Victorian obsession with propriety, which he was escaping for the summer.

1887

On Steamer Crossing Sault Ste Marie, July 4, 1887.
Can take no notice of the date so soon after Her Majesty's
Jubilee. More fog, a great deal more. But the water has kept
smooth all the way. Yesterday the piano had a curious tune.
I have noticed that hotel and steamboat pianos always do
have a curious time of it on Sunday. The feelings about what
may and what may not be done upon the day of rest are
mixed—and on the subject of music they are not mixed only
but curdled hopelessly. I didn't see the face of any of the
people who sat down to our piano yesterday. But each went
through the same performance of apologizing for playing at
all by beginning with the thoughtful prelude of hymns.
Between whiles a restrained and serious interlude of chords
would be played, and then would follow the next hymn tune.
Gradually the pace became brighter, the chords threw off with
much tact a certain amount of restraint and soon I heard a
"Song without Words" by Mendelssohn, the one entitled
"Consolation," which has been used for a hymn, as everyone
knows. This led very naturally into a slow movement from
one of Beethoven's sonatas. Once installed in the realm of
sonata, and you can proceed to forget movements without
danger of alarming your Sunday audience. You must always
remember you are stalking their prejudices. A premature
allegro would act like the crackle of a dry branch. Off the
prejudices would go, and all your labour in vain. But manage
discreetly, and like the unseen players yesterday in this boat,
you can begin in hymns ancient and modern and then end
with comic opera or any other music devoted to the direction
that you choose.

Along the Fraser River, July 8.   The train climbs up until it is more than 5,900 feet above the sea, and then it descends gingerly over the gulches and under the precipices, viewed with scorn by the black pine woods. Had the sun been out on Thursday morning, the splendid terrors of the St. Gotthard would have not reached what we saw from morning till night. All the afternoon I rode on the cowcatcher as we slid downhill without steam, through snow sheds and tunnels (once under a shower bath in the dark, drenching and cold), round turns into a new vista of cataracts or avenues between the pines. Once an eagle sailed up the bank and preened at once on a gigantic log, following the train with concentration in his eyes. Whether he had never seen it before or whether it was his daily habit couldn't be said from his manner. But the cowcatcher is the place. We came on a derailed train, but soon dragged its locomotive back onto the beaten path and continued. The woods burn too much. The fire rushes up the centre of the pine trunks, leaving the outside unscorched and suddenly pouring fiercely out of a hole sixty feet from the ground. The sparks do this, and also the Indian women who wish to clear patches for blackberries. For thirty miles we skirted a beautiful lake, I still on the cowcatcher. Sitting here, the train invisible, you feel something as if you were flying, nothing in front of you but the nearing track, and the advancing point of the cowcatcher that give you no hint of what an imposing affair is trailing in its wake. But this lake was too beautiful. The water unrippled save by wild ducks and loons that kept their self-composure as long as they could, glancing round uneasily at us rattling along the bank and finally starting a long dripping flight to the wooded shores across the water. Over there the trees were burning, and their smoke in the quiet of the evening rose and drew into a long lavender veil that floated down again and lay close over the water. Behind the green strips and snow ridges all melted into pink

and purple, while the sun slanted down between the sides of
every valley and ravine. There was no feeling of being in a
belt of mountains with a limit soon reached. They were behind
each other in any direction one chose to look. Then we left
the lake and glided through the pine avenues again with the
miles of pine hemming us in not too narrowly, and behind
them the snow and rocks hemming them in. We nearly ran
over a pig who remained undecided which side of the track he
would watch the train pass from till nearly too late. "Pigs
always ditch the engine," said the conductor. "If we'd struck
that animal, you'd have had it in your laps and the locomotive
on your backs. Oh, a pig's bad for a train. I don't know why,
but I prefer a cow always." The only inhabitants we had
passed except at the rare stations, were gangs of Chinamen
gathered round a camp resting from work on the railway.

ESMOND HOTEL
PORTLAND, OREGON
Monday, July 11

Dearest Mother:

I notice the steamboats burn wood instead of coal and
puff as they go—a sign of high pressure and cheap engines.
They go very fast, and everybody jumps on and off like a
game. Yesterday we reached the swollen Columbia. Instead
of crossing in the usual way—the whole train going aboard
—we got out and traveled twelve miles up the current and
so into another train on the opposite shore. This twelve
miles was done in twenty minutes against stream, and the
vessel quivers like somebody carrying a big load too long. It
would be interesting to know just how safe that is. I sat in
a place when if a blowup had occurred, I could have gone
harmlessly overboard and got ashore.

In Canada the passengers were colorless and inert. The
hotels and trains here are filled with extraordinary looking

folks. Men with eyebrows as wide as a hat ribbon and
thick blue upper lips. Women covered with perfumes to
whom the train hands are attentive, sitting down by them
and entering into an agreeable talk between stations. French-
looking little boys, well dressed and eating something in
everybody else's seat. Their mammas "deuced fine" women
with the big black eyes and lots of lace around their throats.
You see the Fourth of July happened lately and everybody
went somewhere else for it. So now everybody's on their
way back.

I keep thinking how you would hate nearly all of it.
The only way you could ever come West and enjoy yourself
would be inside a large party of friends who would form a
hollow square whenever a public place was to be entered.

> *Your loving son,*
> *D.*

FORT WASHAKIE
WYOMING TERRITORY
August 4

Dearest Mother:

We reached here last Saturday, i.e., a week ago
tomorrow, and are off into the mountains today. We came
here by stage from Rawlins, a point on the railroad, and
drove from 8 A.M. Friday morning till 5:30 P.M. on the
following day, night included! I thought myself this was
part of the trip you certainly could not have stood. It was
149 miles over the prairie and sagebrush, very much like
the country the Miss Irwins and I drove through two years
ago. I have been here all these days arranging about guides,
horses, etc., etc., which has been a very gradual arrangement
indeed, owing to the fact that the best guides were already
bespoken and the country had to be more or less searched.
We have an Indian (who is hunter), a packer, and a cook

assistant; these last two are white. Tigie, Mason, and West
are their names. Tigie speaks to nobody but evidently
wishes to please; so he works hard. Mason wears spectacles
and regrets that early bad habits have brought him where
he is. West is about twenty-four and much too good looking.
He is much better looking than any of us, but he is suffering
from indigestion just now. I have treated him out of my
medicine chest. In this way I hope to reduce him to a
decently ugly appearance. I shall give him the rattlesnake
antidote internally every three hours. The army has been
most hospitable, and cigars and whiskey and beer and
dinner have all been showered on us. I hope I have bought
a good horse. Probably not, but no one will suffer but
myself. I shall sell him at an advance when I part with him
in the Yellowstone.

Your loving son,
D.

Camp 1, Saturday, August 6.   Reached here, eighteen
miles from Fort Washakie, about sunset. We came over dry
stretches of sage and up and down the strange formations of
these hills and gulches. At one place a line of rocks stood out
of the slope at regular intervals, looking like busts whose faces
had decayed and left the skull. We saw Bull Lake to the left
of us, shining between cool banks that ran down into it, blue
in the evening air. Here we're at the forks of the Wind River,
on a good grass lawn girt with flourishing cottonwood.
Westward, where we're going, the moon country begins again.
Just a little way is a pile, or rather all that remains of the
former level of this plain, flat on top with steep sides that are
slowly crumbling. The approach to the forks last night was
down among stones till the dry sage was out of sight and so
into a shorelike flat over which stood gray trees sparsely
leaved and looking as if they bordered the Styx. The sun in

setting had got wedged in between two different hills and sent a crimson glare into this place that gave it a most unearthly appearance.

Camp 2, by Wind River, Saturday Night. Till noon our road was the same dry waste of sage with bare gravel uplands and hot blue mountains behind. At noon we halted by a stream and had lunch—gallons of tea, which seems to have no effect on the nerves here. All rather sore from yesterday's ride, but getting over it. George Norman and I caught some trout, which we fried in the grease of the bacon. They were very good. Tigie, our Indian guide, partook of them gravely. Then George shot one magpie and I another, and these we tied to the saddle and have just had as a stew for supper in spite of West and Mason's telling us what magpies eat. After all, what do lobsters eat? An Indian is just now paying Tigie a visit. He appeared on his pony and stopped to call. Copley Amory is learning (?) to throw a rope.

Our journey all afternoon has been pleasant, through grass and undergrowth, near the river, which we follow into the mountains. Tigie and his visitor are warming their backs on the other side of the fire. Mason and West are commenting on our magpie diet. Copley is absorbedly swinging a rope round his head, George is attempting to dry his boots, and I am getting bitten by mosquitoes. This afternoon George saw about six wild geese waddling about in a stream. He was desirous to test his horse's taste for shooting; so he fired from the saddle, thereby adding one to the number of geese nobody hurt.

Camp 2, Monday, August 8. A short stage yesterday, and fished in the afternoon. Few fish here. Caught three—one good one—had them for dinner. Went into a lake and washed.

Got up at five this morning and caught one trout for breakfast. The mountains when the sun is rising or setting turn a smoking blue. At high noon they are sultry bleak-looking masses, scant of trees except in the gulches, where the pines show black in the distance. Today we hope for better fishing. We set out for Washakie with but few luxuries, and those we have hastily consumed. Soon the rod and rifle will have to cater for us entirely.

The Wind River comes down a many-winding avenue of cottonwood and thorny undergrowth of rosebushes and wild gooseberries, hedging the water in from the hot levels of sage and stones with a broad green belt. The water is of a smokey green, sometimes streaming turbulently about stony islands, and then running in a smooth-swimming current where the fish are. If you stand on one of the uplands that rise near the river, you can watch it for miles over the plains like a great green serpent.

Noon. Tigie and ourselves have halted for noon meal. In an hour we caught ten trout. Now George and I are fishing again. I have just landed the first—first I saw took with a fly. He measures from the tip of my middle finger along to my elbow. I was afraid the improvised rod would snap, but it didn't, as I left him in the water till I could jerk him into George's hand.

CAMP ALONG WIND RIVER

August 9

Dearest Mother:

An unexpected cowboy has wandered into camp tonight on his way south to Fort Washakie—now ninety miles off—so I'm scrawling you a line by the light of our campfire, lying flat on my stomach. The weather has been so lovely that we have slept beneath the stars without even

a tent over our heads. The river we follow farther and
farther into the mountains is possessed with every magic a
river has had allotted to it. Clear green to the bottom—
rushing and tumbling—cool to go into, cast over, and full of
trout that live behind the jutting rocks under wild rose
bushes. Each night we camp by it, and when we leave it I
shall go into mourning. Tomorrow hope to reach the elk
country. I am very well—very thin—hungry at all meals
and find this sort of thing even more utterly enchanting
than two years ago. Just now the only sounds to be heard
in the world are the crackling of the logs and the tinkle of a
bell round one of the horses' necks a hundred yards away in
the dark. While the serene stars shine down over us. I must
not write any more, for the firelight is beautiful but not
very steady. Good night.

> *Your loving son,*
> *D.*

Camp 6, Thursday, August 11.   A long stage yesterday
—twenty-six miles. We've left Wind River and are at the top
of the large range, just at the beginning of the Pacific slope.
An hour after starting yesterday we found a pool with ducks.
George killed six and a rabbit. We lunched on four of them,
and I caught some trout. Then after lunch George killed three
grouse on our way, at the edge of the timber. Then we
entered the timber and came up and up on the Sheridan
Trail. About five, Tigie sighted an elk and I missed as good a
shot as I ever had. Then we came over the ridge at sunset.
The range to the north stood out over the pine surface, a gray
blue broken into blacks of jagged peaks and corners like ice-
bergs. Here where we stay for two days or so, we have put up
the tent. This morning slept late. Tigie, while after the horses,
killed an elk. We are camped in a clearing of green undergrowth by a very cold spring. (Yesterday we passed by some

snow.) The pines surround us, and down the hill to the west is a splendid range of mountains.

At Tigie's Elk. Yesterday we lunched on wild duck and dined on trout and wild duck. Today we breakfasted on grouse. We'll lunch and dine on venison. This bull [shot by Tigie] must weigh 800. Too bad his horns are in the velvet.

Saturday, August 13. Great God! I've just killed a bear, and I'm writing this by his bloody carcass—6:30 A.M.

I looked down towards Jackson Hole and saw the ragged leavings of the thunder cloud prowling up the slopes of pine hills, beyond which the ice-sharp points of the Tetons glittered with snow and sunlight, and over the basin hung a brilliant golden cloud that swam in the rays, while all the other clouds were black or gray.

As I write [in the evening after killing the bear], we hear the ominous howl of some beast that would like to come into camp, and may before morning. The Ward-Dimmick hunting party that started from Washakie after us came and camped next door this evening. But they realize they are trespassing on our hunting field and are to move on tomorrow. Also there is a horse thief hanging about them and us. Altogether we are in good company what with the bears, the catamount now howling, and the horse thief lurking about in an unoccupied manner. He sat by our fire tonight for about an hour without speaking a sentence or meeting anyone's eye. How we killed the bear I must record tomorrow, as it is ten (very late), and George and I get up at four to visit the bait. It is fearfully cold.

Tuesday, August 16, 8:30 P.M. I return to Saturday's work. We went to bed Friday night, having settled that

George and I with Tigie should visit the south bait in the morning. The weather was uncertain. Sometime during the night I waked and heard rain patting the canvas overhead steadily. Later I waked again in the dull gray and shivered and was sorry we were going to any bait at five in the morning. I went to sleep, hoping Tigie and West (who was to wake us and give us something to eat) would oversleep. But they didn't. My foot was pulled, and I rose and shivered into my cold greasy boots. We had some tea and bread and started.

The way was uphill at once, and in this altitude (the aneroid registers 8900 with a fall in the weather that probably would take 600 off the reading of the barometer) breathing is a desultory operation, and a rifle becomes wonderfully heavy in five minutes. But it was necessary to follow Tigie like his shadow. I tried to make as little noise as he did, slipping by jagged rotten boughs, letting his shoulder go an inch from them and stepping over the twigs that lay thick in the timber. His moccasins slipped over them with never a crack. Luckily the rain had wet the ground enough for the twigs to be pliant; so our boots made much less noise than they would after a dry night.

And so we went over the grass and under the trees till we came to a gulch where a little stream flowed, and Tigie pointed among the trees where the bait was, though it was too far among the thickets to see. We became more silent and snaky as we circled beyond the place to come down on it under cover. Just then the sun rose feebly into a very light blue sky and sent some useless rays across the tops of the pine trees behind us. Now we peered over some brushwood at the bait. It hung there alone, and as we searched its neighborhood a squirrel burst into scolding directly beside us. After the sudden start it gave me, coming in the middle of such a tense silence, I could have flayed that squirrel alive. He would have suggested danger to any moderately intelligent bear. Also

53

some of the gray carrion crow birds that swarm in this country began to talk and caw. So we came up close to the bait and saw it had been torn and mangled by big jaws recently. The other piece near it, but just inside the timber, was untouched. Tigie said that at sunset the bear would return and so should we. We returned our steps somewhat wearily and found breakfast hot.

As we were finishing it, Tigie, who had gone to get the horses into camp, suddenly appeared over the rise to the northeast of camp beckoning violently from his horse. I grabbed my rifle and rushed across our bathroom and pantry (viz., a stony little hole in the thread of water on which we are camped) and up through the wet brush to him. "Bear! Bear!" he said. "Jump up here. Go. Quick." He had seen a bear crossing on the edge of the timber some three hundred yards beyond. So I jumped on the bare rump of his horse and sat there behind Tigie, my rifle in one hand, the other on his shoulder. Away he started, trotting and galloping. My horror was that I should slide off somewhere with a crash and ruin the whole thing. For the way we went was over anything that happened to be in the straight line that Tigie made for the gulch that we had lately left. Down across the stones of dry water channels, up their banks perpendicularly, under limbs of trees bending right and left to avoid them. I have never taken such a ride. Then we came across the gulch a good deal above the bait, and the feeling of hush came down hard on me.

Tigie whispered, "Over there, way over, down." I saw nothing but a wide grass clearing and pines beyond, but I got down among the sparse trees and so did Tigie. Then we crept forward. Tigie put me in front, and as I looked over my shoulder at him for directions I caught the horse's eye as he found himself alone, left behind watching after us with anxious self-control.

54

Then again Tigie said, "There," and crouched against the grass.

I looked across some three hundred yards to the edge of the pines and saw the bear leisurely sauntering along. I had wondered how it would be with me when this moment should come, and now found myself simply submerged in staring—no excitement, at best no shaking of any nerves, but only my eyes misted on that big beast as he rolled along by the edge of the wood. He looked brown and gray, and his gestures were those of a good-natured old gentleman taking a little morning air for health's sake. Now he would wag his head, then gaze at the landscape judicially, then pause at a rotten trunk on the ground, or sit up with it between his paws looking for insects on the damp underside.

"Quick," said Tigie behind me. "He come then—so-so," pointing the course the bear would come along.

I hurried forward nearly parallel to the bear's march and sat behind a good wide tree, Tigie at my side. The sun was now bright as I looked across the intervening grass. The bear arrived at where the line of woodland curved down more in my direction, rounding off the end of the lawn some hundred yards ahead of where I sat holding my rifle and wondering when it would begin to be unsteady in my grip. Slowly the bear came down, admiring the weather and pulling his rotten logs. Then he passed behind a tree that stood in the middle of the open. I looked at Tigie, who nodded. Then I ran forward out on the grass, and the bear's head came out from the further side of my tree. I shifted my course so that he and I were like the opposite spokes of a wheel of which the tree was the center, only I neared the tree as quickly as I could. Each time the bear's snout showed to the right of it, I edged to the left correspondingly. When I got under its branches, I stood up full height (for I had been mincing along in a very hunched up position), and the bear walked out into full view on the other side. He saw me then and stopped short. Well, my hand's steady after all, I said to myself, as I looked at him along my rifle barrel. I remembered how the brown hair on his shoulder looked thick. I heard my rifle crack and saw him fall at once on his head with a slanting kind of rush and near enough for me to see the dirt scatter a little from his claws.

"Shoot, shoot!" screamed Tigie from behind. I did as I was bid, but I was loath to do it—that first lucky shot had been enough. He tried to get up twice, and before he was half way to his feet they rolled up under him and he tumbled in a heap each time, head downwards. But I shot.

"Shoot! shoot!" said Tigie, running out from his tree, and he worked his arms as if he held the lever of the Winchester himself. I felt like a murderer as I pumped the bullets into the poor old gentleman who swayed about on the grass, utterly gone. My last shot went through part of the skull and down into his throat almost to the shoulder, where I afterwards found its flattened remains. We turned him over and rode back to camp, where I found the betting was three to one against my having hit anything.

Camp 7, August 17. Got here in a stage of about nineteen miles. Alongside of Ward again. They've killed elk and antelope. On the way Mason lost his temper badly and maltreated a horse until I was obliged to say what I thought. West says it's lucky my remarks led to no further row. All right. But I should do the same again and take the consequences. When a man hits a horse with the limb of a tree so hard that it breaks over his head and flies ten yards and hits my horse, I shall generally have a word or two to say. What I said was, "Don't trouble my horse, Mason, and I think a

56

milder treatment of your own would be better." That seems to me the least any one could say.

Camp 9, Saturday, August 20, 9 A.M.   Came thirty-two miles. We are on the Snake River about seven miles below Buffalo Fork. Over Snake River is a wide plain, eight miles or so by about twenty long, an old lake bottom, and from it abruptly rise the Tetons gray and streaked with snow. They stood like steeples. The way in which they come up without any heralding of foothills seems as though they rose from the sea. At sunset they turned lilac and all their angles swam together in a misty blue light that was as if a veil had been thrown over them. Caught big trout and had an excellent swim.

Camp 10, Sunday, August 21, Head of Jackson Lake, 7 P.M.   Got here last night after thirty-two or thirty-five miles more. Harmony restored. The Tetons across the lake magnificent. Today I hunted all day for elk with Tigie, 9 till 4, in cross-timber—awful. Tracks everywhere—only two elk, which I missed like a fool. Our friend the horse thief joined us yesterday. He turns out to be a harmless shepherd with a nice dog who eats our supper when we are looking the other way. Ward camped by us again tonight.

Camp 11, Tuesday, August 23, 6 P.M.   We left camp yesterday morning early in order to get start of Ward and get this good camp ground. It is under a clump of nine pines that stand on the bank of Snake River. The Tetons are gone, but down the river is a ravine closed by a big mass of rock and snow that begins the Teton range. The valley here is wide with high pine hills on the west and east. George Norman and I started out at 6:30 ahead and rode over three miles of meadow at a gallop, passing the Ward outfit far to the right. Then our road turned up into the timber. We left the trail once to get a last look back over Jackson Lake and the mountains. The water stretched ᵄway between flat islands and into long inlets very smooth and blue, and to the west of it the ragged Tetons rose still more blue. Then we came back to the trail and rode through a very pretty valley covered with young spruce like a nursery. Below us to the right was a deep rocky little cañon, and cold air came up from the stream that was flowing where we could not see. The morning was clear and cold, and all our journey was done before the sun grew hot. We came here and found an old fire and some tent pegs under the clump of pines. Being first, we took possession, lighted a new fire and so forestalled Ward. I looked about among the grass and found a tattered legend in print which began, "This very fine old rum is widely known. . . ."

By eleven [o'clock] the others came with our harmless friend the horse thief and his dog. George and I fished. He gave up, and I kept on and caught seven by evening, all very large. West and Copley took a walk and brought back some squirrels for food. We are out of the game country. This is the last of the fishing, and next stage brings us in the Park, where no shooting can be done.

Camp 14, Saturday, August 27, on the Wagon Road from Geysers to Falls, 6:30 P.M. We have come a stage of twenty-five miles. We have left the Geysers, and I do not care to see them again. We saw Old Faithful, the Castle, the Giant, the Beehive, and several more. The Giantess we did not see, though she was expected hourly, being some forty-eight hours behind time. I do not like them or their neighborhood. The air has drafts of stenches through it sometimes like sulphur, sometimes like a stale marsh. The ground is drilled with hissing puddles and sounds hollow as you walk, and all healthy plants and grass keep at a prudent distance. At the geysers was an amiable but foolish Englishman in our army who spoke of his connections and of his disapproval of republics.

We caught up then with the buckskin horse thief again, who had left us the day we stayed for West. Then we passed him again on our road today. It's a sort of savage imitation of the way one turns up on people at successive table d'hôtes abroad. Our journey today was tame and a bore. All along the highway, meeting tourists and dust. As we ascended a mountain before coming to Trout Creek, on which we are, the view of the valley was pretty, but that was all. Nothing but regular rounded hills covered with pine. After we had been here a little time, two men and two women drove up and camped thirty yards off. Then came two men, one thin and rickety, the other short, dressed in brown corduroy with hatband eyebrows, and they camped by us. Then came two more down the hill, and trailing after them Buckskin. Altogether we count fifteen souls, all camped together on Trout Creek.

Sunday, August 28, at the Lower Yellowstone Fall, 2 P.M. This is the most beautiful thing I have ever seen. The water falls from where I sit 300 feet into a caldron of rock that lies in deep shadow. Then the spray floats out into a rainbow that melts away into many-coloured moss, until you cannot discern which is moss and which rainbow. The yellow and brown sides of this cañon pitch down from the pine growth that fringes their jagged rims, and so into the green water that one can follow for a quarter of a mile in its turnings until it goes out of sight round a corner. The formation near the top goes into turrets and pinnacles, crowned with little spruce trees. Above all this the river is smooth and shallow. Then a series of rocky gates narrow it down into turbulence, and it takes the first plunge of 160 feet. This one region makes a journey worth while. The sulphur mountain with its boiling pot is curious as one passes—but not worth stopping at. It is about six miles above. "The Shepard party is here!" A curse on people who carve their names at these places. At the geysers they wrote in pencil at the bottom of any little puddle that was cool enough, and here as usual the trees are scarred with their impertinent initials. I hope they'll have to write their names in Hell with a red-hot penholder. The cañon seems so deep that the sky comes closer to the tops of the trees.

Monday, August 29. West, George Norman, and I are now having a hell of a time trying to get down to the bottom of the cañon, with ropes, sliding, teeth, etc., etc. I am at present sitting about nowhere—halfway down the side of the cañon—and George is above, undecided whether he will untie the rope from the last tree or not.

1:40—On the top again. West and I have been clear to the bottom, where nobody has probably ever been before. You get an idea of the vastness of the walls when they are above you. A glimpse of the top of the fall came round a corner, and we could see the spray clearly, but there was not a way to walk up the cañon. George Norman stayed by a halfway pine tree.

In North Pacific Train, Thursday, Cinnabar to Living-stone, Sept. 1. Well—it is over. George Norman and I started with Mason yesterday, and when we reached Gardiner, we bought a huge trunk and packed hides and ammunition away and so let Mason go back to camp. A freighter took my trunk on to Cinnabar. Gardiner is a collection of houses so meagerly built that they resemble theatre scenery for a sensational drama. George and I got something to eat and continued our road, rather dismally. The day was gray and cold, so were the mountains, and both he and I were blue because our trip together is done.

Palmer House, Chicago, Tuesday, Sept. 6. 1 P.M., *Dinner.* God Damn Chicago. (Later—in Chicago and Atlantic train.) Chicago is a great deal hotter than Hell. Nobody who lives there need be discouraged. I put on the garments of civilization in the freight house by the canal, surrounded by freighters who eyed me with fascination. I told them that California was the place to live and that they had better go there and drive out the Chinese. They are all going. My trip is nearly done, and I am very sorry.

During the past two months I have been mistaken for—

1. an Englishman
2. a drummer
3. a bartender
4. a stage driver.

The Englishman leads because I'm taken for one by themselves and my own countrymen at first invariably unless I anticipate the error by employing Western idiom. It is my clothes—for I traveled in a loose comfortable flannel shirt that came from London, and a soft cloth hat. My trousers and coat were also English, and this did it. But in another day or so I shall be back where nobody takes me for anyone but myself, and my period of entertainment will have ceased for a long while.

61

July–September, 1888

―――――――――――――――

WYOMING

NOTHING of note occurred during Wister's third year at the Harvard Law School. He wrote regularly to his mother, telling her about the parties he was going to, the books he was reading, and the music he was hearing in Boston. He did not ask for money to go West, at least in any letter to his parents.

He starts his 1888 Journal on the train and in high spirits. He makes no mention until much later of his two new guides. His old guides George West and George Mason were with him for the second time; Paul LeRose, a half-breed Indian, was new that year, and so was Dick Washakie, a full-blooded Shoshone.

Wister started on July 17 and returned September 18, and he wrote only once to his mother in all that time. His parents worried desperately and spoke of their alarm to their relations. When Wister realized the anxiety of his parents, he made up his mind never to let so much time go by again without more letters.

The 1888 Journal, which is an account of a thrilling and successful hunt for mountain sheep, does not always follow a strict chronology. Here as in other Journals Wister often returned to an entry or an incident that he had not finished in its proper order.

1888

Here begins Western trip the third—may I someday write the thirtieth with as much zest! We have been going most of two days now. Yesterday morning, George Norman and Bob Simes met each other at Jersey City and met me at Philadelphia.

Sunday, July 22. In Rawlins we encountered two deplorable things: a suspended bank which many stage drivers and such have put their earnings in; and a bootblack from the East who wished to black my boots. I found he was on his way to San Francisco, but his partner fell sick of an ague here and was in bed. I got some quinine for him, and he went on one or two errands for us, and made some silver. The stage company may not make any living for itself, but it assuredly swallows the livings of other people. There were three of us, and we had 400 pounds of extra baggage. For the journey of 150 miles we paid $86.20. Moreover, you have four horses and a wide Concord stage no longer. Two horses, and a narrow stage, and half our baggage left behind to follow us the next day. The express boxes from Chicago had now caught us up, thanks to Jack Tebbets, and here we left them behind again, along with all our blankets and all our ammunition. Also, the stage holding four inside and one out, there were some eight or nine to go.

Altogether, the time between our rising and our departure was a black period. We left Rawlins five in number. The balance stayed with our baggage to come when it could. Same driver as last year, and he remembered us, I believe. The other two were a Swede and a young but proficient card player. Both on a contract to build a school near Lander for the St. Stephens Indian mission with money left for the purpose by a good female Catholic. The Swede was honest and sensible. He had the regulation coloring and accent and could not drink the whiskey we offered him raw. Of course his name was Anderson. The card player had bright brown eyes and a wicked, winning smile. He could drink our whiskey. His eyes, he told us, had once been blue, but they turned brown after his attack of measles. Curious, if true. A pack of cards were produced, and he began showing his skill, which was very various and considerable.

We played all fours a good deal and so killed the day, also buying beer at one of the ranches where horses were changed. The gambler was only twenty-three. But he had seen more of life than all the rest of us put together. At stealing rides on freight trains, on top or underneath, he was an artist. We had only his own word for it; but he told us of his many journeys performed thus with too much circumstance and technique for doubting of his ability. There was more room for doubt in the tale which ended in his leaving a game of stud poker twelve thousand dollars to the good. "Well," he said, "it takes all sorts of people to make a world—and we've got Goddamn near the entire quantity." He had played with less fortune at Rawlins on the preceding evening. The first meal by the roadside, he did not come in to, but loafed by the stage and stable with his hands in his pockets, and a singular askew gait, very suspicious to see. Suspicions were fixed, when we looked out the ranch door and called to him dinner was ready, by the defiant way in which he announced *he* wasn't hungry. So we told him to come in and not be a fool. And the Swede Anderson paid for that meal, and ourselves took turn about with those that followed. He did not have a cent.

About six [o'clock] we stopped nowhere in particular with a hot axle. There was (naturally) no water, and no grease either. For grease the rest of my bottle of vaseline went, and for water a quart of our precious beer. We poured it tenderly and with care where needed, and the hissing and froth it made went to our hearts. This performance took near to an hour, and from time to time we halted after for prudence. So we grew more and more behind time, and the next driver, who came on about nine or so, when all warmth had gone and the moon shone cold and brittle, was a crank who lost half an hour for each one he drove. My turn on the box outside came about twelve-thirty or later, and that stage was bitter. The driver said he was numb under his coats, and I had no coat.

I do remember that the world looked very beautiful in the
moonshine, all lines being soft and uncertain and the sagebrush very silver-like—but it was too damned cold for
romance and nature. The look of my own shadow sticking out
of the shapeless black cast by the stage seemed to lower the
temperature. We ate the meal at five that should have been
eaten at one. This warmed me up, and the sun rose. By ten,
after we had all walked down Beaver Creek hill, the day was
scorching. We changed stages at the Frenchman's and broke a
whiffletree soon after. We got to Lander late, although the new
driver (No. 3) made up time in a highly creditable manner.
We gave the gambler potted chicken at Lander—also beer—
and there his carpenter colleagues met him, and that light-
hearted and vicious spirit left us without any sign or word of
formality. At Washakie Paul LeRose was sitting on the front
porch waiting for us.

The officers at the post were most cordial. Quartermaster Gordon, to whom I went at once, ordered us an
ambulance in which Lieutenants Buffington, Parker, and
Trout drove us to the warm spring, where we became clean
again and wore new underclothes. Then we sat up with them
and Gordon and drank his claret. West turned up that night,
and Mason. Both not changed a whit. Sunday we talked
matters over and decided to take a third man, Dick. Later,
Captain Smith, the commanding officer, called and asked us
to dinner, and a very pleasant time he made for us, he and
his wife and his whiskey.

*Camp 5, Sunday Morning, July 29, Headwaters of
Wind River.*　We came here up the narrowing valley, past old
man Clark and his domicile, the last inhabitant we shall see.
Bobby missed an antelope. I missed a big gander with my
rifle, but luckily Paul and George got the young ones by

67

chasing them. They were very good at supper. Here Wind
River leads up into the timber and is gone. This meadow is
the last one. Ahead of us the woods close in. Above to the
right is a glorious fortress of rock half a mile long—hundreds
of feet above the highest timber—and broken into battlements
and turrets by the hundred, with a big stone man sitting at
one end watching the valley. The sun shines along this whole
line, leaving the crevices filled with a pale blue floating colour
while the buttresses stand out brown-yellow in the daylight.
There's another fortress to the left and a long regular line of
wall joining the two, with a green timbered hill rising in front
of it—and so Wind River begins its journey.

Camp 9, Wednesday Afternoon, August 8. This camp
we came to on Sunday, and we had to work to get here. First
I will correct a slight error. Our last camp on the Snake just
below Crawford's shack was not six miles away from the
Tetons but fifteen at least, as every one of this party can now
testify through painful experience. The atmosphere in this
country is like all other mountain atmosphere—tricky. After
a sharp rain last Saturday evening, Bobby and I set out for the
geese which Paul had seen in a slue of the river just above. It
was too late. Moreover, had we shot any, a boat would have
been necessary to get at them, for a large belt of willow swamp
makes approach to their feeding ground impossible. But what
was tantalizing was the sight of five sand-hill crane roosting on
one leg along a sand island, hopelessly out of reach. I never
eat a bird I thought better than the sand-hill crane we had on
the Snake a year ago. May have been self and stomach, but
think it was the bird. Bobby and I returned to camp, drenched
through with the marsh, and found George had caught some
dubious looking fish, whose taste at breakfast was more
dubious still.

68

On Sunday morning George and I consulted the maps and found out just where we wished to go and just where we are now camped—but no thanks to the natives for that. The trouble that morning was twofold; Paul LeRose was having an old man's fit of crustiness (owing to his insides, I think), and he had never been or heard of where we wanted to go. He told us in husky and forbidding tones that he did not know the country west of the Snake. When we made a diffident allusion to two lakes that lay south of Jackson Lake, under the Tetons (we did not dare to call them their United States map Christian names, since the bare idea of a map gives Paul acute nervous trouble), Paul said he had never heard that there were any lakes there. This was his method of denying their existence. Then, how to cross the Snake at this place? Well, we told him to go and find a crossing at once, and in the meantime George and I went up a hill to survey our route but learned nothing in particular except that the prickly pear will penetrate a moccasin. After a while we packed and got away, a crossing of course being found within a mile.

Monday, August 13.   Why all the horses did not break each a leg or two, I cannot explain. I never was in a worse place. Long wet grass and weeds completely hid the scaffolding of rotting and rotten pine trunks that lay across this piece of marsh, and the ground was so boggy that often your horse lurched up to his shoulders in it and then frantically plunged forward and fell against the hidden timber. At the edge of this where trees began and the land suddenly rose steep, we became securely netted. Spikey trunks pointed down the hill, and had to be jumped over from loose stones to loose stones. Any pack horse with pretence to originality of mind chose a separate trail for himself and after following it a while, halted at a good distance off from the rest of us. My horse nearly fell backwards with me, so I hurried off of him into the oozy patch of mud. Getting over this piece of our road (certainly our road, for nobody ever used it before, and nobody will ever use it again) took an hour, and it was not much more than three hundred yards we traveled from the beginning of the swamp to clear going. There we followed up Snake River, which flows nearly due east here before bending south to Buffalo Fork. Presently it spread into the beginning of Jackson Lake, and still we kept along shore.

The lakes we were aiming for, we were pretty sure, lay south of our direction to some degree anyhow, but Paul, the crusty, continued his way in the van. I spoke to George, but George said we were going properly, and to a certain extent he was right. We were aiming generally for anywhere along the two little lakes west of the river, and had we continued as we were going, we should finally have come out (or rather scraped under and climbed through) on the northeast shore of the north lake. That route would have increased our experience of timber if we have not already enough for a liberal Wyoming education.

I gradually grew nearly as crusty as Paul—and kept riding to the south of the outfit, which Paul observed clearly enough but never turned a hair. At last we came to a fork and turned southwest, after having gone round two bays the lake made, instead of cutting south of them and so saving time, trouble, and temper. Dick Washakie's derision of Old Paul waked up now, for he said, "What a ridiculous trail we are taking." Dick, whole breed of Indian, has continual amusement out of Paul, half-breed and white man, as near as he can do it. Paul declines to speak anything but English to the Indians and affects to be without their instinct for trail-finding. But he claims a special white gift of his own for that Art. So Paul took us south, but not enough, and always into needless and very vile timber. So we came to the fork again and

told him to keep out of the timber in the sagebrush, and he
did.

All this time the great Teton range had declined to come
nearer though we had been making for it since starting. At
length we did make some impression on distance, for when
you looked up the valleys between the peaks, you could
distinguish particular trees from the mass and see the water
moving down. Paul had now got to riding about due south,
though we had pointed out to him a sinking of the pine woods,
just at the foot of the two most southern mountains, which
held out promises of a lake or of water at any rate.

As we passed a thinner share in the timber to our right
which looked as if it might get us near the mountains pretty
clear of tree-trunks, I suggested going through that way to
George, who agreed. Paul ventilated some wrath. "Why did
you tell me to keep out of timber if you want to go right
among it?" I diffidently said that I thought it looked thinner—and then added that of course I didn't know the ways of
the country very well and if he thought that would take us
into bad timber, we'd not go. "No, you chose that way and
you shall go," snarled ancient Paul, and in we went. Then I
think he thought he'd box me up—for he said, "I don't know
which way you want to go. You ride in front now." So I did,
and very fortunately I had hit on a pretty good pass between
thick woods—and we all got through without entanglement.
George's horse cut up—dashed him against a tree and banged
his jaw—but nothing really serious. I steered as well as I
could for the dip in the woods below the range, and we came
out on a big sage park. Paul has ceased to be crusty and rode
alongside talking affably on many topics. Then I rode ahead
some way to a ridge to look over if possible, but woods stood
in the way. It had been very hot for many hours, and nobody
had had any water or food.

As I stood on the ridge, I heard far off coming from the dip

71

a faint and sustained roar. When Paul came up, I made him listen. He said it sounded like water, and we went on. He had been very sceptical about lakes and water over here all day, and presently it returned on him. We went up a ridge over which we expected to find ourselves close to mountains and water, and then in front stretched a big yellow waste of sage and cobble stones as wide and flat and dry as the ones we had just crossed. On the farther side of it a belt of pines, and then the mountains rose at once.

"Well, we shall camp without water tonight," said Paul with a cackle of triumph, though not a joyful one.

"Listen again," I said. The roar was just as sustained as before and much louder.

"Oh, that's the mountain wind," said Paul.

Then Bobby came by and said that George said the lakes must be east of us now—there could be no room for them in front. Till this I had kept unshaken faith in lakes and water ahead, but now I passed a bad quarter of an hour during which Dick came by hilariously repeating, "No water! Camp tonight—no water!" and West looked at the belt of pines and saw no cottonwood, which led him to join the chorus.

But where, I thought, in creation is a big mountain range 20 miles long and 1,300 feet high with snow in giant patches and green valleys and no water at all at the bottom? Possible in the moon—but on this planet, nowhere. The situation grew strained, for we seemed now about two hundred yards [from] the rise of the Tetons. Dick rode ahead and came back laughing. "All right," he said. And so we came to a big rushing stream which slipped out of a placid shallow spread above and went into the woods below, foaming down rocks, perfectly clear and not cold. Next day we found one lake ten minutes ride above us and the other lake fifteen minutes walk below us, and water enough to drown yourself in or to float a fleet in—of canoes anyhow. The lake below us is the best of the two—very deep and jammed with trout. I'll detail here the resources of this camp. Of the following fauna and flora all have been killed, seen, or eaten by one of the party: black currants, raspberries, strawberries, red and blue huckleberries (the red new to me, and very sweet) trout, duck, mink, otter, porcupine, beaver, fox, antelope, blacktail deer, elk, moose, and an unknown black quadruped seen by Bobby and not likely to be anybody's dog.

Our camp could hardly be better, and we struck exactly the best place along this water system—below and above us is too much timber and too little pasture. On Monday, winning the matching, I hunted with Paul north—in timber all the time. Late in the day had a good shot at an elk and hit him. He fell down and kicked, and so like a fool when he got up and stood vaguely looking about, I concluded one shot enough and did not fire again. He had not fallen at once but sank down slowly. Well, he got away, and Paul was justly enraged. So was I, but luckily he and Dick found him an hour or so later, and we eat him. I should have probably found him myself; but Paul was so disgusted that with that and his affectation of not being an Indian he lost the elk's trail and got us all snarled up away off—and so we came home.

I don't yet claim to have the hunting training enough to follow a trail with unless there's more blood than this bore— but my economy of shots on this occasion was the act of a chump. Bobby went out with Dick, and maybe he saw a moose. Paul saw one with me, but the moose had the wind of us and left the country.

Next day, Tuesday, Bobby went with Paul, George with Dick. The latter saw not even a fresh track (to the south). Bobby unluckily missed about five animals, including all the venison species in the neighborhood. West and I struggled up the mountain range and found a lake perched about three hundred feet above us and game trail so thick that in spots it

smelt like cow stables. Sounds Western and romantic this—
but quite true. We also found the mountain as mountains
usually are, higher than when seen from the bottom. Going up
took us four hours. Very steep all the way—first grass, then
rocks, and lastly snow and shale. We did not get to any peak
but up to a collar between over which we could look into a wild
country below—and blue mountains far beyond in Idaho.
The view of the basin on this side has given me a permanent
and very accurate idea of the whole country here. On the way
down we saw two otter. Next day our account of this ascent
sent George, Bobby, and Dick up. They took much longer—
having all day—and reached West and myself and afternoon
tea on the lake up the hill. Next day, Thursday, we concentrated forces on young trout and netted some two hundred—making a whitebait effect of them that was quite
taking. I sat with my legs bare in the water on logs too long in
the morning and therefore suffered horribly from sunburn.
Fishing for big trout in the afternoon I fell in to my waist
and neglected to do anything about it. So got slowly and
surely chilled and then sick.

On Saturday, I went off alone to see if any trail could be
found over into Idaho between the Grand Teton and the
next to the north, opposite which we are. But one way
round the lake I did nothing but empale my poor horse in
the timber, luckily not deep, and the other way round I
found also impracticable by reason of timber into which I
did not penetrate. On this ride I spent a long time crawling
over the baking cobble stones and trying to screen my carcass
from three antelope behind sultry clumps of sagebrush. The
antelope grazed on, suspicious but not alarmed, and slowly
grazed their way to a position where nothing but pancake
could have approached them unobserved. So I gave up and
came into camp weary and my sickness not gone but worse
apparently. This day two mink came tearing into camp

together, all among the pots and kettles while all but I were at dinner. They were proposing marriage on the spot—and therefore ignored all other things. Result—she escaped, his skin hangs on a tree. Paul has trapped a fine beaver.

Camp 13, August 20. On Continental Divide over the ridge to the north of our last year's camp. Came here from Camp 12 on a north fork of Gros Ventre when nothing particular happened. Leaving there Saturday morning we were visited by Tosi, big Shoshone medicine man. He was accompanied by his brother-in-law and Master Tosi. He was on a hunting journey. Later we met his fifty or sixty horses, his two dogs, and Mrs. and Miss Tosi, who rode with a bird cage on the saddle. Mrs. Tosi jiggled a papoose.

September 1, Saturday. On Wednesday, besides George's fawn and ramling, Bobby appeared with an ewe. Next day, Thursday, was his in camp, and George and I hunted. We labored up the mountains behind us and along the ridge till far away up the next valley we spotted sheep. Unluckily the sheep returned the compliment; for after we had laboured down to the bottom and halfway up the slope on which they were, we carefully sneaked on to the place where they had been and saw them contemplating us from the extreme top. So we proceeded to labour up this new and equally high mountain. My horse is not up to such work, and puffs and trembles, so that I get off and lead him. Coming down anything, he betrays an uncertainty, whether sincere or affected I don't know, in his knees, so I get off and lead him down also. The result is that I get my share of exercise on any inclined plane we strike. One encounters finer and more frequent specimens of the inclined plane while pursuing

the mountain sheep than at any other pastime in which I
have hitherto indulged.

From the top we now achieved, we looked down into a
third valley similar to the two we had quitted so painfully.
Down it, very small and [word illegible] went the north fork
of Owl Creek, and beyond to the north and west bristled
a horrible litter of ridges thrown together anyhow. Eastward
you could see out of all this into the plains, evidently hot
under the sun. Where we stood it was cold. We had placed
the sheep behind a little rise along the top some three hundred
yards away. To get close, it was necessary to bear towards
them a little down on the side we had come up. The other
side was a precipice footing in shifting stones and shale and
so by jumps to the water at the bottom. Peering along this
side, we saw our sheep evidently on the watch. They soon
gave this up, however, and we started quickly towards
them, screened by a succession of little rises and hollows
that lay between us. We went so far near two hundred
yards and came over the last rise but one into the laps of
an intervening bunch of sheep which we had known nothing
about. They arose like one man and took to diving over the
edge of the precipice. I had a general impression of hind
legs and hopping, and of being at my best in profanity.
Not one of us was ready with his gun or his intelligence.
We indiscriminately stampeded to the edge, and there went
the sheep, hustling down over the stones, sliding and jumping
and dissolving away. We pumped a fusillade down the mountain. They skipped aside from the bullets that came too near,
zigzagging along and growing smaller to the eye as the
departed express train dwindles. Finally, they were mere
white dots, quickly adding distance to the separation between
us. You saw them traveling up a little bank, then you waited
while they went down the gulch beyond it, and come again

76

into view up the next little bank, grown a trifle smaller during the interim of their invisibility.

One only stayed on the mountainside. He may have been hit. George may have hit him. As sixteen shots were fired, so may others. The glory, to whomever it should be given, is not a spacious one. This sheep stopped every little while, and, seen through the glasses, perhaps he limped in a foreleg. We have not seen him since. This performance of ours had several direct results. The lead we squandered on the retreating sheep did not serve to increase their confidence in this part of the country, and the noise we made over it sent the band we had been trying to come up with, and had got within a hundred yards of entirely unsuspected, clear away over the mountains heading the valley at a pace that was smart, sustained, and effective. We looked round and descried them just curving over the final ridge so far away that there remained to them no colour and only one dimension—length. They might have been a handful of toothpicks. Behind them the sky, we now observed, was clotted with black and a wind came down over the breaks, hard and somehow always in your face. I buttoned up my canvas coat, but merely as a matter of form. My gun grew bitter cold in my hand, and my horse had taken to a new way of stepping that thumped me stiffly up and down. Perhaps it warmed him. So we went up towards the head of the valley, watching the big thunder cloud that we trusted was traveling parallel with our course. One last sheep moved away out of sight in front, and it became very much colder.

Two or three valleys off to the right, long black streamers led down from the cloud, waving mistily just over the pines, and if you looked hard, you saw the water come down in them. But still an [word illegible] strip remained between that and where we were, where the air was clear and no drizzling had begun. We went on a little way, and when I looked across again, the strip had narrowed and gray bars of rain were falling between us and pieces of woodland that had been unblurred the last time I had seen them. "Our only hope," said George, "is the wind." The wind was now raging from the storm straight to us. "Thunderstorms," said George, "come up against the wind, so that one may go away. But there does come a point where this ceases to be true, and that point may have come." I put on my rubber coat. When we got to the head of the valley, there was a very much larger cloud coming down on us, you may say across the wind. We turned, following the ridge towards the big needle which we had gradually got between ourselves and camp. Below us, began a new valley at the bottom of a caldron. On the other side of the caldron, the air became thick white; then a sheet of storm came across. The caldron went out of sight, and the hail began at a rate to chip pieces off one's ear. The ground swarmed with bouncing pellets, and they soon filled up the holes between the coating of stones which lay on the hillside.

We got down and huddled each under his horse, and the horse did as much huddling by himself as he knew how. You could see nothing but a general shooting slant of white. All the lines of the mountains were gone. I got the brim of my hat down against my collar, but not before a train of hailstones had rolled down my spine. Then George's science came to him once more. The lightning was constant and getting nearer. We were the only raised objects in the district, and we had four guns. So George got away from the group of horses, guns, and men and crouched along in the hail, and I crouched along after him. Every now and then a particularly ugly crash of thunder would happen, and this would seem to prod George a few feet farther away from the dangerous mass of attraction. I did not at all relish the

78

situation. I was chilled all the way through; my shoes had been cold a long while and now grew steadily wet. I dragged off a limp mass of slush once with my glove, and I pondered on the phenomenon of lightning. But when things got as bad as that, they became good, and I laughed sincerely at the whole business. I turned around and saw Richard's bent head and Paul wearing a most miserable expression and the shrinking horses with their tails tucked in and their heads stuck down and all four feet converging into a point under their middles. Turning again, I saw George, gingerly slinking a little farther away from electric annihilation. This gave me a notion of my own appearance, and I roared enough to have made me warm in any other weather but what was going on.

The hail melted on my rubber jacket and trickled down on my breeches where the seat of them is thin by the constant saddle. So far as the look of things went, it was mid-winter and no sign of spring. The pelting lasted a long time (Sunday, September 2) at the same unslacked rate, but at last it began to fall more gently and wetter, and the view thinned out in front till part of the valley came into sight very faint and with impenetrable hail coming down beyond. Everywhere was white that was not too steep for the stuff to lodge upon. Paul and Dick went off to look over the divide and see if we could go home a new way.

The men came back, having found nothing but precipices, and so we ploughed home the way we had come, slopping down the valley into milder weather where the ground was turning dark again, and where everything not mud and sliding stones was drenching weeds and grass through which brooks improvised for the occasion were taking their way unsteered. The little channels that had contained nothing but dry sand and stones as we came up now boiled muddily down to the main stream, with unmelted hailstones seething in them like a mass of hominy. As usual, I led my horse where it was steep, skating smoothly on the mud that caked on my boots. Once more we toiled up again from the valley bottom into the level of winter. No January ever looked whiter and blacker than the pines and snowfields near the top. Coming down into our own valley I chose a steeper and directer road to camp, having learned now to lead my horse downhill at a run. George took a milder descent, fit for a horseman, and I got home first, to tell of our luck.

We heard four shots not a mile off, and presently Dick came in ignorant, followed by George, displeased very naturally at Dick's leaving him. He [George] had struck a fresh elk trail on his way down, come up with the elk, and shot three, it turned out afterwards, much to his regret. We needed fat badly, and had come to boiling our meat. So George shot at two more, killing all three. He now ordered Dick to return and help pack the fat home. Paul had turned up then on hearing the shots. The slothful Richard resaddled and went his way. It was growing dark, and Paul refused to cut up the third elk, which was left, and still remains, to rot unused where it fell. Two were spike horns and one a four-year-old. All were thin and gave us but little tallow. So ended Thursday, August 30, a most instructive day, full of weather, wind, and experience.

On Friday, August 31, Bobby and I hunted, he with Paul and I with Dick. Each time I lead my horse up these infernal mountains, I wonder why I came at all and determine to keep repeating inwardly that this is the last of it. Then my breath goes so utterly that I can repeat nothing, not even inwardly. Then I come home at the end of the day ready to go again. No amount of training seems to inure you to this climbing, however. It seemed worse up that hill on Friday than it had ever been. Dick was doubtful of finding anything. "Too much shoot," he remarked, "run away."

But presently (it looked halfway up, but it wasn't) we passed very fresh tracks, and the ascent continued.

Some of the formation we crawled by was most extraordinary. Little pillars of round stones baked together in mud and planted on end supported each a single rock of another colour, set transversely upon them. This is a new variation from the colossal mushrooms and columns that sometimes jut from the face of the cliffs. Those seemed carved from a single yellow or red block, but these look as if large children had built them for diversion. The scaly spike of buttress we passed over on our upward career got so narrow at last that I kicked stones down into unseen depths to the right, and Barney, my horse, sent them rattling from his heels to the left. This sounds ticklish, but on foot it is not at all so. In the saddle I should not care to ride over such a place in pursuit of pleasure.

Now and then in a pause Dick took the glasses and surveyed our world. "No sheep," he always chuckled as he handed them back to me. I chuckled also, mirthlessly, for the sake of not seeming behindhand in the humour of the situation. At starting, Paul had been sulky. It was no use hunting today, he said. Dick and I reached the bare top and from it saw a great deal; the head of Crow Creek below, new amphitheatres of falling-off places where auxiliary valleys headed; new aspects of the dignified Needle; new surfaces of mountain tops, and a bit of far off plain murky in blue heat. "No sheep," said Dick.

We went along the ridge one way as far as we could without a balloon and scanned every bulge of pasture and every nook of rock. There we turned to hunt along the ridge the other way, towards camp. Doing this, we came face to face with Paul and Bobby, who had seen nothing in that direction. We all sat disconsolately down together and conversed but little. It was perhaps half-past noon. Time to

81

give it up and go to camp. Time to cross where George and
I had been the day before. I suggested this, but I fervently
hoped nothing so steep would come to pass. Yet here were
Bobby and Paul, each able to count a mountain sheep among
his slain, and I not able to make such boast. We all looked
vacantly at the hills below and around and saw nothing.

Then Paul said, "Well, now, Goddamn if dat doesn't
look as like a sheep as anything." He showed it to me. "Yes,
but it's a stump down there," I said, and applied the glasses.
"Why it is a sheep!" said Paul, "I seen his legs move." And
so did I just then through the glasses, also a pair of very
fine curling horns. We all sat very still among those stones
while the sheep looked up and down leisurely. He saw our
horses above us without much concern but not ourselves,
for he presently lay down near the bottom of a rocky gulch
the far side of which was in sight. Bobby offered to match
me [to decide] who should go down and shoot him, and this
enraged me so much that I declined to match and declined
to go when Paul suggested I should. My rage grew from
Bobby's having already shot a sheep and my having shot
none, nor had any chance to till now. But Bobby's sheep had
been an ewe and here was a fine ram, and also Paul had seen
it and not Dick. So as a matter of fact ill luck was all I had
to be enraged at. Finally we did match, and I lost. Then
Bobby suggested both should go, and I was not too proud
to forego the chance, by a long way! "He is not alone down
there," I suggested, "there is sure to be a bunch." But
nobody took any sort of notice of this suggestion, made as
it was by an amateur from the East. Bobby and I started
creeping down, having agreed that both should shoot together
and toss up if the ram was killed.

The side we went down was a surface of rolling stones
with scanty patches of grass and an occasional steadfast
rock. It was next to impossible to move any section of one's

82

frame without starting a string of stones that gathered noise as they went and finally sprang into a rocky cañon that gave out hollow roars. The grass and the other objects affixed to the soil we traveled by as much as might be, bearing on the loose sand and shale as lightly as hands and feet could arrange it. The distance may have been three hundred yards; the time must have been thirty minutes, during which we worked down that slant and got the rocks at the side of the gulch between us and the reclining ram. Then we lifted up and saw him as he saw us and rose. Bobby fired a trifle the quicker, and both our shots came about twenty yards from him, he being about fifty from us. He walked leisurely toward us, and I don't remember whether we fired at him again or not; for now from behind every rock below horns rose up like things out of a trap door, and we were invaded by sheep. They came straight up to us, evidently not understanding the matter in the least. I saw their big grave eyes and the different shades of their hair and noticed their hoofs moving there, but whether they came by fast or slow or what number there were, I cannot remember at all.

Last year during the long preface to shooting my big bear I was perfectly cool and actually watched to see when my hand should take to trembling. This year the crawl down the mountain, the suspense, and this ambush of sheep, though I had suspected it, set me shaking so as to turn me and my gun useless. I did succeed in getting a bead on the broadsides of two, for I remember following them along a moment before pulling the trigger. They crossed over our ground, dived down and up the little cañon over the next ridge one hundred yards off, and some, but not all, disappeared to reappear farther away, and so at last Bobby and I stood alone. The sheep that had not come up again from the first disappearance will never be accounted for. The

two men were running along the top of the mountain. They
went out of sight, and we heard them firing repeatedly. Bobby
and I still stood so disgusted with our performance that
silence reigned. I thought I heard a struggling in the little
cañon close by and went to examine, finding nothing. As
I came back, Bobby exclaimed at a returning sheep. Sure
enough one was coming back over the ridge, but higher up.
Then Bobby saw another coming the same way but at a
little distance from the first. This one I never saw, and he
disappeared from Bobby's view and remains unaccounted
for. I began to fire at the other one, who turned out to be
wounded. Mindful of my elk experience at the Tetons, I
proposed to pump away at that animal until he fell once
for all or my lead gave out. So I fired and missed him and
fired and missed him.

The improvident Bobby's cartridges had already failed
him. Though warned by George not to start out for a day's
hunt with only five shots, that is what he had done. I had
brought sixteen and now hauled out one of mine for him, but
it was .45–90 and he uses .45–70, which neither of us had
thought of when he asked me for ammunition. I had hit the
rock just above the sheep's back, then seeing where it struck,
I had fired too low and shot just between his legs. He had
walked about at first but now paused, wavering and swaying,
his mouth dripping blood. Bobby called out he was going to
drop, and so it looked, but the elk stuck in my head and will
continue to stick there as long as I go hunting, so I fired
once more. The sheep dropped dead. Paul and Dick came
over the hill, and at my urgent suggestions Bobby trailed
down the cañon taking my rifle. If one sheep came back
wounded, why not another? Then the men and I came
together at the dead sheep, and during the cutting him up
it turned out that they had not shot him as we supposed,
but one of us. They had fired parting shots after two sheep

they saw running away, had missed them, and on their way back had jumped up this wounded fellow and turned him back into our gulch. We finished cutting him up, he was very fat and heavy, and Bobby returned having not sighted the other sheep he had seen come back. Pretty surely he was wounded too, or he would never have come back on his tracks. I offered to stay with Bobby and hunt him up, taking care to obviate any reluctance that Paul and Dick might evince at prolonging their work, by assuming they should go to camp with the meat and head. But Paul at once doubted if the other sheep be wounded at all. Why did he come back then, instead of running out of the country like the others? In order to stay with the wounded sheep.

This highly developed devotion shown by the mountain sheep places it at once among the front ranks of intelligent mammals, and not far behind the human species. Yet tame sheep are not conspicuous for their powers of thought. In my experience of other stampeded game, I have never seen the well ones stay behind to comfort the wounded ones with their company, but in my ignorance of the habits of mountain sheep, I could not dispute Paul's dictum on this point. After some more talk from me of taking the doubt and staying behind to see about the sheep who had played the nurse so faithfully, Bobby decided he preferred to go home; so home we came, with one sheep out of five, and thirteen shots fired. Bobby and I have decided that whichever kills another ram gives up his claim to the head we have. If neither gets another, we match for it.

September 18, Tuesday. On Sunday, later, Dick received a visit from three of his countrymen. After they had gone, we found they were one of the Sheepeaters, Tigie, and his brother. Tigie knew who we were, but having nothing to say to us except good day, he followed the Indian fashion and did not say that. West, George, Bobby, and I spent the day in riding up the head of Bull Lake. Had a fox hunt after a coyote who was nearly run down. But some bushes saved him. Today we go to Washakie, thence to the railroad. Good-bye, Wind River!

October—November, 1889

WYOMING

ON his return East from the successful hunting trip in the summer of 1888 Owen Wister went to work in the law office of Francis Rawle and Robert Ralston, 402 Walnut Street, Philadelphia. In 1890 he was admitted to the Philadelphia bar.

The incident to which Wister refers as the "Waln-Strong catastrophe" near the beginning of the 1889 Journal involved Maurice Waln, an Easterner who was murdered by his cook while hunting in Wyoming. The Waln family and the Wister family were lifelong friends.

1889

402 WALNUT STREET

July 15, Monday

Dearest Mother:

Your most delightful letter I have just read, and it is the first day for several years that I have had the slightest desire to be in Europe. Partly the things, but chiefly the people, you've been seeing in Paris, stir me to wish I was there. But I'm not. Before I give you my chronicle, I'll say what I can (all I know) of my plans for the remainder of this (for me) most *manqué* holiday. Being virtuous disagrees with me completely—probably on account of my stomach's unfamiliarity with the dirt—and of course the summer won't really have been a fizzle if I by hook or crook manage to light on some substitute for Wyoming that shall stow away the health I imbibe out there.

Well, I shall be at Butler Place till about the 25th—

in and out of town during the steaming day but conversing
with your widower during the evening. When I go to
Ned Tibbits for a few days chiefly because I've not seen
him for so very long and don't want more time to slip by.
I had better stay here and get through with my work,
but I'm compromising by "taking my work with me,"
though one knows exactly how much that means. Then
(when Miss Fox tells me I ought not) I shall try for
some outdoor life during August. It will be on the edge of
Maine and New Brunswick about twenty-four hours
from Boston—fishing and river and wood existence.
If Miss Fox says don't go anywhere in particular this
summer, I shall return from Tibbits, make Butler Place my
headquarters, and behave toward the widower like a somewhat vagrant daughter. Now don't ever speak of this to him,
for on this matter he is very naturally not in my confidence.

And now my chronicle. Mrs. Roosevelt asked me to
renew our acquaintances by spending a few days, including
the Fourth of July, at their house at Oyster Bay. She
promised music and Walter Damrosch. But I had other
and better plans, so sent my regrets. I left here on the
25th of June—a Monday—with Louis Biddle—arrived
at Boston, I descended on various pals, and that night
assisted at a most genial dinner of classmates, held at a
famous fish tavern down the harbour, where we steamed in
a tug accompanied by a harp and violin picked from the
streets by Emerson at the last moment. George Waring
and Fred Stone were the only others you know much
about. Gillig was expected but didn't turn up. I must
have allowed champagne to get further ahead of me than
I generally do, for Waring told me the next day (which
was Commencement) that about midnight I took him
outside the building to a somewhat vast and solitary [word
illegible] of stones and undergrowth and with my hand

to the sky remarked—"How much more beautiful the stars are out in these mountains than they are in the East."

Your loving son,
D.

Pittsburgh, Fort Wayne, and Chicago Ry., October 9. As this particular trip West is mostly by myself, I shall begin by putting in my diary minute items—just to see how much interest such may gather by the lapse of time.

Between Laramie and Medicine Bow, October 11. Pacific time at Council Bluffs and Omaha. Failed to see Jack Tibbetts. Man at station remembered me. Nine miles out of Omaha lost two hours over a drunken signalman, who showed the wrong signal and had a fight with the conductor—we made time today however. Talk in smoke compartment far superior today—no damned drummers. But two sheriffs who had just been catching horse thieves. One is from Rawlins and has had lots to do over the Waln-Strong catastrophe. He tells me they have not got the man.

In Stagecoach, October 12. Got into Rawlins this morning at 3:10 A.M. Got in parlor in company with a very long gentleman, at 3:45—called at 6:30. Nothing in parlor to wash in except the spittoon which didn't have any water in it. Breakfast, and off at eight. This is not exactly a soft journey. Stage driver sulky at my big trunk—ignored him. Two years ago would have tried to be winsome and whisked him up. Came up nearly to Crooks with Noble, the cattleman. Very pleasant time. But in truth this stage ride is an awesome thing and doesn't improve with familiarity. Now night is coming, and it's going to be cold. But think I have enough things. Sat yesterday in smoking car with one of the gentlemen indicted for lynching the man and the woman. He seemed a good solid citizen, and I hope he'll get off. Sheriff Donell said, "All the good folks say it was a good job; it's only the wayward classes that complain."

FORT WASHAKIE

October 14

Dear Mother:

There was an occasion when we were in Paris when my superstitious father imagined I was going to let you come home alone, and remain inside some trombone in Germany myself. It's just possible some such notion is lurking about him now. So please, if you observe it, assure him my plan is not to become a pioneer or a settler, even to winter here, but to return and complete the index of the law book on which Rob Ralston and I are at work and continue to walk down Walnut Street in the A.M. and up Walnut Street in the P.M. Now I must go and pay my respects to the wife of the Commander and the various other dignitaries of the Post.

Your loving son,
D.

Fort Washakie, October 15. Got here at six [o'clock] Sunday. Found West standing to see the stage come in. Since which time he has been my host in a way I can't persuade him to abandon. Spent yesterday in preparations and calling on the people at the Post. All were very pleasant and cordial. I got in terms instantly with the commander thus. He said, "You know, sir, I don't sympathize with you men from the East who come here and shoot our game." "Well, sir," I made answer, "Did you but know how little of it I shot, you would symphatize with me very deeply." He has offered to send an ambulance and a doctor for me if I get hurt. I told him that was a most comfortable idea to start off with. But he'd do it. Dined with Parker and sat up till twelve. Saw Stagner, Speed Stagner, who strikes me as the finest specimen of a male I've seen in this country.

Smith's Ranch, October 18. Horse Creek and Wind River. Got here at four [o'clock] yesterday—twenty miles. Played cards till ten, quite a gang here. Weather cloudy today—walked up to the ranch with West. The country is slowly filling up with people—i.e., a new cabin is building just above here.

November 19. Same luck here as everywhere. Gone all day up and down and nothing to show. The game has been hunted so hard by the Indians that it leaves any country into which an outfit comes. So today, regretfully, very regretfully, for the time has been delightful in spite of poor hunting luck, I say au revoir to them—the most enchanting mountains—and shall count the months until I can return to them. Wish I could spend the winter on North Fork.

> Would I might prison in my words
> And so hold by me all the year
> Some portion of the Wilderness
> Of freedom that I walk in here.
>
> The black pines lie far up the hills,
> The white snow sifts their pillars deep,
> And through the cañon's misty rifts
> From the cold West the storm clouds sweep.

92

Serene above their moving shapes
One star has burned into the sky,
While here in the gray world below
Over the sage the wind blows by,

Rides through the cottonwood's pale ranks,
And hums aloft a sturdy tune,
Among the river's tawny bluffs,
Untenanted as is the moon.

June–September, 1891

WYOMING AND YELLOWSTONE PARK

IN a letter dated March 1, 1890, Owen Wister explained to Oliver Wendell Holmes that he could not join the Judge in Europe that summer. Wister's mother was in Europe traveling with her mother, Fanny Kemble, and would not understand it if he did not join them. "So my holiday with you melts away. So also will any Western scheme of outdoor life—I am about certain. The shock that the murder of Waln—out in my country by his cook—gave my parents, has been lately revealed to me. And I find that it is so nearly more than they can go, to have me vanish for six or seven weeks unheard of, that I'm baffled out of being able to draw the line between selfishness and resigning what I love better than anything on earth—and love more and more each year I live."

But in the summer of 1891 Wister, who was still a lawyer and had published no Western stories, was able to go to Wyoming again. This was perhaps his crucial trip, for, as we see in the 1891 Journal, his ambition to write Western fiction began to stir. More and more in following years the Journals became a writer's working notebook.

One of the incidents he witnessed and recorded that summer—the deliberate gouging of a horse's eye—turned up three years later in the short story entitled "Balaam and Pedro," published by *Harper's Magazine* in January, 1894. Rewritten, it became a chapter with the same title in *The Virginian*. Theodore Roosevelt, to whom the novel is dedicated, asked Wister to omit the description of the actual gouging from the book, though it had appeared in the magazine. "Roosevelt," Wister says, "was almost fierce about it. We argued about it for several years."

1891

June 9, Morning. Last night in the smoking room was bored by a humorless Southerner from Chattanooga who talked to the conductor and me of how best to make dollars and how times in Chattanooga were going to be slack. There is no escaping these fetid commercial bores. Every state in the Union seems to spawn them, and they infest every mile of railroad in operation. Their song is always the same—booms in Kansas City, dead times in Omaha, skinned Yankees in the South, capital moving to Denver— and outside these facts that nobody but a fellow brother of the spawn cares to hear, their minds are a howling wilderness.

If it was said to what is called a "good American," he'd say it is these people and their ways that build the glorious prosperity of this country. Well, it isn't these people. It isn't bogus land booms that flare up and vanish, and it isn't the selling of a worthwhile or worthless mountain to somebody else for coal, that makes the glorious prosperity of this country. That's the most these commercials do, and [what they do] does not enrich the country. It merely robs Peter to pay Paul. These people produce nothing, improve nothing, and help nothing, except when they help themselves to somebody else's money by menacing—cheap, juggling on the one hand, and silly credulity on the other. Still, all this is old, only nobody has said it out, hard and clean, and indeed what would that accomplish except making any "good American" who reads it angry for fifteen minutes.

But let me say something I have never seen or heard said, and that is that the faces, the minds and the talk in these commercials in the Pullman cars, are inferior to those in the conductor who takes the tickets and the brakeman who swings the lamp. These latter are not forever squatting on the alert to make somebody believe something that isn't true and fall into a bad bargain in consequence.

Slowly today crops and trees and grass and farmhouses grow more and more rare. Then I looked out, and the round green hills were gone and the big empty country had begun. There came two bunches of cattle and cowpunchers circling among them. At this beloved sight I almost cheered aloud in the car. The strangest sun set; don't let me forget it. Over the bare plains in front, and all around us, a sluicy downpour of rain, the clouds brick red and luminous against the horizon, on which the sun, a blurred fluffy ball of yellowish light was resting, while continual streaks of blue lightning quivered down straight across the looming disc. Now, the rain has gone, and on a platform when we stopped just now, I looked westward and saw the sky still light, and the silhouette of the long monotonous hills clear as a knife edge against it.

After two years, this glorious, this supernatural atmosphere meets me again better, clearer, more magical, even than I remembered it. As for every word I could get together that would give the faintest notion of its beauty and its effect on the observer, that can't be done by me and hardly done at all, I think. I'm going to try in "Chalkeye" however![1]

Chadron, June 10. Reached here at 2:15 A.M. this morning. Then up and breakfast and off on this train which takes from 6:30 A.M. till 7 P.M. to go 192 miles. It has one passenger coach behind a miscellaneous assortment of great

[1] [No manuscript of this title has been found.]

freight and stock cars, and the engine is always just around the next curve and can be identified only by the jetting black smoke it shoots heavily up. I don't object to the gait of this train. It oozes along through the draws, and the sun blazes comfortably down. I sit on the back platform and find it great luxury to stare at the things I know so well. Not a house, not an animal. But the train goes so slow that the birds sing louder than the noise it makes.

Every now and then a cracked, dry watercourse up through the mounds, and on its bank black, stiff, little pines whose trunks and boughs are twisted in leaning contortions, as if they had been lazily stretching themselves and caught forever midway. Now and then a stream, whose little green valley is choked with cottonwood and bushes. Then a bald station and "town," ragged cattle, wire fences, wooden mansions suggesting that firmness and permanence of stage scenery. Then more trundling, with occasional trestle work over a chasm along which a lonely trail winds below. We're too late, nearly an hour. But I don't seem to care. Sometimes the country makes you think of a face without eyebrows. The occasional windmills look like stage setting too. So do the solitary meaningless sheds one passes. All seem constructed to be shifted at a moment's notice. Then a man with a huge broad hat comes by driving a team slowly, and apparently from nowhere to nowhere. I was amused at a pencilled legend on a way-off forlorn shell of a cabin. Supper time.

Now we emerge into a wider country and no more birds or rocks, or anything. This is the country without eyebrows. I wish John and Ned—oh, I wish!—they could see all this and say the pictorial thing. Can I apply acid to my English, tell nothing till the sharp cutting metal is left? Just now the landscape is jammed with deserted forts and breastworks.

99

All of the glacial period. What is the colour of this? Dusty green and light brown—buff. I'm rejoiced to recognize in the air once more the full pungent aroma of the sage.

THE VALLEY HOUSE
DOUGLAS, WYOMING

June 11

Dearest Mother:

This town of Douglas is typical and not unlike the pillar of salt near Sodom. The saloons are harmless solitudes where young ladies might sew. My dispatches are likely to become scarce now. I can't tell exactly when you'll get another. Possibly not for three weeks. For now I can jump off, my baggage having turned up. I go for a while to Cheston Morris at his ranch, then come back through here and so by branch trains and changes to Rawlins, having met Lawrence Brooks, Charles Penrose, and Bob Ralston.

Your loving son,
D.

Douglas, June 11. The Valley House. All is as I had expected. I'm going to note it down, however. The one-track silent railroad and buildings. The town at one side, an acre back. On the other side, a stretch of land, prickly-pears, grease plant, cans, here and there a cow's skull, would go down to the muddy, wrinkled river sliding quickly along, and barren bluffs beyond it. The town, though laid out at right angles with wide streets, is a hasty litter of flat board houses standing at all angles, with the unreal look of stage scenery, always that same artificial soon-to-be-changed-for-something-else look.

Here and there a taller square brick building destined for commerce that never came. On a bottom bench of sand and sage above the town, a large brick schoolhouse that will be mostly empty as long as it lasts. The streets, though having oc-

casional board walks, present no defined shape and are empty
of horses and men. A clump of men here and there round the
open door of a stable or a saloon. But stable and saloon are un-
troubled with customers. Rebellious very young babies squat
on the board walks and howl with rage at the parent voice
within. The town reminds you of a card town, so aimless and
unsubstantial it seems. Douglas is a type. It was once the
terminus of the railroad. That fact turned a few acres of desert
into a booming hilarious drunken town in a few hours. There
were corner lots, and there were the brick buildings. Then the
terminus went fifty miles west; and this little sordid hustle of
artificial prosperity went as it came, passing like some small
blizzard into lands unseen.

There stands Douglas like a pillar of salt, a monument to
the reckless animal spirits of the American vagrant. There are
no mines here. Farming is impossible. The cattle traffic lan-
guishing and needing not a center here. There was absolutely
nothing that could possibly make Douglas a real place. The
bleak country is in tune with this. Douglas is surrounded by
the monotonous rises and rolls of sandy sagebrush desert, on
whose ridges break and show the grim ruinous fortified rocks.
Beyond and far away to the southeast, tall hard-looking peaks
that suggest neither forests nor streams among them. I
hinted at the bank that Douglas must be quieter these days,
and the swift assurance I got of the great business done here
left my impressions deepened. Then I sat among freight at the
depot and talked to an employee, who told me the whole
story.

Douglas had boomed, Douglas was dead. I spoke of the
schoolhouse. I found the walls were cracked so that in winter
the few scholars had to be dismissed, as the cracks let the wind
through, though they had been stuffed with raw cotton! There
are six saloons here. The man who spoke, though handling
freight for $50 a month, spoke excellent English, I mean edu-

cated English. Each saloon paying $300 a year for its license. But they sent the second teacher away from that school for lack of funds.

I passed a diverting evening with Dr. Richards and the army doctor, hearing remarkable stories round the stove in the hotel. Stories of bear and of the habits of wives of post traders. And one of Col. Andy Burt and Judge Fuller.

News of my trunk! Am relieved. It's on today's train. So I go on. My freightman told me how living at Douglas was dearer than at Chadron. For during the boom wholesale dealers East had furnished goods for which they had never been paid, so that now they recoup slowly and charge an additional per cent to the buyers here or west of a certain line. Douglas has 350 inhabitants, [including] 50 children, and these 50 are all who go to the three churches, Episcopal, Methodist, and Congregational. Hard to identify the latter, as it resides in a decorous shanty marked "Boot and Shoe Store." Well the train has come and so has my sack, a little untied but I hope that not otherwise changed. Mr. Richards very pleasing and civil. He has a son at St. Paul's.

At Tisdale's, June 13. I reached Casper at seven [o'clock] the night before last, passing desolate deserted Fetterman and Wolcott's station. Saw George Mitchell, who piloted me to a bargain with a pleasant sandy-faced little scrub for his team. Hotel food, vile. Town of Casper, vile. Left yesterday morning in buggy with tough pair of little horses. Off horse a very delicate kicker indeed. Came here, sixty-five miles, at 7 P.M. Dreary country, bad, worse, if possible, than Rawlins to lost soldier. No water except poisonous wells. My scrub knew all the people I do, and beamed when I mentioned Chalkeye, who it appears got a windfall of $5,000, went East, and is married. I didn't tell him I aspired to be the author of a

102

book called "Chalkeye." He gave me news of Tom King and was enthusiastic about West; [he] let me note for future use his talk of roundups.

Four days nearly without water. Old bulls lying down to die, and left so. Cattle at evening with eyes sunk through thirst. Little north breeze springs, ah! They throw their heads and tails in the air and stampede. All people jumping for rocks to get out of their way. The cattle have smelt Willow Creek on the breeze and travel on the trot till dawn, when they break into this ranch pasture. Old Tisdale routed out and furious. But when he hears how it is from the foreman, is very helpful. Cattle water to their heart's content.

This sort of event could be worked up splendidly. Also, steers travel faster than cows. When they get too far ahead, cowpunchers turn them off trail and they fall to grazing. When they're put on trail, they know what "travel" means. We killed a rattlesnake. We saw a few antelope. Powder River is a beastly stream.

But Tisdale's ranch stands where good country begins. There are cottonwoods in the bottoms, and the river twists out of the dreary empty plains here and gets among pleasant sunny bluffs, and timber lies only a little back from it on steep hills. Morris left here twenty-four hours before I came. So did Tisdale. But they'll be back soon, so the German (or Swedish) cook said.

I spent the night, and am now much at leisure—very pleasant delightful leisure. Rose at five, breakfast five-thirty. Then the four men went off in various directions. Cook's at the house. My scrub is loafing by himself, as I am. The day was cool till lately, with the clear sky and the "light that never was on sea or land." This can transfigure even such hopeless god-forsaken country as this at the south edge of Tisdale's, and make it seem like a piece of Paradise, though a flat one. Wish I could draw. Writing is so wretched. But I am bound on this trip to lose nothing. Former experience has taught that you can hardly make a journal too full. I hope I shall be able to keep it up and get down in notes, anyhow, all the things that are peculiar to this life and country.

The ranch buildings on the river make the usual flat cluster of low brown cabins and stables and corrals, and fences all brown. One gets the effect of universal logs. Irrigated garden behind, irrigated area of grass in front. Ditches dry, but their carrying will start this evening when the water will get down from Willow Creek. Little incipient trees in grass area, beyond which, fence. Earth very dry. New gawky unstable iron pump at kitchen door, sunk (they say) not deep enough. Horrible water spits out of this. Smells like dead things, but is only highly chemical. River muddy and chemical too. There's a cellar and a dugout. Scott and Dickens and Shakespeare in study, with heaps of magazines. All cosier and more comfortable than many ranches I've seen. Much ground fenced in. Thousands of acres. And Tisdale has the water rights of Willow Creek. The land is particularly green this season.

Riverside, June 16. On Blue Creek. It stormed Sunday afternoon, and all yesterday. Lay about, reading and sleeping. Rode over here this afternoon to get mail. Prospect of a troubled night. The beds are said to be turning with an energetic colonization.

Riverside, June 17. Shared bed with Tisdale on floor. No bugs there. Not much sleep either. Today the surly weather is gone, and again comes a cloudless sky, and the birds piping. No mail came. On way here yesterday, passed emigrants on their way from Black Hills to Oregon. Three slow-crawling wagons ("prairie schooners") with their white

104

tops and long teams. A woman riding straddle, several other women and any amount of children. The women do this work, and the children are begotten and raised along the journey. A miserable population. These people, it seems, have been moving in this way pretty much all over the continent west of the Missouri, settling nowhere. Comment on them in the cabin last night was severe.

The bed, as usual, a tray of rough boards on four legs, filled loosely with half-folded blankets and greasy mounds of canvas slung over them. This particular canvas stained with the blood of a man who was killed here in the spring. Here is part of his history: A good and boastful rider, who could break any broncho. Forged, and was sent to penitentiary. His sister got out a petition, and he was let out. Then he came back here to work for the Bar C (or the NH or the EK, or some outfit in the neighborhood). He said one day how he would show his way of breaking a colt, which was to ride him at full speed and throw him suddenly. So he got on one, and they watched him fly over the grass for two hundred yards or so. Then he leaned, seized the hackamore on the right side of the pony's mouth, and jerked it hard down, swinging the pony to the right, who instantly rolled over and up with the man still sitting in the saddle. But as they looked, he sat strangely, and tilted backwards, crooked, with his head on the horse's rump, his spur caught in the single cinch of the California saddle, and so holding him on. They took him into the cabin when they got to him, and he died twelve hours later, never speaking. His whole insides seemed to have been crushed to pieces, for when they came to put him in a coffin thirty-six hours later, he was so swollen that he had to be jammed and packed down. His grave is up on a rise of ground. I rode by, with a look at the little wooden post to mark it. His sister is coming to fetch the body away.

By the trail north of here lie the bones of an old fellow

found shot some years ago. It is suspected his employer, whom he had left the morning he was found, shot him. Teams come by constantly, but he has never been buried. This is not thought well of by Smith, who says it is a disgrace "T'have lef' him there thet way like a cow." Lately someone went to appropriate his boots, Government boots, but on picking them up, the bones of the feet fell out on the ground. So the boots are there yet alongside of the bones. Also someone has set the head on a stake.

Mail still not here. We shall stay another night here. Just had a delicious bath in Blue Creek. Some of Smith's conversation: "That's a terrible plain woman Hank's got. All driven and dried up. Looks like a picture on one of these shoo-fly boxes. But she's jest as joyous as one of these leave-me-alones. Old Westfall hates her. He calls her 'that buckskin son of a bitch'. . . . Got that boy Mose down at the EK yet? He's a Jew. Got the oldest-looking head in the world on him. Looks as if it'd wore out four bodies. Put him in a tent with that head stickin' out, and you'd swear that he was a hundred years old. . . . Old Gregg's a cunnin' man. Wanted a woman. Couldn't get none in this country as was willin'. Went out to England and fetched one along aback. Told her he had a large interest in the Powder River Cattle Company. Well, she comed and learned he had an interest. Had a cookin' interest in the roundup sometimes. But she couldn't find her way out of the country. Had to stay with Gregg. She'd been raised under a wharf there in Liverpool, and like as not she'd have struck west if she started out for England. She's here yet." In all this I omit many pungent expletives.

Still we wait. It's 6 P.M. The NH man strums on a guitar, and on Smith's open magazine a bedbug has just fallen from the ceiling. This strikes me as unjust. If I can secure one blanket tonight, I shall secretly sleep outside.

106

Back at Tisdale's, June 18.   Did sleep outside, along with Tisdale. During the evening a second bedbug dropped from the ceiling, just missing Smith's head, and falling on his book, as he sat by the lamp. This is evidently intentional on their part. Very cool and pleasant going to sleep under the moon. Was waked by the sound of imminent horse's hoofs—Coable with the mail. The river had been up, he explained. I wrote a line to Morris to be taken to the roundup. I trust it will reach him and bring him soon.

Taking the mail for the men at Tisdale's ranch, we left Messrs. Smith and Coable. We had two extra horses with us. I rode one, leading Syd, my horse of yesterday. Tisdale led a big sorrel, an outlaw because of his bucking habits, whom he proposes to make into a team horse. We came along comfortably by the Carrs' ranch on Middle Fork, passing three vultures who sat on some high bluffs with wings spread out to catch the sun. A curious sight.

When we passed the last gate on Carrs' ranch, Tisdale roped the horses we were leading, pretty close together, and started to drive them in front of us. The sorrel got a little way ahead on the trail and decided he was not coming with us. So he ran up a steep sultry hill towing Sydney after him. Syd was conscientious and had not a thought other than to follow the trail, but he was weak and had no other choice than to follow the sorrel. Tisdale drove his horse up after them, and they turned and made for the gate we had left. Down and up, into crazy ditches of baked mud and so back to the wire fence which stopped them. I came slowly after, not much use at this work. Then we started again, and in about two hundred yards up goes the sorrel on the other side of the steep little valley, straight among the red ridges above, dragging the harmless Syd after him.

Tisdale's horse, while he was dismounted at the gate, had

put his foot inside the bridle rein as it lay along the ground
dangling from the bit. The horse was stupid about lifting the
foot to free the rein. But I thought Tisdale unnecessarily
violent about this. To make the horse lift his foot, he jammed
his heel down on the hoof just where the hair begins, and after
several kicks the rein came free, upon which he dug his heel
into the other foot above the hoof, filling these actions with
the language appropriate to them. Then we set after the sorrel
and Syd, who were not on the trail but now climbing high
among the rocks. But the sorrel soon saw the place was too
steep and returned on his tracks. Then we chased them up and
down, I not doing much, and Tisdale forging heavily after
them, for his horse began to tire and breathed painfully. My
horse was tired too, for the ground was very broken and pre-
cipitant and the sun blazing down.

At length the runaways got far ahead of us, and I left
Tisdale kicking and cursing his horse, who was now able to
walk only. I took the high ground, pretty level and free of
holes, to keep the sorrel in sight, and Tisdale kept in the trail
below in the valley, his horse being too done up to go uphill.
I stopped, and he at last came up with me. The sorrel and the
kidnapped Syd were now away off still going over the uplands
at a good steady gait.

Tisdale dismounted and kicked his poor quiet beast, who
stood quite patient. He kicked its ribs, its legs, its jaw, and I
saw that red foam was running from the bit. I saw Tisdale
was insane with rage. "I'll have to ask you to swap horses for
a time," he said to me. "This —— brute's given out on me.
They'd never got away if he hadn't given out. Just refused to
go, for no reason whatever. No call to give out." Then he
resumed his kicking the animal and jerking its head. I jumped
off as soon as he said "swap," very anxious he should do so and
leave his wretched horse in peace. Beyond urging him to take
my horse at once and go, I said nothing. I felt like remonstrat-

108

ing, but I failed to do so. Tisdale seemed to forget about his intention of swapping. He continued to swear at his horse and kick it, and then I noticed him make several vicious grabs at its eye. Then he got into the saddle again, and the brute walked slowly forward with him some twenty yards in the direction of the vanished sorrel, leaving me dismounted and watching Tisdale's heels and fists beat the horse without pause. It stood still, too weak to move, and I saw Tisdale lean forward with his arm down on its forehead. He had told me that he would kill it if he had a gun, but he hadn't.

I watched him, dazed with disgust and horror. Suddenly the horse sank, pinning him to the ground. He could not release himself, and I ran across to him and found only his leg caught. So I lifted the horse and he got his leg out. I asked him if he was hurt. He said "No" and got up, adding "I've got one eye out all right." The horse turned where he lay, and I caught a sight of his face where there was no longer any left eye but only a sinkhole of blood. I was utterly stunned and sickened at this atrocious cruelty, and walked back to my own horse and sat down, not knowing very well what I was doing. Tisdale's horse struggled to his feet, and he mounted, and the animal wavered slowly away with him. Then he came back to me and asked for one of my spurs. I gave him both at once, with the idea of saving further brutality, for the spurs were not severe and all horses here answered to them from training. It turned out as I hoped. The blinded animal walked forward without any further violence in the direction of the runaways. I sat still where I was.

My first resolve was to ask for horses and quit this ranch at the earliest moment. I did not feel like eating the bread of a man whom I had seen perpetrate such a monstrous thing. I watched him grow distant, then followed him at a distance. We never saw the horses again, and so we came slowly home here across twenty miles of baking desert. Now and then we crossed some gulch where Tisdale was obliged to dismount and lead his horse down and up. It was too weak to carry him through these heavy places. Once it fell with a heap as he was leading it up a steep bank. I never spoke to him, nor he to me (after the first half of our journey). At first he would turn back and make some remark, but I answered only in monosyllables. He became silent, though I don't know whether he knew or knows what I was thinking. As we rode, my position became more complicated to me. I tried to think of other matters, but this damnable thing I had seen done kept burning like a blister through every thought that came to me.

Moreover, my own conduct in making no effort to prevent or stop this treatment of the horse has grown more and more discreditable to me. But, the situation was a hard one. Here was I, the guest, and the very welcome guest of a stranger, who had done all he could to make me at home because I had come to see his friend. He could have told me the horse was his horse, not mine, and I was riding another of his. And I should have done no good, and reduced the relation between us two solitary people to something pretty bad, with nothing to do but sit together, eat together, and sleep together. No getting away, unless I requested to be driven the sixty-five miles to Casper, and then here I would have come to see Morris and gone away not seeing him and think of an explanation! So my worldly wisdom, for I think this is all a low argument, prevailed over the higher course.

June 19. Still Morris does not come, and still I sit (though as little as I can) with Tisdale. The man's conduct yesterday has given me a lasting disgust. I cannot talk to him. I don't know what he thinks. Whenever he addresses me, I answer with perfect civility and coldness. Hand him the things at table and then it stops. His manner to me is pleasant, but

he says very little now. I don't know what he thinks. He told
the men at dinner about how the horses got away from us, and
he spoke about his horse giving out, but not a word about the
eye. He didn't even suggest that the horse had enraged him.
So I conclude that at least he prefers not to dwell on that
episode. I wonder if after a time I shall laugh at this situation.
Old Keyser (the German cook) was sick with rheumatism in
the bunkhouse today, and I administered potent mustard
plasters to him. During this he said, "Vat vas dat droble mit
de horses?" But I gave him a very cheerful, innocent story.

June 20.   Last night Morris' continued non-appear-
ance made me doubt his having got my letter, in which case
he would not be here till the roundup came, a week at least.
So I told Tisdale that if Morris did not come today, I should
like to be sent to the railroad, if he could do so. This was arranged in a perfectly smooth manner (Tisdale retains his
friendliness if not conciliatory tone, and it's all damned awk-
ward). But today, to my great relief, Morris came, having
got my letter a day late. I put my intention to have gone away
tomorrow on the excellent (and also true) ground that I could
not possibly impose myself for two weeks on a stranger's
hands, no matter how hospitable he was, and I underlined
Tisdale's hospitality with care. This Morris naturally accepted, and all I have to do now is to be civil but taciturn
when we three are together!
   I find it still utterly impossible to be cordial to Tisdale, or
treat him in the least on the terms of before the horse incident.
If he thinks anything, I imagine he sets me down as a capri-
cious and moody crank. But I seize every chance to be civil,
as you would to a stranger just introduced to you in a club by
a friend. Nothing disgraceful an acquaintance of mine has ever
done has nauseated my soul like this. The man who cheated at

cards; the man who pretended to be my sincere friend and came to my room every day and left it to blacken my character; the man who treated the Cambridge waitress in that way —none of these people's acts have had the sickening effect that the sight of that wretched fainting horse having his eye gouged out has had. I wonder if I take an exaggerated view? If any man who reads this will think I am overstrung? By God, as I rode back over those dry steep gulches, I found myself once or twice hoping the horse would fall and kill him. And I remain the moral craven who did not lift a finger or speak a word.

Some confidences Otto the cook made to me today let some light in. He knows nothing about the horse, for Tisdale turned him into the pasture at once on arriving. But Otto, talking to me at this kitchen door and observing Tisdale down by the river beating a horse with a stake over the head, called my attention to it and went on to say no one in the territory had such a name for cruelty. That the two hundred or so men who had worked for Tisdale at various times all spoke of it. He then added that sometimes Tisdale gouged an animal's eye! I was deeply astonished, of course. I begin to conclude from five seasons of observation that life in this negligent irresponsible wilderness tends to turn people shiftless, cruel, and incompetent. I noticed in Wolcott in 1885, and I notice today, a sloth in doing anything and everything, that is born of the deceitful ease with which makeshifts answer here. Did I believe in the efficacy of prayer, I should petition to be the hand that once for all chronicled and laid bare the virtues and the vices of this extraordinary phase of American social progress. Nobody has done it. Nobody has touched anywhere near it. A few have described external sights and incidents, but the grand total thing—its rise, its hysterical unreal prosperity, and its disenchanting downfall. All this and its influence on the various sorts of human character that has been subjected to it has not been hinted at by a single writer that I, at least, have heard of. The fact is, it is quite worthy of Tolstoi, or George Eliot, or Dickens. Thackeray wouldn't do. Well, I shall finish "Chalkeye" and then will see about the frog and the bull.

Now Morris has come, I resign my helm for ten days, and it's a relief. I wish I could say a few choice unutterable things about the moonlight night. Something novel in the line of word-painting as to moons. But somehow I can't seem to think of anything that strikes me as remarkable. Here sit I by the open wood fire, and the open door, on the night of Saturday, June 20, 1891. It's cold and still. You hear the river where it comes shallow over stones, and far across the wide silence the neigh of a horse. Tisdale's in bed inside the house. Morris is in bed outside. And I sit serenely here and stare at the moon that will be full tomorrow night, and which now possesses and controls these barren ridges and spaces and makes them turn beautiful beyond word or belief. "Night of the few large stars."

I have tested the power of the moon by consulting the second hand of my watch and reading a letter with rapid ease. But that's a poor mathematical way to talk or think about such magic. And all through the still air, the clean sharp odor of the sage. Not dusty, as it smells at noon, but cool, like something a fairy would give you to make you suddenly well. Nobody, nobody who lives on the Atlantic strip, has a notion of what sunrise and sunset and moonlight can be in their native land till they have come here to see. One goes back to "The light that never was on land or sea." If he had been here, he would have put a footnote and said "except in Wyoming, U.S.A."

Tonight there's a Porcellian dinner at Cambridge. Just these days in Cambridge are days I have loved dearly. But I have had a bigger share of them these times than most. And though the year never comes round to them but I am sad with pleasant recollections, I'm resigned, and would rather be here than anywhere just now. Yes.

June 21, Sunday. The longest day of the year. I wish it was arranged so the sun didn't take to setting earlier until September.

June 21

Dearest Mother:

Here's another chance to give you news of me, but there is no news really to give. I've not seen anything, but seen the days go in most agreeable passivity. The only thing I do is to jot down all shreds of local colour and all conversations and anecdotes decent or otherwise that strike me as native wild flowers. After a while I shall write a great fat book about the whole thing. When I feel enough familiar both by time and knowledge. There's a story I've already begun, some fifty pages of manuscript lying at home. That is intended merely as a trial trip.

P.S. If you write to my grandmother or aunt, please speak about *The Dragon of Wantley*,[2] I want it back if no publisher they can get at will take it.

Your loving son,
D.

Buffalo, June 25. Reached here on Monday, riding from 6:45 to 11:15 A.M. to Hesses' ranch, where we stopped several hours and had a good meal. Then at 3:45 we started and came in at 6:30. The whole distance was forty-four miles.

---

[2] [*The Dragon of Wantley* (Philadelphia: J. B. Lippincott Co., 1892) was a fairy story to which Wister gave the playful subtitle "His Tale."]

Owen Wister's Hunting Party
in Camp at Jackson Hole, Wyoming, 1887

Seated (*from left to right*) are George Norman and Copley Amory, his companions from Boston, and George West and Jules Mason, guides. Standing are Tigie, the Indian who helped Wister shoot a grizzly bear, and Wister himself, pouring a drink from a flask into Tigie's cup. (*Photograph courtesy of Mr. Amory.*)

Wister's Party at the South Ford
of Snake River, 1891

The rancher Charles Smith, the guide George West, and Wister's Bostonian friend Lawrence Brooks take their pack horses across the Snake to follow the old Sheridan Trail.

Owen Wister at the Age of Forty

Citizens of Tombstone, Arizona, 1894

Wister wrote on the back of this photograph (which he took during his search for material for *Harper's Magazine*) nothing more than "Tombstone Court House—Mr. Swain *et al*." According to the Arizona Pioneers' Historical Society, those pictured are (standing, left to right): Billy Bradley, deputy sheriff; Mr. Swain, the county attorney who took Wister to the Parlor Saloon; unknown; A. H. Emanuel, clerk of the court; unknown; William Ritchie, jailer; Nate Hawke. Seated on chairs: D. K. Wadwell and unknown woman. Seated on steps: W. C. Steahle, attorney; M. D. Scribner, county treasurer; A. W. Wentworth; W. D. Monmonier.

Passed a place where Morris said good-by to Henderson for
the last time. Henderson had been the only man who would
cope with certain "rustlers" on the EK outfit. They had run
the preceding foreman out of the country. Henderson went up
to the roundup, and when they came to the EK wagon, he
told them to pack up their beds and go. They were not going
to eat at that wagon. Moral force prevailed, and they left.
But later on, Henderson was entering his cabin unarmed, and
he found six of them waiting. So he was shot through the
heart. We passed Mr. Canton, Deputy U.S. Sheriff.³ Very
quiet, very even voice. Does less shooting than any officer in
his position, but he is feared by all hands.

BUFFALO

June 26

Dearest Mother:

This isn't the town of the same name in New York.
I reached here on horseback, riding forty-four miles and
was not particularly stiff. Rode next day with perfect
comfort in the afternoon. There is a military post here—Fort
McKinney—most beautifully situated at the edge of the
plain against the Big Horn Mountains. These are quite
high, and the whole central ridge of peaks entirely covered
with snow, over which the sun sets. It has been very
pleasant to sit on the porch of one of the officer's quarters
and watch dress parade. The band is good, and the whole
scene, in the fine weather there has been, very beautiful and
wholly unlike one's usual notions of this country. But for
this uniform and the flag, you might imagine yourself in
some country across the globe. As a whole, the scenery of
these Big Horns does not (to me) compare with Wind

³ [Frank B. Canton was with Major Frank Wolcott in the
"invasion" of Johnson County, Wyoming, during the 1892 cattle
war.]

River. There is too much empty desolation always in sight.
It's just the particular moment of sunset when the light
that never was on land or sea, except in Wyoming, turns
not only mountain and plain but dry ditches of mud and
ash heaps into objects of enchanted splendor; then you
see a sight that puts anything I have ever seen into the
shade. The dress parade makes a harmonious addition to
the even drill, the simultaneous flash of shifted arms,
the music, the one gun, and the flag fluttering down—I
assure you it's worth looking at. The town of Buffalo, of
course, is something horrible beyond words. They all are. But
I'm so busy watching the motley blackguards I meet, that
I'm in one continuous state of concentrated amusement and
interest. If you want some impression of Buffalo's appearance
and all the other towns too, think of the most sordid part
of Atlantic City you can remember. A general litter of paltry
wood houses back to back and side to back at all angles
that seem to have been brought and dumped out from a
wheelbarrow. You would die in a moment here. Today
we ride away again, for brief fishing, and so back to the ranch,
whence I go to the railroad and so to Douglas, which I expect to reach on July 3 and from where I shall write to you.

Your loving son,
D.

June 26, Friday.   Buffalo is a shade better in its appearance than most of these towns. It stands on Clear Creek
(well named) which comes pouring and sliding from the Big
Horn Mountains only a short distance away. The town itself
has less of that portable appearance so prevailing elsewhere.
There are some neat little cottages and a number of brick
buildings, also a flour mill. The stages come in from Douglas
and from Belle Fourche. Fort McKinney is two miles away to
the west, almost against the mountains, whose cañons open

116

just above it and whose snow peaks are in plain view behind the lower timbered foothills. We went up there with the doctor in the afternoon and were very cordially entertained. The officers made us stay to dinner. We chiefly saw Ames, Richardson, and Major Fretchet. He plays the banjo extraordinarily well, and they made me play the piano for them. Their hospitality was of a quality that sent Morris and myself away through the moonlight riding at a splitting gallop all the way into town. No Eastern horse could have gone over such a road at such a pace without breaking his neck, or his rider's neck, but my horse did not even stumble once.

Our visit to the officers started us off on a highly picturesque night, during which I was rejoiced again to encounter my friend of Riverside, Henry Smith. He is the real thing, and the only unabridged "bad man" I have ever had a chance to know. He is originally from Texas and pronounces Spanish very prettily. He has been "run out" of every country he has resided in. His last coup was some eighteen months ago to persuade his friend Russell to borrow money from every man he knew and take him traveling to foreign parts on the proceeds. They disappeared suddenly. When Smith returned here this spring, he had been to South America and all over Europe. He could come back because it was not he who borrowed the money. Russell's whereabouts are not known. Smith is at present stealing cattle or, more likely, mavericking.

Before I forget him, I must describe Smith's appearance. A tall long-nosed, dark fellow, with a shock of straight black hair on end, all over his head. Blue overalls tucked into boots of the usual high-heeled pattern, and a slouchy waistcoat. He is so tall he bends down over almost everyone as he talks, and he has a catching but sardonic smile. His voice is unpleasant, very rasping, though not over loud. The great thing is his eyes. They are of a mottled yellow, like agate or half-clear amber, large and piercing, at times burning with light. They

117

are the very worst eyes I have ever looked at. Perfectly fearless and shrewd, and treacherous. I don't see how an eye can express all that, but it does. I have sat and talked to Smith, or rather listened to him, he's brilliant talker in his vagabond line, and he has found me what I set out to be in this world—a good listener.

And all the while he talked I watched him as intently as I have ever studied the day before an examination, noting every turn in his speech and every lift of his head. He is not a halfway man. Not the Bret Harte villain with the heart of a woman. Not the mixed dish of Cambric tea so dear to modern novelists. He is just bad through and through, without a scruple and without an affection. His face is entirely cruel, and you hear cruelty in his voice. How do I know all this? Because I know something of his past and present, and I have heard him speak for himself. He has attended to scores of men and women in his talk and never to one without a corrosive sneer. When I come to my Castle in Spain—my book about Wyoming—I shall strain my muscles to catch Smith. I'm getting to believe mixed characters are not the only ones in the world.

July 3, Friday. In train leaving Casper. I was much struck by our manner of departure just now, ten minutes late. The train hands were doing nothing. Merely sitting on the platform or leaning against the doors of the station. That is all they had been doing for fifteen minutes, and I looked out of the window and wondered just when, and owing to just what, we should leave Casper. A man said, "Well, let's get out of this town." Apparently the conductor. Another in blackened overalls rose. Apparently the engineer. He walked towards the head of the train out of my sight, and immediately we began to move. Some parties in the baggage car just in

118

front are firing pistols at the telegraph posts. Six shots and not a hit. Three more. Now comes a jack rabbit. Four more. "I guess the rabbit's safe," a passenger observed in the car. [Now it is] 8:50, shooting ceased and stopping at Inez, and empty is the shell of a station among the sagebrush, pronounced "Eins" by the employees. I've heard of this sort of thing, but never before saw it.

We stopped, not for passengers, but to hunt jack rabbits. There is a greyhound on board, and with him the conductor, a brakeman with a six-shooter, and one or two passengers are scouring the plain in search of game while the train waits. I am sorry to say they have not been successful. If I had my Kodak handy, I should snap a picture of this train, and call it "Waiting for Jack Rabbits." For the past two hours the country has been very familiar to my memory; looking at the various canyons in Casper and crossing Deer Creek, recalled most vividly [the country I saw] in 1885.

BETWEEN DOUGLAS, CHEYENNE

July 4

Dearest Mother:

I have not enjoyed my days and hours like this since I was last here. Nothing can make me forget the homesickness I feel for it every day when I am in the East. Getting into court and arguing or doing some hard work of that sort does not cure the nostalgia; some only just stops it for the moment. I am exactly as enchanted and enthusiastic as I was in 1885 when I first saw all this. Of course I cannot write long letters or descriptions anymore, because there is nothing new or more to describe; and also, now I'm forming "literary impressions," and you must know how that shuts one up. I have discomforts of the most uncompromising sort every day, but they simply amuse me, and the

other day I rode fifty miles without a trace of fatigue
next day. Often lately I've slept on the board floor or else
outside the door of some cabin I've come to in journeying,
having no pillow and no sheets but only rough blankets—
because either the beds were occupied by fellow mortals
or by large, active bugs. At one place, these intelligent
creatures crossed the ceiling to the appropriate zenith and
dropped there like falling stars on one's knee or open book.
Often there's been no supper or dinner but greasy bacon
and coffee made of gavel and gum. But I don't mind at all.
Half-past nine is late to go to bed and half-past six is late
to get up. Five was the hour while I was among the ranches.

Yesterday in Douglas a storm came while I was at the
bank writing to Aunt Fanny. The rain fell as if one were
beneath the sea. Then hail came, all as big as marbles,
many as big as walnuts. Then the evening cleared, and the
Laramie mountains came out stoney and blue, cut into the
air like diamond edges. You would have said, "Oh yes! the
Dolomites!" But never any Dolomites had such atmosphere
and such colour to bask in. A cow looked into the bank's
window and attracted my attention and the cashier's to
the beauty of the scene. I am, as you have read, on my
way to Cheyenne—Ralston and Charles Penrose are there
waiting. Tomorrow unless the unforeseen has happened,
Lawrence Brooks comes along from Boston, and we all go to
Rawlins—then on to Fort Washakie, where I expect to
arrive on Tuesday, the 7th. It's my own wish to be in one
party with Ralston and Penrose. Four is too many to hunt.
We shall travel continually together, and if Bois Penrose
and another man also join them (as is possible), I shall ask
Bob to come with Lawrence and me if he will.

Your loving son,

D.

FORT WASHAKIE

July 9

Dearest Mother:

What will interest you far more is the new regiment composed entirely of Indians.[4] Their commander, a Captain Ray, old, fiery, and most interesting, talked to me last night for two hours about it. He is heart and soul in it and his views of the Indian question would cause you the keenest joy. It's queer to see these Indians walking about in military uniform. Captain Ray says they have a better notion of discipline than many raw Americans. This I find so surprising that I can't quite believe it. I think it's the view of an enthusiast—Captain Ray declares there's no such thing as discipline through the length and breadth of the American people. Agreeing with him, I still feel somehow that an Indian's brain is remote from hours and drills.

We are now delayed by the trickiness of the people here who have horses to hire or sell. The night before we came, they (some unknown person or persons) drove the horses West (George West) had brought in for us away— we don't know where! This was done supposing we were in a hurry and would have to buy horses to get away. But we are in no hurry and don't care if we wait a week. Also I have remarked casually to all people I talk with that tomorrow I shall telegraph to my friends at Rawlins who are coming to join me to buy horses for me there. This has already produced a certain effect. A man (whom I suspect) starts to hunt our horses this morning "to help West," as he said. You see, he counted on our getting horses through him, or his friends, then when Ralston & Co. came, West's

[4] [The opening lines of this letter have been omitted because of their uninteresting character.]

horses would be found and they could take them. But he has been woefully disappointed. I have told Ralston to get his horses at Rawlins. It's annoying. It proceeds from the desire to take advantage of Eastern strangers. But this time it failed signally.

Your loving son,
D.

Smith's, July 16. Came here Tuesday, fishing on the way, chiefly whitefish. West has gone to hunt the two missing horses, and we stay camped here. Yesterday had a rough walk in Warm Springs Canyon, and nearly lost my horse, hunting for the Natural Bridge. He fell over three times as I was leading him, out of sheer exhaustion. Finally he fell and could not rise. It was 5:30, and I was retracing my two hours terrific climb, trying to get out of the trap I had got myself into before the daylight should leave me. Often I had to lead the staggering horse along through the creek with water up to my arm pits. I tried to ride him across one particularly deep pool, but he fell and rolled, wetting me completely. At the last fall he made when he failed to rise, he rolled up the whites of his eyes, and I was pretty anxious. Then I took off the saddle and blanket (which being drenched weighed 100 pounds at least) and left them, coming out of the canyon at 6:40, and leading my horse all the way down the mountain to Wind River. I was quite played out several times, but luckily had my flask. At Wind River I mounted bareback, crossed, and galloped the five miles home. My horse having recovered from his exhaustion.

Today we hunted for a way to reach the saddle, and tomorrow I hope I shall bring it out. We also went to real Natural Bridge (for the one I had seen and been disappointed in was not the right one) and found there were two! A very remarkable and beautiful place, but dangerous. It was impossible to get down to the water there. But we shall try tomorrow, for I greatly desire a photograph of this place.

Still at Smith's, July 18.   Yesterday West and I went down into the Warm Springs Cañon from this (south) side and found the saddle. A hard climb, particularly one ledge of rock where the cliff was brittle and one had to turn. Once down at the water, I took off my breeches and paraded up and down the cañon in a costume somewhat leaner than a Highlander's. I waded and stumbled among the rocks over which the water poured and then went sliding among the slithering shale slants above till I came on the saddle. West and I then took turns carrying it and the blanket up again and out. A hard pull, but only one hour and five minutes.

Today Brooks and I went to the Natural Bridges and got down to the water without difficulty. What a wonderful stream and what a place for charm and beauty! It is nameless and almost unknown as yet. Also, for the average tourist, it is hardly accessible, and somewhat dangerous. But when you have a steep cañon with a stream which inside of two miles gives you a chasm much more magnificent than the An Salle, and throws in two natural bridges, not to speak of being full of large trout and delicious for bathing, you have something that would be speedily ruined if it were anywhere near the hordes of summer sightseers. But, thank the Lord, it is nameless and unknown save to Indians, cowboys, and horse thieves, and it flows down through its pine forests and cliffs entirely at peace. Some day, no doubt, when civilization crawls here, this poor creek with its cañon and natural bridges will echo with the howling of the summer mob, who will have easy paths made for them, and staircases, and elevators perhaps too. There will be signposts directing you to Minerva Terrace, Calypso Garden, Siren Grotto, for every

123

unfortunate ledge and point will be saddled with a baleful name rotten with inappropriateness. I hope at least some of the photographs I took will succeed. I took off my breeches once more and waded under the lower bridges from one end to the other. It is not very high, from 30 to 50 feet, I should say, but at least 75 yards long (through) and on top about 100 acres, but so much up and down hill that it is hard to judge.

Foot of To-wu-tu-tee Pass, July 24. Came here yesterday and just at the Fork of DuNoir met Bob Ralston and the Penroses by great good luck. They had reached there at ten the preceding night from John Lee's ranch.

July 25, Saturday. We passed just above here where Wind River falls into this valley through a beautiful gorge reminding me of Trenton Falls a little. Dick guided West, Brooks, and me pretty zigzag. There is no trail, but only game trails, often useless, and exceedingly steep and obstructed with fallen pines. At the lake we fished and lunched. No trout under twelve inches, and, had it not been windy, we should have caught fifty, I think. This lake is the true headwaters of Wind River and a remarkable, beautiful, and lonely piece of clear water, rippling on the top of the range between smooth pine forests and straight sharp lines of rock where the snow still stays. Many geese and duck, but far out of range.

Meadow Creek on Yellowstone, August 9. No more devilish marshes, but fallen timber, and mighty uncomfortable. As West perhaps would say: "Am mighty resolved to try no more cross timber." Also, the beastly fool of a horse Shanghai left the whole bunch of horses and ran back where we had only left an hour and a half ago. We waited from 10:40 till 2:45 before we got started again. After that we took to the shingle on the lake shore and soon found a good trail and came along very fast till five, when we camped here. After sunset the lake was too beautiful to be described. All done by the light, for the sheet of water is in itself merely pretty and wholly lacking in distinction.

The one touch of greatness is that from here—shining above the tame round hills with their endless pines—you see the distant Tetons. Their glittering pale blue peaks with the snow hanging to their sides where it can. For the Tetons to show over the Continental Divide at this distance proves them very high.

There is ice on the pots in camp every morning now. We are pretty high, for the lake is 7,441 feet. Saw wild swans and "large flocks, very large flocks of grey geese." What I liked in the late sun tonight was the intense sense of solitude and distance from things in general that one felt. No books, no smoke, just the shores of green pine and the warm saffron sky with a clean icy moon cutting through it, and some wild duck quietly watching me from the water. Four deer came to feed in the low ground beneath our camp this morning.

Have thought of a good opening sentence for "The Adventures of a Bad Shot," if I ever write that series of sketches: "No man tells the truth about himself and his gun." I should like this autumn to finish "Chalkeye" and write "Raymond and His Three Lives" and then start on "The Bad Shot." The title is good, and a magazine might take it. I keep thinking of themes and good titles of books I shall never write in all probability. E.g., "The Demon Lover," the old ballad carried out in modern style. "Fallen Timber," good old New York families trying to be like the fashionable set there. Then my castle in the air, "The Tenderfoot," but this I think I shall really do someday.

Tomorrow we shall not reach the falls, I feel perfectly sure, though we are now in the region of good trails.

August 11, Tuesday. No, we did not, by any means, though we are there now. But it is too late tonight to continue.

We came down the river and camped on an island near the mud geysers where we had originally intended to ford. Good fishing, but some of the trout wormy. Lots of outfits, and people passing on the road and children screaming. This park is an immense thing for the American bourgeoisie. Popper takes mommer and children in a big wagon with two mules and their kitchen and beds, and forth they march hundreds of miles and summer in the Park. Nothing like this ever existed before, I think.

Next day, yesterday, we rode ahead to the Falls Hotel, all new, stopping by the Sulphur Mountain where George Norman, and Copley, and I stopped in '87. Lunched at hotel and read a large mail at the brink of the falls, which with the cañon are more marvelous in their beauty than my four years of imagination and memory had been able to picture. It is very much the most beautiful thing I have ever seen or expect to see. In the evening dined with Smith and West at hotel. But this can't go on, for our money is small, and to-day I made the horrid discovery that money can't be had here by telegram, on which I had been counting since Dick left us. Brooks and I are now going to Yancey's in quest of a hunter who shall quickly take us to mountain sheep.

YELLOWSTONE NATIONAL PARK

August 11

Dearest Mother:

The fact is, the Yellowstone River is most beautiful. Yesterday afternoon we followed it down from where it

flows out of the lake. Blue, clear, and the bottom always
visible, though sometimes pretty deep. The whole current
sliding serenely along about as broad as twice the Wissahickon, wild fowl, ducks, great white pelicans floating in the
quiet turns. Then above the water, green sloping hills beautifully wooded with pines that open into smooth rolling spaces
and close again, and all utterly solitary.

Occasionally a jet of steam among the trees—not an
engine, but some lonely geyser or sputtering pool with
a becoming mess of strange-looking gum boiling and
groaning down the scaly crater. These things are not beautiful.
They are admirably interesting, but they smell bad—very
bad—and I mostly pass them by. But when you know that the
mysterious uncertain pillar of steam coming up and waving
among the woods is merely a geyser, you don't object to it
at a distance.

Then after some fifteen miles of this flowing, the
river narrows in between wooded banks like Trenton (only
you feel the whole thing is bigger), and then the water
becomes rapid and finally plunges white over the first falls
162 feet, and a fine generous mass of water too. A waterfall
of the first and highest order. And the deep green ravine
it goes into is also the best. But when you come to that
second fall and the cañon breaks upon you, then there's
no use attempting to say a word, and the noble fall you
have just seen is swept out of your mind instantly.

But what you see is like some unearthly legend, but
without a particle of terror of destruction about it. The
lurking threat—a grand sort of threat, but always with the
implied comment, "What business have you here?"—that
is Niagara, and that keeps one from ever becoming personally
attached to Niagara, is here entirely absent, and yet there
could not be more dignity. The place is at once romantic,
exquisite, and wholly sublime. The South is not in it, nor

anything of Homer, but you can easily believe Monsarrat
is round the next corner or expect to see the Gods stretch
a rainbow somewhere and march across to Walhalla.

I am reminded of certain of the most beautiful passages
in Wagner's trilogy—those moments when the whole
orchestra seems to break into silver fragments of magic—
sounds of harps and the violins all away up somewhere
sustaining some theme you have heard before, but which
now returns twice as magnificent as it was earlier in the
evening. If you can recall the song of the Rhine Daughters—
or the last few moments of *Die Walküre* when Brunhilde
falls to sleep among the rocks—those passages are inspired
by the same thing which vibrates in this cañon.

Certainly no mountain sea or lake which I have ever
seen in any country is so singularly and so divinely lovely.
I think the Lake of Lucerne and the Lake of Como from
Bellaggio two more of the "top notches" of natural beauty
—but each of these is more beautiful than other lakes I
know in degree alone. This fall and cañon have the
quality of being like nothing else one ever saw or thought
of. In fact I can't get nearer than to say again they are as
different from all other falls and cañons as an old legend
is different from all other stories—a modern genius can't
invent one. All this must be Hebrew to you. But it was this
marvelous power that bowled Mrs. Lawrence over when
she looked at it, so that she had to sit down. Did she ever
try to tell you? She said to me, opening her eyes staring
wide, "When that sight came over me I——I was so
emotionée I had to be helped to a log."

I can hardly stop talking about it, for the more I
dwell upon it, the more wholly irresistible does it grow to
me. One could never weary of looking at it. Yet the
tourists scuttle through here like mice. They come, they
lunch, horses are brought. They tremulously mount and are

128

conducted a few hundred yards along good paths though steep ones. They return in about forty-five minutes, speak of having "seen the young eagle in that nest down by Inspiration Point" (this callow nestling produces a deep impression; everybody has spoken of him today)—then they huddle their bags into the conveyance and rattle dustily away to the next spectacle. That is what most of them do. Almost nobody stays more than one night!

Your loving son,
D.

Yellowstone Falls, August 13.   My visit to Yancey's has proved very successful. On [my] reaching Yancey's, the old man with his long gray hair above his ears came out, and I made myself known as a friend of Barringer and the Penroses. He was delighted and at once proposed a drink. Then two old reprobates appeared down the steep hill in a buggy. They were from Gardner's, going to Cook City for the opening of a new dancehall. A very pleasant evening. I find that Moses Brown drifted by Yancey's last year, and Yancey also had had General Brish. Also he told me that Teddy Roosevelt was down on the first and Barringer on the second, so the whole place seemed swarming with acquaintances past and present and to come. Very satisfactory. Yancey knew of two good hunters for sheep, and Keeney took a message to one for me today to Gardner, James Woody. "What he says, he knows," said Yancey. He came at 1:20, and I made an arrangement with him for a few days. He is to go with Roosevelt. I increased Yancey's respect for me by making a most lucky shot with his rifle, a 300-yard shot at a white stone on the hill.

Near the Hoodoos, August 18.   We are camped in upland open country, good sheep sign, recent, also bear, but unluckily horse tracks also. The game has been hunted out of here, and we must move.

September 11. I am pausing among the mountains to lunch and write this up to date. I am hunting alone, which I prefer, though my eyes are not quick to see game. In a week, Wind River, and these mountains, and all, will be behind me, and I am sorry to think it. I look forward to the winter with unmixed dislike. Not unmixed, for there are a few people I care to see and who care to see me, but Philadelphia is not the place I should choose either for any friends or myself if I could help it. Today is very beautiful, and I like to dwell on every detail of what surrounds me. My horse feeds by a swampy cold little spring, where the soft ground shows the recent tread of elk. A steady gentle wind is making the pines sing. The other sounds I hear being the furious scolding of a squirrel in a pine up the hill just behind me and the coarse call of the various mountain jays who fly across this opening in the woods, inspect me, and pass on; while here I bask in the comfortable sun, a willow bush for my head, my feet in some sagebrush, and look down and up the little green draws that come down through the pines to meet just here and make a brook which flows into Gros Ventre below. Could I "say to the passing moment stay!" I'd surely say it now.

October–November, 1892

WASHINGTON

ON July 2, 1892, Owen Wister began a puzzling journey to Cinnabar, Wyoming, just to tell George West that he could not hunt with him that summer. Wister kept a journal of the trip (he was back in Philadelphia on July 14); but it does not explain why he made such a short trip or why he could not make a longer one, and thus it has not been included here.

"Dick Penrose came to see me off," Wister wrote. "I explained to him that I had abandoned the idea of spending the summer in the mountains. And to tell the exact truth, the thought of this long and hot journey, for nothing, in a way amuses me. Making the decision was not amusing, but once made, there is something modern and globe trotting in traveling 2,500 miles to say you're sorry you can't come." In the station at St. Paul he noted Railroad Labor Agency advertisements reading, "Ho for the great mines of Minnesota. 2,000 hands wanted at $2.00 a day. Fare free."

In October of the same year, Wister was able to go to the state of Washington, where he stayed with Mr. and Mrs. George Waring and hunted wild goat. Waring, a Harvard classmate of Wister, kept a small general store on the remote Methow River.

1892

Ruby, October 11. Through this tall country of wandering ploughs we came to Walla Walla, a town of dust and poplars. The rain falls so seldom that when the wheat is sacked, they leave it in great piles lying out under the sky till it can all be shipped. So at every way station lay mounds of these wheat sacks. The delegate fireman Taylor sat with me in the smoking car and told me of the Palouse Indians in this region. They are much civilized, the squaws virtuous, and the men pay their debts. This, said Taylor, was the result of the Church of Rome.

Beyond the slight discomfort of atmosphere, the smoking car on these Western trains is the place to enjoy one's journey. For it contains the local colour of the districts passed through. You have probably a judge and two or three politicians. They know the conductor and call him "Bill." He sits with them and despises the humbler passengers. These are both men and women. In our car between Pendleton and Spokane was a foreign family moving from Iowa, parents and children, with rags and bags bundled up around the stove. They had brought three little guinea chickens in a box, which was tied on the platform. These the conductor fancied and bought on the way. Then there were miners drifting in search of new country and asking where they had better go. Young men with pets are common. One in our car had come from California, and [he] produced a fat ground squirrel who sat tamely out on the newsboy's baskets for miles at a time. At Riparia we came on the Snake River once more, now quite large, and a stream where steamboats run. The river flows between vast bare hills, and is imposing but bleak and austere.

Winthrop, October 16. Taylor [the fireman on the train] was raised in the west corner of Virginia by Saltville, his father very well off, having something to do with the salt works. Taylor has been a self supporting animal since he was thirteen. Near Saltville in the mountains is a deep basin with good grazing, steep walls, and but one practicable approach. In this place, called Ward's Cove, lived a father named Luster with seven sons, six feet high or over. They hunted, distilled whiskey, and hunted. Every now and then they would descend on Saltville and do it up. But next time they came, they paid for any breakage. They sold their whiskey and told the officers they did not understand the law that forbade their making it. They argued the ground was their own, the corn was their own, and why could they not do what they wanted with their private property? Being seven brothers six feet high, they were let alone with their logic.

Rees Luster seems to have been somewhat hard to deal with. People pastured cattle during summer in Ward's Cove, paying the Lusters for the privilege. One man's cattle was sold out by the sheriff, who came up to get them. He found what he supposed was the right bunch and was driving them down, when he met Rees. Rees expostulated, but the sheriff was not to be convinced. He would not believe they belonged to Rees, which they really did. Rees offered to take the sheriff back and show him the right cattle, but the sheriff refused to go and was driving the cattle away without further argument. So Rees shot him.

Down at Saltville they got a posse to come for Rees. This the Luster brothers heard of. When the posse arrived at Ward's Cove, they found nobody at home. They hunted about a little but decided after a while it would be pleasanter to return to Saltville. As they were leaving the cove by the single outlet, a voice hailed them. "Hello." It was Rees, sitting above them, under a pine, sitting quietly with his rifle across his knees. He asked what they were doing, and they said they had just been taking a ride and now were going down to town.

"Haven't you forgotten something?" inquired Rees.

"Well, yes, we did have an idea we wanted you."

"Come and get me, why don't you?"

But the posse preferred returning to Saltville, and left Rees sitting by the pine, with (of course) his six other brothers a little farther inside the wood.

They took a fancy to Taylor, and he used to go up to Ward's Cove and remain there hunting and drinking with them for months at a time. He played the fiddle a little, and they used to have dances up there.

October 18. I was called at 5:30 at the Hotel Spokane and brushed my teeth in the forlorn sunrise. It was too early for breakfast, and I got a cup of coffee at the station, taking hard-boiled eggs with me in a paper bag. The train started at 6:10, and here too was the judge, the lawyer, and the conductor—their familiar friend. We ran at first through a dull pine region where there were many rocky ravines, and through them a new road along which the raw telegraph poles gleamed among the dark trees and seemed like things flayed alive, so staring fresh was their colour. At noon I reached Coulee City and found to my dismay that there was no stage connection until Monday. This was Saturday, and Saturday's stage leaves at the usual hour of seven for Port Columbia and Ruby—my route. But all stages so manage that the passengers must spend the night at the Hotel Grand, and I was in for two nights and a day, with Saturday afternoon thrown into the bargain.

They gave me a room—No. 9—about the size of a spittoon, and I was glad to see as little of it as possible. I washed in the public trough and basin which stood in the office between the saloon and the dining room; and I spent my time either in the saloon, watching a game of poker that never ceased, or in wandering about in the world outside.

October 9. This morning the game was still going on. The bartender sweeping the office waked me, and I arose and made a toilet as usual in the public trough. I spent the morning in a walk to the little Coulee. It was like walking out of all such towns as these. The houses end at once but do not seem to grow distant as you proceed through the sand and brush of the desert where they lie. Blowing over this waste came sudden noisome smells from the undrained filth of the town that huddled there in the midst of unlimited nothing. It is a shapeless litter of boxes, inhabited by men whose lives are an aimless drifting. When the railroad continues, the freighters and stages will connect elsewhere, the commercial travelers to the mines, with their sample cases of watches, jewelry, and cigars will no longer patronize Hotel Grand and its cockroaches, and these innocent insects must die.

Judge Holmes said to me last September at Burnly that America's special contribution to art was the painting of infinite ennui. This was new, and our own. If Coulee City and its thousand twins have got into art, they surely support this notion. For Coulee is too dead even for much crime. The ceaseless poker game was a cheap one, and nobody got either drunk or dangerous. People have been killed there, I believe, but not often, most likely not lately. There is but one professional woman in the whole town, and from what I heard the men say, she is a forlorn old wreck, so unsightly that even her monopoly brings no profit. In such a sordid community, this fact shows stronger than anything else how poor and torpid existence has come to be. It is the "Big Bend" country, and treeless, shadeless, leafless, featureless, with one gaunt exception—the coulee that gives a name to the town.

You travel for miles over the dull sterility, where to surmount the rise of waste in front of you merely shows the next rise you have to surmount, and where the only variety in fine weather is the wind. This occasionally rushes through space, raising a primeval dust that blinds the landscape out for a while and makes a certain relief. The poor dry weeds are yellow, the ground is yellow, and you cannot even see a bare piece of rock to break the mean similarity of the universe. Then, three yards in front of you, you suddenly see down seven hundred feet into a black parched chasm that gashes the plain in two. There is no warning. A couple of steps shows you the whole unearthly thing at once. This is the Grand Coulee, about sixty-five miles long. The rock walls are sheer in some places, while in others you can make a descent and cross, even with a wagon. The bottom has brush, desert, marsh, dead lakes, mosquitoes, and scorpions in it.

October 10. Left Coulee City at seven [o'clock]. Four inside stage: the two Hebrew drummers, and a man I had treated in the saloon, who turned out to be going to the other end of the line as driver at $30 a month. A rain had laid the dust a little. But after some fifteen miles it again became choking. Far worse than any I have ever seen between Rawlins and Washakie. About five we came to Bridgeport, a store and a hotel in construction, the rest of the town on a map only. Here was the Columbia River—a restless rapid river with rapid current, flowing among dismal hills. I thought of Stevenson quoting the ballad at the leper's island as he rode away: "The most distressful country that ever yet was seen." The loneliness of Wyoming, even at its worst, has an attraction for me, and I have become attached to it, but this country chills the imagination of the heart.

We went along the Columbia and had to round some hills on a steep and shockingly risky road. The Hebrews were chattering with anxiety. By dusk we came to the night's stopping place, Port Columbia. I must do this sorrowful region the justice to say that at sunset, for some heavenly moments, it turned to Paradise. Even the deplorable country at Coulee City was transfigured and grew soft, as veil after veil of purple light floated across it, melting the bareness into beauty. Port Columbia is like Bridgeport, a store, a hotel, some sheds, and all else invisible except on maps. At the wooden edifice, post office, stage office, and hotel, passengers pass the night, taking a tea or breakfast which are not attractive. But I had a room to myself, to which I retired early from the company sitting down in the general wash, dress, and wait room.

October 11.   The stage we now took was an open one. I sat by my Coulee friend, the driver, anticipating a new Hebrew drummer who joined us here. But he was not inclined to dispute, and turned out a humorist of a low but successful order. We crossed the rapid Columbia at once, on a rope ferry that seemed to me rather unsafe. Entering the valley of the Okanogan we went some six miles and crossed that stream on another ferry equally unsafe. Last season in high water a rope snapped and instantly killed a driver.

The scenery greatly improved. Hills surrounded us, water and trees were always in sight. We passed some cabins and at one found a watermelon patch, where the Hebrews descended and brought some fruit just ripe and very cold, which we all ate en route. After nooning at Millott's, where we had a really decent meal, we passed the down stage. "Haf some gin?" sang out the humorous Hebrew to the driver, and held a flat bottle in the air, which was filled with water. I shall never forget the driver's expression of countenance. He pulled up and said, "Well I never *do* refuse." The bottle was handed him amid total silence, and I did not dare to meet anyone's eye. He uncorked it, looked at us, and said very kindly, "My regards, gentlemen!" and tipped the bottle well into his jaws, removed it slowly, and said, "I'll be son of a bitched!" in tones so utterly disconcerted that we all shouted for a minute. He recapped the bottle and drove on. "That's one on me," he

said, "but I'll fix somebody before sundown." This episode
was worth ninety miles of stage, even in the Big Bend country.
The humorist surprised us once again as we were near the
journey's end. We picked up a venerable old man who was
walking to Ruby, and the driver, feeling good-natured, offered him a lift. After he was seated among us and before any
other word than "good day" had been exchanged, the drummer said, "And my friend, vat vas your views on the immortality of the cockroach?" Coming after Hotel Grand this
seemed fine and timely.

At Ruby I left the stage, which went on to Conconully,
six miles. Ruby is an ungraded street on a steep hillside in a
slit of a valley, quite beautifully situated. On one side of the
street the houses are away up above the road, and steps
descend from the saloons and stores at intervals. At the
bottom of the town is the Concentrator, to which travels the
running flume along the hill above the housetops. When you
are unused to it, the apparition of two black buckets passing
each other in mid-air in a pine forest is startling. Of course
these were what brought the quartz from the mouth of the
tunnel above to the Concentrator below. These buckets take
their eccentric journey clean over the mountain.

October 12. Greene, George Waring's stepson, and I
on a buckboard and King, Waring's neighbor, on his horse
ascended out of Ruby, and drove through the mountains all
this fine day some thirty miles. *Post tenebras lux.* The miserable Big Bend desert and the company of Hebrew drummers
now changed to excellent companions and most lovely scenery.
Our course lay through plentiful woods, still green, and many
little streams ran among them. We journeyed on, marking the
hour of time with moderate pulls at the bottle, and by night
arrived comfortably at a cabin where lives an old vagrant

called "Arkansaw." We turned the horses loose, and Arkansaw hailed us cordially from his cabin door. He looks about sixty-five, torn, ragged, rather Rip Van Winklish, with long and most unkempt hair hanging grizzled on his shoulders. For he is a fiddler, and considers that the proper way for an artist. We gave him plenty of whiskey, and he played to us till late, all sorts of old-fashioned airs and dances. He had fiddled his way across the continent and taken his lifetime to do so, had seen the days of Indians, buffalo, and the days in California, when for a night's fiddling in a mining camp his fee was $100, and he always got it. He was perfectly blithe-hearted and penniless, though by his stories, he must have handled millions.

October 13. At about eleven we drove up to George Waring's gate, in the rain. My huge journey was done, and I was glad indeed to see him and his new venture on the frontier. They had worked on a new flag to fly for me, a boar's head vert, on a white field,[1] but the weather was not for flying.

October 14. George was anxious I should get my hunting as soon as possible, as October being half over, snow is a thing more or less imminent. I told him goat was really all I cared for, George regretting that his many duties and cares kept him from going with me. This day a little melodion was brought out and set up in the dining room; and now I play for them what I can, especially in the evenings. The weather cleared, leaving the valley shining with yellow autumn and the high peaks all in snow.

[1] [The emblem of the Porcellian Club, Harvard.]

November 2. One of my particular long cherished wishes is now accomplished, and I have seen and killed a mountain goat. This puts the necessary tincture in my trip to make it completely successful, and no fault to be found.

November 24, Thanksgiving Day. Last week the snow persisted, and I grew alarmed. I decided that when Harry Greene should return from Conconully, he should drive me out to Ruby, at once. But Mrs. Waring persuaded me to remain for a dance that occurs tonight, and for which Harry and Bob are now busy dressing in the next room. On Thursday it snowed again, and though before that everybody said the older snow would go, it did not, and now we have about a foot, and the mercury at $9\frac{1}{2}$ this morning. But I am going to travel out by a freight team. I decided this because George has freight at Coulee City waiting, his whole winter outfit for the store and nobody willing to risk the journey now that winter seems to have begun in dead earnest. Maxey came in from Allensburg and hesitated. So to turn the balance I threw myself and freight in for him to take down, and this did turn it. So if he can get ready, we start tomorrow, for a four days' drive. This will be a new experience at any rate. My hides are all packed, and my warmest clothes out against need. I fear it's going to be horrible getting up in the morning, for we don't stop at houses, but anywhere when the water and wood are handy.

November 25. The dawn was not a gay one but interesting enough as a picture of customs and manners. We drove down in the sleigh by a cloudy moon, and this morning of my departure it snows, though not as if for all day.

141

November 27. En route. Snow everywhere and a cold slow drive. This is the second night. The first passed at a cabin in the timber country, called Leasy's, eighteen miles; last night here at Wateous', fifteen miles. We came out of the timber country with the suddenness of an explosion into this godforsaken waste. I was glad to have suddenly seen Cheval, the right-hand man of the fire-eating French Marquis, whose name I forget. He was very pleasant, and so was his wife; and the dinner we ate there was really worth the sum paid for it, twenty-five cents, which is a rare occurrence.

The first night at Leasy's was miserable. A dirty horrible little cabin, a frowsy old man, a pipe-smoking old woman whose dialect was the only good thing about her (she said to "much" a person etc.), and besides these a visitor who is there from across the Methow. Besides these were three dogs, three cats, and lice, I think. So after a mean supper Maxey and I made our beds outside on the ground under a shed. I will say that our hosts urged us to make ourselves comfortable in the cabin, but though they were kind, we preferred cold to filth. The weather was, and is, most mournful. The pine woods were so heavy in snow on their branches that they were gray in the landscape, like ghosts.

Last night here was better, and Filer, with another freight team going from George Waring to Coulee, has overtaken us. Now, for the rest of the way we travel on the Big Bend country, which, seen across the Columbia from here, with the wide desolate valley lying between, looks more utterly dreary in the snow than it did in October in the dust. Maxey's night leader has just kicked him and nearly broke his leg, but chaps saved him. He told me of a signpost in the Big Bend that originally read simply "35 miles to Central Ferry," but travelers had successively added their impressions of the Big Bend: "45 miles to water," "75 miles to wood"; then a wit had finished, "2½ miles to hell." Yet at the World's Fair, innocent gazers will see huge specimens of wheat and other grain grown "In the Big Bend Country." Watson here tells me the people who selected these had to hunt miles for each single spear, and I've no doubt it's quite true.

Night.   After crossing the Central Ferry we ran into a snow storm, and all afternoon we crawled along through the dismal country. Now we are passing the night in a ruined schoolhouse that stands in the middle of viewless desolation. Snow one foot deep. The horses are tired and tied around the wagons. We have fortunately in this schoolhouse a little stove, with no door, but it burns the wood we fetched from below, and keeps us warm, while the wind blows through between the gaps in the logs and the snow falls through the roof. We fried some bread, made coffee with water from an old alkali well outside, and I cooked some salt side. This all sounds most uncomfortable, but it's bliss compared with what camping in the snow would have been, so I bless the schoolhouse. A pile of quite good desk benches looks incongruous in this ruin. Whether we make Coulee City tomorrow or not, in the evening, is a doubtful thing, and I fancy that getting up in the morning before daylight is not going to be luxurious.

November 28, 6:30 A.M.   It has begun to get daylight. I got out of the blankets at four and was pleased to find it not so cold as I had anticipated. I made the fire easily and so had not long to wait to be entirely warm. At 4:30 I yelled to Maxey and Filer, who arose with cheerfulness, and now we have had breakfast, the horses have had oats, and most are harnessed. It remains to water them at this dubious alkali well, hitch up, and go, all which will be done creditably early. The water in the pail froze in this sieve of a schoolhouse, last

night, but the weather is really mild, and very husky too! I
wish I felt sure we should reach Coulee City tonight.

Coulee City, 7 P.M.   I am glad to say that we did, but
it was a hard day. Soon after we started, there occurred what I
suppose was the sunrise. That is, the leaden-coloured east
turned a clotted sore red for some five minutes and then
deadened out again into a cheerless gloom. We drove for
miles without seeing a bush as high as one's knee. The dead
grass barely showed above the snow, but here and there a thin
yellow bunch of spears that were taller emerged and stood
leaning in the air that was too still to wave them. A heavy
white fog bank extended to our left for miles, ragged and mo-
tionless, and above that came a bank of cloud like blue ink,
and above that always the leaden sky. We ran into the fog,
and then it came on to rain.

We passed Foster's Creek, visible by the bare willow brush
that marked its course, and here and there was a deserted
cabin or a forlorn wire fence, then nothing again for miles but
snow, fog, and huge black rocks standing alone, looking like
buildings. At Alkali Wells we learned we had thirty miles still.
We pushed on till 12:20 and then nooned by a large rock,
giving the horses oats, and eating cold bacon and sour bread
ourselves. My blanket and buffalo coat were sopping with the
rain, which now stopped.

We passed Haines's lakes, puddles of alkali; these and occasional badger holes en route blackened the snow and made
a variety. As we reached the beginning of the descent into the
Coulee, the fog lifted so we could see extending beneath it the
horrible country this town lies in. I thought it horrible by
sunlight, but this afternoon it was ghastly. The gaping holes
in the earth, all of the blackest rock, and endless in their extent, made a labyrinth of cuts and very large crevasses as

144

far as you could see. The world's surface was nothing but huge cracks, and these looming under a dismal bank of fog.

As we crossed through the bottom of the Coulee, the mud from recent rain was as awful as the dust had been before, and rising out of it shapeless mounds of stones, forming squares and alleyways, between which lay the mud. So we reached Coulee City just after dark, and I was actually glad to get to this hole. The civil landlord Mr. Bisbie was pleasant and carried in my baggage, spread my sodden blanket and coat to the fire, and treated me to a drink of whiskey. I have reason to believe the hardest part of my journey is over. Maxey and Filer, my companions in the discomfort of the last four days, say they never traveled in more wretched weather.

Between Coulee City and Spokane, November 29. Now I am in a train once again, and leaving this Big Bend desert behind me at an encouraging speed. These coulees are a sort of Leviathan scenery, wonderful, unlovely, and repulsive. A hard rain set in by and by, and in this I departed. Maxey and Filer came to the depot, and we parted there. The final picture of Coulee City, with its board boxes standing among swamps of muck will remain to complete a picture of utter horror I shall not soon forget. When a country and a town are so livid in desolation as this, they seem to fascinate me. I must see if something can't be done with them.

When I think of the amiable Maxey and Filer traveling back with their loads through the dismal country we all came through together, I pity them indeed. It's pleasant to think how good-humoured we all took each new discomfort. The beastly weather, the scanty food, the lack of much shelter— all these things furnished us with nothing but mirth. I can see Filer now, ahead of Maxey and me on the road, driving his six horses through the rain and, as he stood in his freight wagon, jumping now and then into the air to warm his feet or beating his arm against his body. Both these men are simple and pleasant natures, and I grew to kindly like them in the four days. That line of Virgil's about looking back with pleasure on hardships that are passed by well deserves the immortality it has gained, for I don't know a truer line in all poetry.

And now already my night at the ruined schoolhouse has become a purely pleasant reminiscence, though when I saw the building as he halted by it in the snow, my heart sank. I looked through its walls much as through the ribs of a wreck, and it struck me that my journey was truly a rougher one than I liked. I'm glad to think the men thought it was rough too. Filer said he had traveled across country a good deal, but never in worse weather, and both declared several times each day that if they had guessed what they were going to have to put up with, they would not have come to travel Waring's freight for three cents a pound, or any sum at all. They're doing it for two, and George is certainly lucky to have his supplies in.

December 2. A week ago today I left George Waring's. We are now running through the huge vividness of Dakota. But still the wonderful light is here and invests the monotony with charm.

A passenger in this car has *Harper's* Christmas number, in which my eyes were feasted by the sight of my story of Lin McLean. It has been well illustrated. And my wish now would be to hear the passenger say something about it. O Joy, O Rapture, I did! The army officer I had talked with about Custer picked up *Harper's* after lunch. Just now I found it lying on the seat opposite his and began turning the leaves. "This looks like a good number," I observed to him with diplomatic subtlety. He remarked he liked *Scribner's*, and I continued turning the leaves. "I read a story in there," he said—"Mac, MacKay, or something." Then he laughed, and I inquired (with continued subtlety) what it was about. "Oh, it's a cowboy," said the officer. "There!" opening at one of the illustrations, "Lin McLean. That's it. He went East." Then this excellent officer, this truly discerning critic, told me the story all through. "And he gets back to Rawlins," he concluded, "and tells the bishop that he guesses the fellow that wrote that about the elder brother 2,000 years ago had things about right." Then he roared. "Oh, it's a good cowboy story," said he, and I, preserving my incognito, remarked (with final subtlety) that I should have to read it. There's encouragement for you, O Wister!

February–March, 1893

TEXAS

IN February, 1893, Owen Wister and Harry Groome, a contemporary and a Philadelphian, went to Texas to stay on the
ranch of Fitzhugh Savage, also a Philadelphian. It was entirely a pleasure trip.

Savage bought cow ponies, schooled them at his ranch
(Seven Springs, near Brownwood), and sold them in the East
as polo ponies. Frank and Dick Conover, whom Wister had
known at St. Paul's School, owned ranches within riding distance of Seven Springs, and they often came over for rousing
bachelor parties. This set of Texas bachelors frequently
played polo in the afternoon, a game that they taught Wister,
and played cards and drank whiskey at night, activities in
which Wister held his own.

1893 (Spring)

February 22. At Brownwood, Savage and Frank
Conover met us on the platform. The hotel was not uncomfortable, and Brownwood is a fair specimen of these board
towns. But Savage astonished me with its morals. The munic-
ipal authorities are all church members, and professional
ladies are run out! Also I read a regulation forbidding anyone
to throw paper or refuse in the streets or alleys, except in the
barrels or boxes placed for the purpose. This is not much like
Lander, or Casper, or Buffalo! But there are breezes of hy-
pocrisy in the air, and I am inclined to think that Virtue in
Texas is not more rampant than in other states. Many families here are so religious that they cannot possibly dance.
But they have assemblings of young men and maidens that

are called Play Parties. At these a song is sung, quite harmless throughout.

February 21. We left Brownwood on Tuesday morning, February 21, under a fine sun. After a little, Savage gave the reins to me and I drove 4-in-hand for the first time in my life. Such an experiment with Texas ponies seemed to me highly precarious, but it answered well enough. Our team, "A," "Ink," "Ellis," and "Molasses," behaved wonderfully and took us along so we caught up with the stage at the dining station. While dinner was cooking, we waited in a sort of sitting and bedroom combined, into which the host had showed us. The bed was not made and was in rumpled disorder of quilts and sheets. Savage asked the host to join us in a deer hunt, but he was not able, he said, because his wife was sick. Upon this there was a movement among the quilts and sheets, and we perceived the lady herself, wrapped among them. We had been loudly conversing for twenty minutes without the slightest suspicion of her presence.

After dinner, with a new team of Texas ponies we went on. We had so far never been outside a lane between wire fences. When there was no longer any lane, we still were surrounded by the wire fences that enclosed enormous pastures through which we passed by a succession of gates. The live-oak and mesquite still clothed the country with seeming orchards. In the leafless mesquite frequent bunches of mistletoe grew, and their green showed far as we drove. Sometimes the ground was stony and almost impassable, while generally it was of earth, brown and dry; the smaller growths being cactus, cats-claw and broom-weed. The air was extremely springlike, but no wild flowers had come yet. We had finished our forty miles and reached Savage's Seven Springs Ranch at about four. To me it had no appearance of a ranch, but of a New England farm, owing to the prevailing effect of orchard.

Savage's servant is a negro weighing 280 pounds, named Homer. His foreman is married and lives in a little house a hundred yards off. Then there are several hands living in a third building that stands near the stables and corrals, and which in Wyoming would be called the Bunk House, but which one of the hands has christened "The Boar's Nest" because inhabited by bachelors exclusively. In this part of the country you come upon that miserable prudery about words that seems almost fabulous. In the presence of a woman you cannot use the ordinary words for male animals of any species. If you do, it is an insult. Thus you must allude to the "male cow," the "male hen"—though I believe that "rooster" is permissible. When one reflects that this bosh is the code of the most degraded and worthless class of American known, namely the cracker, the "poor white trash," the ignoble breed that was despised by the nigger in the South, and which has come here to Texas where it remains as sordid, ignorant, and incompetent as it has always been in whatever region it has infested, the thing becomes highly ludicrous.

Savage took me to a neighbor, a Texan of the second generation, I think, Bill Montgomery. Bill and a wolf trapper sat in the cabin, and the trapper during conversation appealed to me to say if this were not a splendid wolf country; and on my frank confession that I had no experience in wolf countries and was not a judge of what was a good one, he was astonished and amazed for some time, and laughed and said, "Well, well, you allow you don't know a wolf country!" Savage explained to me afterwards that this was because he could not conceive of anybody's being so ignorant as that. Delightful! In Wyoming you seldom find a citizen now-a-days so unsophisticated. A cowpuncher may despise you for being ignorant of his accomplishments, but he knows that many people are.

152

Bill Montgomery gave us a quiet meal but was very urgent and hospitable. Savage could not induce him to talk about his early journey across the Staked Plains, a region I am anxious to be told of. As soon as Montgomery felt I was a sort of audience for whom he was being invited to perform, he froze up, not out of malice, but inevitably. There is never any hope of extracting songs, anecdotes, or anything from people of this sort. You must sing to them first, and by so doing gradually lure and warm them till bye and bye out of sympathy they will unconsciously dance for you.

Texas life breeds sayings and doings enough to fill a volume. For instance, on the road to Brownwood there used to be a sign: "See Cross-eyed Jim before you sell your hides." The gentleman himself put it up, as that was the name he was known by; but today he would not care to have you call him by it, for he has become civilized. It is Texas fashion if any man has a deformity to name him accordingly. One Ace Brown had a hump back and was known as "Camel." A man lame from being shot in the leg is "Crip" Jones.

I have come upon a unique song, which a boy wrote out for Savage, and I transcribe it faithfully. Only a cowboy could have produced such an effusion. It has the earmark of entire genuineness.

1.

As I walked out one morning for pleasure,
I met a cowpuncher a-jogging along.
His hat was thrown back and his spurs was a-jingling,
And as he advanced he was singing this song.

Chorus

Sing hooplio get along my little dogies,
For Wyoming shall be your new home.
Its hooping and yelling and cursing those dogies
To our misfortune but none of your own.

153

2.

In the Springtime we round up the dogies,
Slap on the brands and bob off their tails.
Then we cut herd and herd is inspected,
And then we throw them on the trail. (*Chorus*)

3.

In the evening we round in the dogies
As they are grazing from herd all around.
You have no idea the trouble they give us
As we are holding them on the bedground. (*Chorus*)

4.

In the morning we throw off the bedground,
Aiming to graze them an hour or two.
When they are full, you think you can drive them
On the trail, but be damned if you do. (*Chorus*)

5.

Some fellows go on the trail for pleasure,
But they have got this thing down wrong.
If it hadn't bin for these troublesome dogies,
I never would thought of writing this song. (*Chorus*)

I have heard more stories of cowardly murders here than I have ever heard before. And it is a serious thing to be a witness against any man, for he or his brother or cousin will shoot you sooner or later. In fact a man who is likely to be a witness at a trial not yet come off is likely to be killed by some unknown person as he sits by his lighted window in the evening. Sometimes these proceedings have a touch of the ludicrous. There was a versatile doctor who was helping dig a well. He was down at the bottom and just beginning to be raised out by the man at the windlass, for he had lighted the fuse of a heavy blast. But the man at the windlass had some months previously assisted at a lynching; and the brother of the lynched man had ascertained the names of all the parties, and came into the country from up north, and just at this particular moment was watching the man at the windlass from behind a bush. It being a good chance, he shot him dead, and the doctor halfway up the well plumped down again on the hissing fuse. His screeches produced no effect on the parties above; but he had a happy thought and bit the fuse off in time.

There is to this story, also, a moral. About three years ago this part of the country was in a high state of disorder through cattle-stealing and other crimes. In eighteen months there were thirty-four murders. It began to be a common thing for people to receive a paper giving them ten days to leave the country. If a man was noticed to be "eating too much beef without owning cattle in the country," he was sure to get his ten days' warning; and the results that followed upon neglecting the hint were so uniform that a man upon being given ten days to quit was heard to exclaim, "I'll let 'em have nine days back." And accordingly he left at once. Thus many people left land behind them which they would not be likely to return to, and from this quite a business grew up. The owners of lands so vacated would receive a letter from their district written by some well-wishing citizen who, "supposing they had no further use for their domicile," wrote to say he would pay them so much for the land and improvements. This was frequently done.

In fact, people began to receive notices of ten days at such a rate that one, Ace Brown, one of the citizens who often wrote making offers to buy their deserted places, began to be looked upon with interest. About this same period there lived a pony whose history is not a common one. He was ridden by a negro named Jim. Jim was on the black list for being suspected. Nothing was definitely (or legally) known against him, but his reputation was bad on many counts. Jim rode the pony out one morning, and in the afternoon the pony returned in good order but without Jim; and the saddle was bloody. Some few days later the remains of Jim were found; and it looked as though he had been shot on the pony's back. Then Ace Brown took him and rode him. And again one day, the pony returned in good order, but Ace was not in the saddle. They found Ace hanging to a tree which overhung the road he had traveled. And later it grew plain that the rope had been adjusted as he sat on the pony, which had then been driven from beneath him. The pony was taken north by Savage and is now owned in Philadelphia.

One of the neighbors here—Jim Neil—received a ten days' notice but suspected it was not genuine and decided to stay. Of course, he took precautions. Wherever he went he "packed" a six-shooter and a Winchester along with him; rode on high places; avoided thickets, and did not go through gates, but took fences down instead. Thus he was never troubled and is here still.

He is fond of putting up jokes on strangers; and one evening when he took supper here, Groome and I tried to make ourselves out in conversation more ignorant of the West than we are, hoping to draw some stories from Mr. Neil; but we drew nothing. He is always after Thoroton, it seems, and on one occasion told him this story.

They had a dance somewhere—one of the regulation dances where the babies are all brought and piled in a corner while their parents jump about to music. After the thing had got going full swing, some unknown person got the babies and changed all their clothes—putting the linen of Mrs. Jones's little boy upon Mrs. Smith's little girl, and so on. In the dim light nobody noticed, and all went home with the wrong baby. Next morning there was the devil to pay, and for a week the whole countryside was busy exchanging and identifying babies.

156

Thoroton believes this for a fact. Savage told me it was all Neil's invention. I maintained Neil's invention is not up to that high level and that he read the story somewhere. The other day he was over here again before I was up in the morning, and I shouted out to Savage to tell Neil that he got the baby story out of the back of an almanac, which Savage did. Neil said that it must be in the almanac for next month, then. But he admitted that he had heard the story down at San Saba.

To devise a trick of that completeness clean out of your head while you were talking to an Englishman would indicate most unusual powers; and I think, that if the thing did not actually occur, somebody thought of doing it while they were actually at a dance with the pile of babies in sight. Then the flight of imagination would be one of which even I might be capable.

Saturday night was something I have not seen since I lived in Cambridge. Groome, in a stiff white pair of duck trousers, was master of ceremonies. He was superior to most and equal to any I have seen. Such occasions as these were once common and also appropriate for me. And though they will grow less and less so, I trust the time will be long before I cannot on occasion still rise to the necessary pitch and join in. But for a company of people of thirty and upwards, we conducted ourselves like the finest species of undergraduates, and it was most beautiful to see. Next morning we walked a quarter of a mile in pyjamas to the water and went swimming.

March 25. A pleasant visit at Frank Conover's. On Thursday night we unexpectedly caroused to such a note that next day I was nearly obliterated, and poor Frank was entirely so. At two made my final farewells, to Savage, Thoroton, and Conover, and drove twenty miles to a Mr. Atkinson's, where we passed a pleasant evening and comfortable night. Working for the Atkinsons is another Englishman who shows unmistakable signs of once having been a gentleman. *La voix c'est l'homme*, and his was gentle and civilized, as was also Atkinson's. His name is Philpot, and, O Heaven and fig leaves! A Texas family he worked for in San Antonio could not manage to call him this; and by them and their associates he was obliged to be known as Price! He answered to the name of Price, because Texas ladies could not possibly say Philpot and feel pure.

New Orleans, March 28. Before Texas is too much a thing of the past, I will write a few final notes of incidents highly characteristic of that community.

There was a negro named Brock in Brownwood, a kind of pimp as many of them are. He had been employed as messenger between a man and a certain married woman. This got him the woman's confidence, and she employed him to gather cavaliers for her. She seems to have been both gregarious and mercenary. One evening she had told him to supply her with a companion, and finding a likely young male in a saloon, he struck a bargain and brought the male into the lady's presence. She screamed, and the male immediately filled Brock full of bullet holes, for he was the husband. But where poetic justice fails is that this husband and wife are now peaceably housekeeping together. Boccaccio or Balzac could have used this theme and embellished it to advantage.

TEXAS VOCABULARY

To come up dead to die.

Little old applied to anything, e.g., a little old pony; hard to say what it means.

Like getting money from home delightful, easy.

Trifling poor, mediocre.

Bobble mistake, blunder.

To puny to be ill.

To break it off in a person to get the better, to outdo, to spring and bind.

To fog to hurry, to scamper, to go quickly.

A-goin' and a-comin' thoroughly, completely.

Bugged up dressed up.

Vara 33⅓ inches, Mexican.

Front name first name.

Spot cash ready money.

Yearlings steers, 1 year old.

Long yearling 18 months. (Anything is a yearling till it's 2.)

2's and 3's steers of 2 and 3 years.

Stag not cut till late, has a coarse head.

Doga anything in stock that's triflin'.

Loafer large wolf (Spanish Lobo).

NIGHT HERDING

The personnel needed to control while driving, say 3,300 head, after the cattle have been broken in to traveling on the plains is the cook with eight men around the herd. One of these is the boss, or foreman, who receives $100 a month where the others receive from $35 to $40. The boss takes his turn night herding and is not unlike the captain of a ship, ready to turn in everywhere on an emergency. There is also sometimes a second boss, whose position is one of difficulty on account of jealousy. His pay is about $45, or was from '83 on. Sometimes there is an extra man to herd the horses ridden by the other men. He rides in the wagon in the day time with the cook, who drives, and at night he herds the horses. This is unusual, however. Commonly the men take turns looking after the horses by day and at night hobble them. Each man has usually four horses, which form his "string." When traveling, the horses as a rule travel ahead of the herd.

If the herd is one gathered on a range and moved out, it dislikes to move and will try to get back to the range; also, if it is a bunch gathered by twos and threes from different ranges, and where some may be yearlings just separated from their mothers, the difficulty of holding such a collection together at first is of course greatly increased, and perhaps twice the number of hands may be needed. The herd may be made up, like a river, of two or three big tributaries and then others thrown in here and there to make the balance. Under such conditions many get loose and have to be left till next year, when perhaps $1 a head may be paid for gathering them in. A roadbrand is the brand placed high up along the back, generally a single letter put on with a stamp iron, so that when the stock is crowded together this brand will not be hidden out of sight but be easily seen from its position, and also because it is fresh and hence conspicuous.

"Milling" is to circle the herd when it threatens to stampede. By driving the animals at right angles a circular motion is sustained, and thus a spiral motion is made as the herd proceeds across the plain. It seems that a mere nothing suffices to cause a herd [to] stampede. An old cow will snuff once, and the bunch starts off like lightning, as if this had been a prearranged signal. Then the two ways to stop them are, first, to have three or four men on one side continually turning them, keeping along with them and so bring them around behind the rest, thus making an ever contracting ring till the whole is a mass of animals pivoting on its center; or a man takes the lead (which is very dangerous, because one trip means death under the hoofs of the following cattle), and he rides ahead, turning on a wide circle and contracting till the rotary motion is produced. Second, if the bunch has stampeded, let men ride along each side after two or three of them, keeping them from scattering and yelling to them as they go until gradually, two or three miles after, the herd quiets down.

160

Sometimes if a man finds himself in the road of an advancing stampede, he can jump to the ground and by waving his slicker cause the cattle to sheer off to either side and pass him. Thus he will create a little hollow of safety walled in by rushing animals.

All this is concerning the trail herd. In delivering a bunch of 100 or 50 to the trail herd before it starts, it is not essential (as later when trailing has begun) to let the animals lie down at night. Pens are used, and inside these the men on guard ride among the cattle and prod them or otherwise keep them on their feet. This is because, being on their feet, they make a continual movement and disturbance among each other; whereas when all are bedded down and utterly quiet, the starting up of a rabbit, the passing of a dog, or the striking of a match will be very likely to startle them and stampede them at once. Singing to quiet the cattle is important. The more restless they are, the louder or more inarticulate is the singing, no words being used at all, but only a strange wailing. But as the cattle grow quiet, the music gathers form, and while the herd lies quietly at rest on the plain, the night herders are apt to sing long definite songs as they ride round and round the edges.

June–December, 1893

=========================

WORLD'S FAIR, WYOMING,
YELLOWSTONE, ARIZONA,
SAN FRANCISCO, PORTLAND

THE second half of 1893 found Owen Wister discussing with Harper and Brothers a contract to write for them on his next trip West, though he had not yet given up the law profession. He traveled twice to the World's Fair at Chicago that year, as well as to Wyoming, Arizona, and the Pacific Coast.

On June 16, by previous arrangement, Wister met Theodore Roosevelt and other members of the Boone and Crockett Club (a group of men who hunted American big game) at the World's Fair, where they had dinner in a cabin on a wooded island near the fairgrounds. "We dined well and simply, camp fashion," wrote Wister. "Delicious fish and beefsteaks. Theodore wanted to have simple drinks also—whiskey and beer. But Deering and Chanler struck, and I seconded them, and so we had champagne. A lively dinner."

Later in the summer, after returning to Philadelphia, visiting the Fair again with his mother, and striking West, Wister met Frederic Remington in Yellowstone Park. Remington had been asked by Harper and Brothers to illustrate the Western stories. On the trip with Wister was John Stewardson, a Philadelphia artist and lifelong friend who in 1892 had illustrated *The Dragon of Wantley*, Wister's fairy story.

The Journal entry for October 8 at Fort Bowie is memorable because for the first time Wister mentions riding with Corporal Skirdin. He says of him in the Preface to the Collected Edition: "I rode many miles of desert and mountain with Corporal Skirdin—born in Arizona, cowpuncher, scout, everything, and just then in the Second Cavalry—detailed to companion me in my wanderings. He seemed to me a sort of incarnation of my imaginary Virginian; he ratified my imagination."

1893 (Summer–Winter)

Philadelphia, June 18. Whenever I felt sufficient
energy during the journey home yesterday and the day before,
I continued writing "The Bear Creek Barbecue," which is
turning out as it should. I read the nearly completed MS to
two plain-talking critics over brandy and soda last night at
the club—Savage with his Western knowledge and Cresswell
with a just sense of mankind—and they commended it. Cresswell made one or two wise suggestions by which I shall profit.
My mail downtown contained two excellently welcome letters
from Mr. Alden of *Harper's Magazine.* One accepting my two
stories "Balaam and Pedro" and "Em'ly" and enclosing three
hundred dollars for them, which is twenty dollars for a thousand words and good enough pay at present; the other hoping
I would not desert the Harpers for "rivals" and inquiring if I
had "really" been in Texas lately, as the editor was anxious
to do modern Texas in the magazine.

Success has of late fallen to me so amply for so little output
upon my part that I feel superstitious—as if it had thundered
left!

> O Muse of mine, if such a Muse there be,
> Lean from thine airy hill and bid me speed.
> Give me God-speed, my Muse, and hearten me
> For noble ventures; all thy help I need.
>
> Beckon me, gracious lady, wave me on;
> So in the lists I shall behold thy smile,
> And, when mid din of joustings I am gone,
> I'll hear thee singing in my heart the while.

These are halting verses, and don't do credit to the Muse or me.

Dined at Manheim with father and mother. Tom was there. Read as much of "Barbecue" as was finished to them. Went in town with Tom, who had a great plan for a drama we are to do together—a very strong situation for end of 2nd Act, which is our starting point. Moral of drama: Westerners must come East to spend their money. Tom likes "Barbecue" but complains my style isn't brief enough. I want a leisurely one. But Tom may be right. Finished "Barbecue" at Club, sitting up till two to get this off my mind. Then it became so much on my mind that I slept poorly in a hot room.

June 23. In train returning from New York. I went today to see Mr. Alden at the Harpers. I told him of my present literary plans, which seemed to suit his notions. The novelette about Chalkeye, he spoke of as possible for the Weekly if, when it should be written, the Monthly was full. And the longer book, "The Course of Empire," he at once suggested would do for the Monthly. May I live to do all this as it should be done—and much more! Alden was flatteringly jealous of my giving stories to other people—and when I delicately stood on my will as to this, he said, "Well, don't give the *Atlantic* any Texas stories." So I made him that promise. He said he was maturing a scheme he wished to propose to me, but he could not today. Asked if my journey West was laid out.

Afterwards, I went to Scribner's to get news of the story I sent them. A week they said would see one attended to. They were highly civil and "Knew my work."

June 27. This afternoon in the heat of rushing from one preparation for my journey to the next, comes a telegram from Alden of a momentous import. It says: "I have an important proposition to make which would if accepted by you modify your whole summer campaign and so ought to see you before you go West." This certainly means business. I answered I should call on him at ten tomorrow but feared plans could not be materially changed. They can of course, if the proposition is important enough—and we shall see what we shall see. I shall try hard to manage *both*—go to Wind River with John Stewardson, and do this other also. But this may betoken so great an impetus to my hopes and aims that Wind River must be foregone. In that case, I shall send [George] West some money anyhow, as I did last year when I disappointed him (and myself too, God knows!). He will not have lost anything by my failing him at this date. But I know now how entirely he depends on my salary. So he shall have as much as I can afford, and bless him.

June 28. In Broad Street station, 7:25 A.M. This is going to be a very long day, no matter what other sort of a day it is. My hopes of a compromise are even more strenuous than yesterday. I want some camp life and exercise and have been counting on it to drive the gout away that has been haunting my hands and head and throat capriciously for the past two months. If I can only persuade Alden to let me begin it, whatever he wants one to do, in October and not now, I shall feel that the cake was to be had and eaten, after all.

In the return ferry boat. I am returning by the eleven o'clock train, after a condensed and satisfactory interview. If I can write what is wanted of me, I shall certainly have eaten the cake and had it too. Alden wants me to do the whole adventure of the West in sketches or fiction, as I find most suitable in each case—taking Indian fighting, train robbing, what I please. He suggests articles of 7,500 words on an average, and to pay me $250 apiece—or on a basis of $30–$35 a thousand. He is at present paying me $20, which was an increase from $12. He also is willing to send Frederic Remington along with me if I desire it! He said that Remington was a very companionable fellow—but that I should do as I liked. He wanted the first MS by September 1. The series should begin through February, after "Balaam and Pedro," and continue through the year till at Christmas he should want—but here I interrupted and said that for Christmas, 1894, I had a Texas story in view called "The Partners"—so there he acquiesced. I told him of my summer plans and how unwilling I was to relinquish them and why. And this resulted in his giving me a generous "leeway," and I am to try and give him a MS of this pure adventure sort by October 1—and stay West, if necessary.

Events in my literary life have crowded so thick of late that I am a little bewildered. But one thing I plainly see— that one of my dreams to have Remington as an illustrator is likely to be realized in a most substantial manner. Alden wants my studies to pause for a while and says that after a series of pure adventure the studies will have a wider popularity. I insisted that I believed in my studies and had no wish to be interrupted or discouraged in my road through them to the final goal of "The Course of Empire," and he entirely assented to the desirableness of the scheme, saying those other would merely put in abeyance meanwhile. So now my next duty is to hunt material of adventure voraciously.

It occurs to me that if "Balaam and Pedro" is designed for January, I must try and have it postponed and write an intervening link at once—Alden, I'm sorry to say, finds "The Bear Creek Barbecue" too much of a link to be published alone. He said it was "admirable" to lead up to sequences and would do in the book, but not alone. His judgment bears out my mother's entirely—I told him simply to keep it by him till its time came.

My day yesterday was as busy as a day can well be. Everything was done however, and we had our quartet,[1] playing *Rienzi's Overture*, Brahms's *Symphony in E Minor*, Boccherini's *Minuet*, Mozart's *Symphony in G Minor*. Then I came in town and passed a good satisfactory night. From 7:30 till 11:15 this morning, it was trunks and checks and downtown and persons and hansom cabs, and at last our party of three got off quite serenely, meeting at the station when I had arranged all things and nothing was left but to sit down in the train. My mother is tired, but she is going to enjoy herself I hope and believe. Molly Moss is a great person to have along.

The chronological trap I have fallen into with my Western stories is rather a nuisance. If Alden won't wait until I can write a missing link in the Virginian's story, Balaam and Pedro will leave him apparently killed before he has fallen in love with the girl who subsequently is to marry him because he was killed! This tangle will not hinder the links appearing in a book, orderly; but I want the double benefit of their coming first in the magazine, and so my next week is now booked for scribbling at the Fair. Not a bad combination, though; and if I can write a story that shall be in itself complete enough to be published alone, and not fall into the trap of "The Bear Creek Barbecue"—which Alden admired but said needed a sequel and could not start alone—why all may be well.

June 30. Mrs. Darrack's. Our journey is smoothly over. My mother had a better night than usual for her in trains and was much better this morning and full of conversa-

---

[1] [This is the first mention of the eight-handed piano quartet. The other members of the quartet were Mr. John Ingham, Miss Molly Moss, and Mary Channing Wister, Owen Wister's cousin, whom he married in 1898. They played regularly during the winters, apparently starting in 1893 and continuing until Wister's marriage.]

tion. The day is hot and hazy. We got off at Grand Crossing; a man carried the extra bags the few steps to the Illinois Central Ry., my mother marching with my rifle over her shoulder while I carried her two valises. We must have looked like the Janissaries or something.

And now if I were doing what I ought, I should start on that story to send Alden—but I'll make believe it's impossible to write romance in unchanged sleeping-car clothes and cinders in one's hair. I'll pretend this is true and do absolutely nothing but be grateful our journey is so well over and take a bath.

July 9. I don't believe my story would have got itself done but for the gout and a cold laying me up one day wholly and part of two more. Now it's finished and goes to Alden tomorrow. He writes he'll put it in November if it'll do. I repaired to the Hunter's Cabin and wrote a false start on "The Winning of the Biscuit Shooter." I ripped my false start open, rewrote it, and went on in much better vein. Heard programme of American music—Arthur Foote's nice, Chadwick clever, MacDowell fanciful—but none of them much. "My Old Master's Island Phantasy" I thought the best. The truth is, no genius has had time to come here yet. When he does, there'll be no lack of applause. We know our poets—our Hawthornes and Emersons, our Lincolns and Sheridans. There are enough of us even now to recognize the real American composer, if he existed. Who says the West is not a theme for poets?

Theodore Thomas playing Wagner—I walked up to him yesterday and briefly explained I'd like him to dine.[2] He had never seen me before or heard of me, but I mentioned Paine

[2] [German-born conductor of the Chicago Symphony Orchestra.]

and Mrs. Gilliespie, and he came, under the bewilderment of monstrous fatigue. I sat in his room first, looking over scores while he changed his clothes, and out of the window were the caravels riding the calm lake. I took him to Old Vienna, and he was hard to unbend, but by nine o'clock I had many of the thoughts of his heart, and he talked about his children and Brahms and America.

He called Offenbach a "musical prostitute," and I asked if the expression did not admit what I claimed—"Oh, yes, he had talent," said Thomas. I told him of my plan to write an essay about Offenbach called "A Musical Outlaw." But Thomas objected. Said he could respect the outlaw. I see his point and shall bow to the judgment. Thomas' attitude toward his art is austere and fine.

I felt greatly complimented at the freedom with which he talked to me. Now and then I challenged his bitter criticisms of this country and told him a hundred years were not enough for everything. He met me squarely and even modified what he had said, and we damned New York and politicians together. He said (my pet thought) this country is great and prosperous in spite of politics. In a cafe where we went, the singers recognized him and sang to us exclusively. I left Thomas entirely radiant and cured of his fatigue, surrounded by twenty dozen Liederkranz enthusiasts to whom he introduced me, and we rioted amid smoke, beer, and light music.

July 13.   My days at the Fair are nearly over. It seems odd how quickly we human beings grow accustomed to the superlative and take miracles as matter of course directly we have seen them. Only two or three times before in my life and never to such an extent have I been moved and impressed as here; yet now it all seems as usual as Chestnut Street. I

171

wonder if the unpleasant superlative things, such as battles and the face of death, grow common too so one drifts on without caring or thinking much?

September 15.   On Limited eastbound, between Harrisburg and Philadelphia. I have let two months of travel go unchronicled till this last lap of the home stretch. But returning home from the West and Wind River this year is only a sort of parenthesis. In two weeks I shall go on my travels again; meanwhile just now this train is too rough for writing, and my neglected journal will have to wait a little longer.

October 4.   Limited Express between Fort Wayne and Chicago. Awake my journal and regain some punctuality if possible! I am some three months behind, and return to the first missing link at once before taking any further notice of the fact a new Western journey is begun than to record it. Thank the auspicious stars, I shall see the Fair today once more for a last glimpse.

July 14.   Was a chaos. I made a journey to Chicago and had our trunks all weighed and checked to Rawlins. There was no time to go to Savage's race, for which I was sorry. The laundry people did not return my clothes and kept me there nearly an hour in a heat that I should think would destroy all their employees before they could wash a handkerchief. Saw also a little more of the Fair and dined [outside the city] with Mrs. Darrack, leaving at once for Chicago again.

Reached Northwestern depot at 10:05. Our train went at 10:15, and I was to meet John Stewardson here. He had not come at 10:14, and after the train had begun to move he appeared, running. A few years ago this doubt up to after the last minute would have disturbed my peace a good deal while it lasted, but a contemplation of the worst that could happen —traveling to Rawlins alone and being overtaken by John in about six hours—rendered me stoic. It was a narrow shave, though, and I had his ticket. If he had had mine—but I provide against such possibilities.

A Russian was in our train, regularly seeing the country, with a Baedeker for the United States. The first we had even heard of—excellent, careful, accurate, and minute. Immeasurably better than any homemade book of the sort I have seen. These are generally plainly in the interest of various railroads and hotels, and vulgarly written. Our Russian was not much. But the heat out of Omaha made it impossible to enjoy anything or anybody. A violent burst of storm and lightning cooled us off, and the night was really cold.

July 16.   Early morning showed us the true land and light and desert. And John was entirely amazed, to my great delight. He had never dreamed or conceived of such sights, and [he] talked about it all morning. You could not have another share your enthusiasm more than John did mine for that first wonderful vision of space. We had the afternoon at Rawlins and made all our arrangements.

July 17.   The stage was worse than usual—worse than ever before—and all my old driver friends gone but Hank and Mills. I remembered what a vile cheat of a meal we have always been served with at Bull Springs, and I laid in beer and some canned things. At Bull Springs there was no dinner at all of any kind, not even a swindle. It seemed the people there expected to be replaced this week and were going away.

"Consequently," said the man who tends the stock, "she ain't cooked up anything." We failed to appreciate this sequence, but didn't care, having beer and groceries.

John rode outside with our second driver for the stage and came in reporting him a jewel. Said John: "He has all the expressions you make Lin McLean use, and a great many others you can't print." Three people inside one of those miserable two-horse stages they use now make a poor combination for sleeping. There is nowhere for anybody's legs, and all to do is to be thankful you are not four.

It was a relief to walk down Beaver Hill in the sunrise. The view under the early light is unimaginable. I sat beside the driver, whose name was Hunter, and he certainly was a jewel. He entirely sympathized with the horse thieves and rustlers over in Johnson County and told me there were four men who ought to be killed—Wolcott,[3] Canton, Irvine, and the other I forget. He was handsome, and with that fascination that so many of his kind have. He mentioned he had never had any luck with women, and of course we exchanged views and notes upon this inexhaustible subject. George West, who had known him in Lander, told us afterwards that Hunter was a cowpuncher noted extremely for his successes. So this modesty was as beautiful as it is rare.

I had promised John one good meal at Birkenshaw's, and we did not get it. We passed there too late for breakfast and too soon for dinner. The breakfast was bad, and Hunter's drive ended here, additional misfortune.

The new driver was without qualities. At Birkenshaw's an ambulance met us, and off got a respectable person who shook hands, and I remembered the Rev. Coolidge, Indian and clergyman. He was on his way to meet the Bishop of Wyoming. I was greatly disappointed to hear Bishop Talbot

[3] [Major Frank Wolcott, who was Wister's host in 1885 and who led the "invasion" of Johnson County in the cattle war in 1892.]

would not be at Washakie till Sunday when we expected to be gone up Wind River, and I wrote him messages on my card.

At Lander was one old acquaintance, Crawford, the signal service and weather bureau man. The government had offered the telegraph line between Fort Washakie and Rawlins for sale, 150 miles; Crawford bid $5 and got it. He can hardly help making some money I should think, but he looked shriveled and dry. Perhaps he sits on a heap of gold all night. Between the Agency and the Post, West came riding to meet us, being he said, impatient "for a sight of my face." His is almost the most lovable nature I have ever known.

At Washakie there were some old acquaintances: Mr. Moore, Captain Ray, Tigie,[4] now sergeant in Company K of the 8th and one of the best Indian soldiers, and old Washakie, ninety-odd years old—tall, splendid, a wonderful figure of a man. This was Tuesday evening. I went at once to call on Captain Ray, whom I found on his porch with two lieutenants, Norman and Miller. I asked promptly for an ambulance to go and get ourselves clean at the Hot Springs, which we accomplished. In the evening later, John and I both called on Captain Ray and were presented to his wife and asked to dine next evening.

Wednesday was filled with preparations for camp, and some photography. The squaws have to be surprised; they will not permit a "sitting," having the superstition that anything which takes the image away takes some control of the person. Old Washakie was pleased to have his picture made, and I stood him stark straight with one hand lifted. Three Indian soldiers made a request through Burnett to be photographed and were taken in a row. John was delighted with all that he saw and luckily had Burnett to be cicerone.

Each day, Burnett was going back to his place, and never went, and John had the benefit of his knowledge of the In-

[4] [The Indian guide who took Wister on the bear hunt in 1887.]

dians. He told a striking experience of being invited to attend the funeral of an Indian. They went into the mountains with all the dead man's belongings. They came to a deep chasm, down which they threw the corpse, and stones on top. Then, one by one, the man's effects—his blankets, pots, all he needed to make him comfortable in the next world. Lastly they came to his horse, his live horse, and Burnett objected. The squaws became angry, but the men of the family seemed inclined to listen to Burnett's protest. There was some consent, and they began to turn homeward, when the squaws raised fierce yells of fury. The horse had a blanket thrown in front of his eyes and, before Burnett knew it, had been led to the edge, where an Indian gave him a cut with a spear and he sprang, the blanket falling from his eyes. Burnett says that the horse turned and gave one look back at the party as he descended to his death.

If one knew all of Washakie's life, there would be an interesting and strange matter. Two incidents show something of him. He had given certain orders about having his tent moved. His mother-in-law (one of them) countermanded these orders; so Washakie had her killed. Lately, they began ploughing 320 new acres in the Reservation. Washakie was away hunting and, hearing of this, sent a messenger fifty miles to order the strip to be planted exclusively with watermelons. He had tasted one and liked it.

West had our horses near the old milk ranch, with an assistant he had brought down in case our party had been three. Originally I promised West the same salary of $100 a month if we took no one else, but it seemed better to him to get a second; and he preferred this at $75 a month to the other arrangement. The man's name was Wilkes, and he was a discharged soldier. West had been having him work at his ranch —reported him good-natured and a good cook—so we engaged him at $40 a month. While I was attending to these matters

176

John saw more of the Reservation under Burnett's guidance.

The Captain made himself most pleasant, talked much of Indian fighting, especially the campaigns of '73 and '77 along the Missouri. His opinion of Custer was of the worst, and if the stories he told us were not greatly coloured with prejudice, Custer was not even courageous, unless he was having the best of it. One of his habits was the card-sharping habit; and Ray told of a certain young New York officer whom Custer had played with and ruined, taking from him as winnings a cheque of $900 belonging to the government. This was on General Stanley's '73 campaign. Ray told of a certain raid upon a Cheyenne village on the Kansas (?) river Custer had made deliberately against orders, and nearly got himself and his command lost but for reinforcements that hurried up seeing what the mess was—Custer was found trembling and white as a sheet!

This is so contrary to all I have heard that I cannot but think Captain Ray prejudiced. He was on General Stanley's staff, and saw plenty of engagements and skirmishes in which Custer had part and on one occasion heard Stanley say to him: "You are the most insubordinate and troublesome officer I have ever dealt with. You may consider yourself under arrest, and take your station in the rear." What a comment on popularity, if all or half of this be true!

Captain Ray told some entertaining stories of a bibulous paymaster. He traveled with a secretary named Charley and a "jimmy-john." On one journey the stagecoach was overset on a mountain, a man's leg broken, and the stage demolished. The major was supposed to be dead among the ruins; but he poked his head out and cried to his distant-flung secretary, "Oh, Charley, is the jimmy-john hurt?" At Fort Robinson (?) he had a German as orderly, who was supposed to attend to the officer's business when the officer was drunk. One day the Colonel and some visitors from New York arrived at the paymaster's quarters and found both master and man hopelessly intoxicated. Later the reckoning was overheard: "You damned scoundrel, didn't I tell you you were not to get drunk unless I was sober?" "Yes, sir, but ven vas I going to haf my chance?"

The Captain, finding I was a literary fellow, promised to give me experiences for narration the next time I should call. John and I went over to Lieutenant Howard's and found he had gathered a company to meet us: Dr. Welty of the Agency, Dr. Raymond, and Lieutenant Miller. We had a pleasant time, and I made some excuses for West's not turning up. We soon found our recent host was not greatly beloved by his officers, and they sang us a song about him, made to "Ta-ra-ra-Boom de Ay." I was, of course, discreetly neutral and only said that so long as I had received nothing but civility and attention from Captain Ray, that was all I could speak of. But I got an idea he was not a pleasant person to deal with as a brother officer. West came in late to make his own excuses.

July 19. Our outfit started to wait for us at Bull Lake crossing. I told West that if I did not come the next day, it would be because I was ill, felt badly, and was afraid of another attack of erysipelas.

Of Bull Lake I heard an Indian legend. Now and then people hear a strange sound of moaning there. This is perfectly well established, but the actual cause is not. Some believe it is wind far in the cañon. But it occurs when no wind is blowing, and is impossible to place. Sometimes it seems subterranean. The Indians say that once a herd of buffalo which their tribe was pursuing ran over a rock wall and were drowned in the lake, in the deep bottom of which the old bulls still mourn for the upper air.

In the afternoon Howard and the doctor and I met at the target range, where John joined us and we tried our new sights, 100 yards off hand. After my first—a 2—I put the other four in the 4. Barringer's invention is an admirable sight, and I promised to send a set to Howard. I was feeling worse and worse and was foolish to be out in the sun. I thought I could pass through this threat by ignoring it. I went to bed and waked with unmistakable erysipelas though slight.

FORT WASHAKIE

July 25

Dearest Mother:

I have had a letter from Alden, and he considers "The Winning of the Biscuit Shooter" "first rate"—so that will be in the November number. They have now made a contract with me, all that I could wish. At my choice the series of stories begin in their March or their April number. If a MS is ready by October 1, then in March. But they must have one by November 1 at the latest.

My pay is to be $35 a thousand words for eight or nine stories of "Thrilling Dramatic interest," to be illustrated by Remington, who goes to any ground I may think necessary. Afterwards my royalty on the book is 10 per cent retail price. They attach more importance to this than any of their ventures for 1894, and will advertise it in the widest possible manner. The only thing that bothers me is getting the best material, and I have already written for reassignments to several people. I have some facts collected in Washington state last year that I think will do for No. 1, and I shall work them up at my ease in camp.

Your loving son,
D.

July 29

Dearest Mother:

We are now without misadventure at the top of
Wind River and the foot of the mountains, and the next
stop has become uncertain through hearing on our arrival
last night that the Indians were hunting where we had
expected to; and if that is really true, we should find all the
game driven away. But it makes very little matter where we
go, as there is sure to be game somewhere sooner or later.

On our way up the river (day before yesterday) John
went out with West after we had camped and shot a young
mountain sheep in a cañon, which was a delightful piece
of luck. Also we had no meat, so it served its purpose in all
ways, as by tomorrow we shall have completely devoured it.

Yesterday John and I fished all day along Wind River,
catching a few trout and overtaking our party here at night.
In a few moments somebody is going down to the post office
[word illegible], so I must stop.

Your loving son,
D.

July 31 till August 9. We stayed at Fish Lake. I was
more anxious to write than to hunt.

Barringer's sights have done a world for me; and I have
gained a confidence I never had before. There were shoals of
trout in Fish Lake, and I caught one that measured 21¼
inches. The last night there, John and West camped away at
the Lake of the Woods, bringing back a doe antelope in the
morning, for our meat was out. I finished "A Kinsman of Red
Cloud," in which I developed the story of the half-breed told
me by Captain Ray. I had to make a beginning for it, as his
facts take up the story at its climax. All that led to this the
Captain did not know, and I have no doubt the truth would

be much better than my fiction, which but for one invention is pretty commonplace.

August 9.   We went along the Divide to camp on the Sheridan Trail, two miles down the Pacific side from the summit. We passed through our old camp of 1887, and there, still in the ground and not one missing, were the stakes we had stretched our bear hides on.

There was ice every morning now, and getting up was cold, and washing at the frozen edges of the stream still colder. We remained at the head of Black Rock a day and found a way over round the steep lava ridges and down to what we thought was Buffalo Fork. We went down a good trail along the supposed Buffalo Fork and then over a ridge and down through abominable cross timber to a stream, and I imagined it was Pacific Creek. But when we were near it, the size showed us this was Buffalo Fork and the other a tributary, and a long important one, between it and Black Rock—something I have seen on no map and never before heard of.

September 8.   We waked at Cañon in three inches of snow, and drove away rather cold. Lunch at the Norris basin, where who should I meet but Frederic Remington! When I told him my name, he said he had many things to say (he had just illustrated "Balaam and Pedro"). I had many things to say to him, and we dined together at the Mammoth Springs, where I found most of my mail washed ashore. Some I shall never find.

Remington is an excellent American; that means, he thinks as I do about the disgrace of our politics and the present asphyxiation of all real love of country. He used almost the same words that have of late been in my head, that this continent does not hold a nation any longer but is merely a strip of land on which a crowd is struggling for riches. Now, I am a thin and despondent man and every day compel myself to see the bright side of things because I know that the dark side impresses me unduly; but Remington weighs about 240 pounds and is a huge rollicking animal. So to hear him more caustic in his disgust and contempt at the way we Americans are managing ourselves than I have ever been was most unexpected. This Friday night we sat in the little drink room with Captain Anderson, who is a man greatly after my heart. I was delighted to find how energetically he watches the Park.

My mail contained all kinds of news. They were well at home, various acquaintances were married or dead, but no friends. Scribner didn't want the story I had submitted to them, and quite right they were! I can make it much better. Grinnell wrote me concerning a paragraph in my White Goat article for the Boone and Crockett book. The story deserves wider publicity than this journal. It shows the Englishman beautifully.

In that article I have put what Thompson, my guide, said to me last year about the Marquis of Lorne falling off his horse at the Queen's Jubilee. An English publisher had written to Grinnell to say he would take 500 copies of the book if this could be omitted in a special edition, as it would hurt the feelings of many of his readers, especially as he published for the Marquis' wife and sister. Grinnell was indignant, he said; but as 500 copies would help greatly, etc., etc., he had consulted Theodore Roosevelt and Winty Chanler, who made themselves responsible for my wounded author's feelings. But my author's feelings certainly need no salve here, as I hastened to write Grinnell. Such a delicious adventure is worth the expurgation of a hundred treasonable paragraphs.

During the journey to St. Paul, which was hot and odious, Remington and I discussed our collaboration and many other things. He made a good criticism on the first two pages of "The Promised Land," which I accepted and profited by. In fact Remington's artistic insight is quick and clear and forcible.

At St. Paul our company parted. He went on in an earlier train, and the Smiths stayed to rest a day. John spent the afternoon with his classmate Ted Howe, and I pegged away at "The Promised Land" up in a bedroom at the Ryan House.

September 15. I reach home, leaving John for a week in Chicago. So our Western trip, John's and mine, began and ended at the same place, just like a work of Art.

September 26. Over to New York and my editor—present shaper of my destiny. It appears "Red Cloud" can't be in the series, even if accepted, or "Promised Land" either, because not made from material gathered by special journey. That's entirely right, for Mr. Harper is paying me high wages. But had I known it, I should certainly not have spent so many days in a tent on the Rocky Mountains, holding a pencil instead of a rifle. Still, it's perfectly right. Said Alden, "Your story is very bloody." "You're not going to get much American Western adventure without blood," said I, "and if you find that bloody, what will you find 'The Promised Land' which I bring you today?"

> It was too much in the slime, sir.
> You don't want Police-News crime, sir,
> 　　Robbing mails
> 　　And breaking jails,
> Ditching some poor locomotive.
> What's all that without some motive,

> Some true human fervent thing,
> Simple as a mountain spring?
> Well, my gracious Master Alden,
> Gracious in that me you called on
> To procure
> Literature
> For the potent Harper brothers
> When you might have called on others.

Then I told him that I certainly was anxious about my punctuality now. I had hoped these two MSS would put off the next day of delivery till December 1 and that it seemed to me I could not possibly get my material and write eight stories in time to finish in November '94. I explained that though I should go West at once, as soon as I heard from Captain Edwards in Arizona where I was to come, the finding of material would take some weeks before I could write at all.

Well, it all came out happily. I was introduced to Mr. Harper, and Mr. Harper was highly urbane; and I need not feel hurried, and I would try and give them something by December 20, and the series might run over in 1895, since the stories were not to be published as a series but as isolated stories; and if it proved a success, why there might be a second volume. So all this was full of purring, and I parted with Mr. Harper, who asked me to think of a title for the volume, as titles were of vast importance. And I told him my mind was already for some while concerned with this, and we both smiled farewells at each other. But I had a practical compliment from Alden. "Em'ly" I found, was to be in November and not Christmas. "The subscriptions come in after the November number," said Alden. The story I wrote him in Chicago will go in the Christmas, and this I like all the better, for it places the three in chronological order. "Em'ly" seems

184

a luck stroke. One or two sub-officials in the office made allusions to it that were most encouraging. I corrected proof and lunched with Alden and Charles Dudley Warner, whose writings have always given me great pleasure.

September 28, Thursday.   Next day I had satisfactory news from Alden. I had told him to let me know before I went West if the two stories would not do, as I would offer them elsewhere. I felt pretty confident of "The Promised Land." Harry Mercer had told me he could not praise that beginning too much, and John Stewardson had said it was very interesting, and then as a final test I had read it one night to Agnes Irwin and Mrs. Gillespie. Both had decided in its favour. I told them I was trying it on them, and should be happy for any amount of damning; I wonder how other men would do.

I certainly have profited enormously from having several intimate friends who bear nuisance of my MSS and speak their mind at the end. I wrote every word of "Hank's Woman" over again because of what Harry Mercer said. I can't remember a single story that has not gained by my adopting the criticism of one of these several long-suffering friends and making (often several) changes. So Alden took both stories and sent me $400 for them.

Monday, October 2.   I made all final preparations. Captain Edwards had written me to come to Arizona and see people there from whom I could gather the sort of information I sought, and Frank Michael had also written from San Francisco most encouragingly. I dined with John Stewardson at the club. At home next morning I played a perfidious trick of saying I should probably be back to dinner. I have always hated leave-takings, and they grow worse and seem more useless.

Saturday, October 7. Captain Edwards had written me to telegraph my arrival at Bowie Station to Major McGregor in advance, and I had done so; but arrived there, I was at a loss just what to do, or look for, and therefore ate my supper. After it, while getting my baggage from the train, McGregor himself walked up and asked if I were I.

We drove the thirteen miles to the Post, and I found my host greatly to my taste. He had a keen Scotch humor and discerned nonsense in anything or anybody at sight. He had enlisted and risen in thirty years to Major and shortly will be Lieutenant Colonel. He began before the war; served through that, and since has been always on the Pacific slope, and a very hard life, one winter losing four children through inevitable exposure.

FORT BOWIE

Sunday, October 8

Dearest Mother:

The Post is built in the exact heart of Apache Pass, a rather notorious place once where the attacks on the overland stage caused the creating of the Post. Now there is no more of either stage or attacks. Sahara cannot be more desolate than what you see here. From my window I look out through a gap into the plain of San Simon east—and west down to the other side of the Pass to Dos Cabezos, thence to the Dragoon Mountains. The names are good, all of them. I have met all the officers, who are, as always, cordial and glad to see me.

I shall not be here very long, partly for fear of wearing

out my welcome, partly because I must get to my real host
—that is, the officer who caused me to come here at all and
who has been preparing for my coming and as whose friend
I am entertained here. If you will address a letter to me care
of Captain F. A. Edwards, San Carlos, Arizona Territory,
it will reach me about six days later.

Your loving son,
O. W.

Sunday, October 8.   I lay idle, receiving the calls of the
officers. On our way here we passed a cabin, and the owner
was walking along the road to it; she was a young girl,
freckled, sturdy, in a sunbonnet, and round her waist a
cartridge belt and six-shooter. We paid her a short visit, and
she struck me as a capable person.

All this week, however, my education in the matter my
journey was taken for progressed at a good rate. The last day
Fowler and his boy and Rob, and I with a Corporal Skirdin,
who had had a singular pathetic history, explored a cave. We
were an hour in its passages but found no end.

Sunday, October 15.   I left Bowie, being sent in the
afternoon in an ambulance to the Station. Here I passed the
night at Tevis' Hotel playing whist till ten with the ticket and
telegraph clerk and a drummer.

Monday, October 16.   We had seven passengers and
the driver as far as Solomonville in the three-seated stage.
An abominable hot ride down the flat valley. Dinner at
Solomonville, which is a fruit-bearing, blooming fertile place,
under Mormon irrigation. My company for a little way was a
woman with a baby, and a Mexican sheriff with one leg, long

hair, and a six-shooter he carried ready, reposing on my over-coat. He was going to Thomas for two prisoners. At Thatcher I heard a lusty dominating voice outside giving the driver directions and chaffing the sheriff. "Who's riding in your bad company?" it inquired, and the canvas flap raised. "Why that's a decent man!" exclaimed the speaker, seeing me. "It's as much as your reputation's worth to ride with that fellow," he said. He had a short gray beard and a strong shrewd face. This was the Mormon bishop Leighton, owner of the stage line and of the whole Gila Valley community.

We reached Thomas by nine, where an army doctor from San Carlos greeted me and told me I was expected by Captain Edwards. There was no bed for me at the near Mormon Hotel, and he kindly offered me part of his own, but the landlady gave me a room over the way, where I went to bed at nine-thirty, being promised breakfast at four before the stage started.

A voice called at my door next morning and said the stage would go in five minutes. I jumped up and found it was 4:25. I flew over to the hotel, but no breakfast was there, and nothing but a blear-eyed Chinaman who said he would get some in twenty minutes. I paid my bill for the supper and lodging and departed in a rage. It was entirely dark and rather cold.

The voices of the other two departing stage drivers sounded through the town—"All aboard for Bowie," "All aboard for Fort Grant"—and so I drove away. I had the stage to myself and slept on a sack of barley that was in with me, while daylight came into the Gila Valley. After a while there was a shout from the bushes, and we halted. An Indian came out to the stage entirely naked but his breechclout, and his clay-colored body and long black hair looked strange in the dawn and the desert surrounding. He received from the driver a little sack of something he had commissioned to be brought

188

from Thomas for him the day before, and we went on. Each side the road we passed Indian huts, which are built of brush, and round-topped, looking like large hollow disks of hay. Some had old torn rags of canvas or blankets flung on them to help the solidity of the home, and from several came Indians and squaws to receive the little sacks or to give the driver ten cents to buy them this or that in San Carlos and fetch it on his return.

Captain Edwards came out of his quarters to meet me, and I was glad to take a bath and chat at ease. This Post stands on a sand terrace above the meeting of the San Carlos and Gila. Down the river some five miles is a rough cañon through these sharp hills, and among the flats and bluffs lie Apache huts, all of the same hayrick and rag-bag construction. The sun blazes down like a curse, but the nights were cool, and the light at sundown turned the whole bleak country into soft prisms and lakes of color. Also the moon, which we had at the full, rode so bright and strong that the cañons shown clear in the mountains, and only the large stars shone in the sky.

During the next days the officers and I called on each other, but they were dull people except Captain Myer, whom I like greatly and saw much of. He came to Captain Edwards' quarters quite often night after night, and we talked and smoked till taps. I learned a great deal from him and Edwards, and never before found out or saw so much of Indians. The chief of scouts was a certain Merijildo Grijaloa, a Mexican stolen by the Cochise band of Chincahaus when eleven years old, escaping when he was eighteen, since when he has been in Government service as scout and interpreter. I rode with him nearly every day and all over the country, buying the well-made and pretty Apache baskets, which are pronounced the finest original work we have, and hearing drop by drop much I came to learn. Had Merijildo only been aware of how extraordinary his own life had been, I should have had material for a volume of romances; but everything to him was either half-forgotten or a matter of course, and it was by dint of unremitting questions and repetition that I got him to tell me what he did.

By day I would thus catechize him as we roamed about the Gila Valley and talked to the Indians; and in the evening when Edwards and I returned from the unentertaining company of the mess, my military information would increase over the pipe and bottle. Edwards was more patient and good-natured over my endless questioning than it seemed possible for a man to be. Several times I sat down and made him dictate to me for two hours together, and half a dozen times a day I came to him with a new bushel of questions.

The day was like this: Early, by six-thirty, Edwards was up and out to his skirmish drill along the sand and brush by the river, coming back to wake me at eight, and we breakfasted. Once, to see and understand the thing, I went to skirmish drill with him. After breakfast he had some routine duties, and between times we gossiped in his room, enjoying each other's private comments on the doctor and certain under officers who did not please either of us over well, and I would take notes and also sleep considerably over a book I was reading. Then I rode with Merijildo after lunch or loafed and took notes of this and that item I happened to see as the hours passed.

I also went to stables with Edwards and conversed with several horses, dogs, and cats who met us there. From stables the Captain inspected the Kitchen, and I with him. After Kitchen inspection we had a little whiskey and then a dinner, and the evening. Two Issue Days came round while I was at San Carlos, and I watched both and learned the details of that business. Towards the end of my visit two companies arrived from Whipple Barracks to exchange with the two here.

There was a Devil Dance among the Apaches the night after their arrival, and a wild sight of remoteness from our day it was, with the fire and the figures, the tomtoms, up among these barren hills under the full moon. When it was time for Edwards to start with his troop for the assembling and regimental drill at Grant, I was more than half sorry this was over.

Friday, November 3. We went over the road and up the hill, where a paymaster had been robbed of $28,000, to Cedar Springs and camped on the graves of seven Mexicans —they were not marked in any way. Barney Norton, of Cedar Springs entertained Edwards and me all evening with the paymaster robbery and old Tombstone days and the trouble between the Earps and Clantons. His talk was a lively comedy of Tragedies and full of local color. I regretted having to go away and leave such a mine unexplored.

Saturday, November 4. We rode into Grant, seeing as we came out of the hills the dust of other approaching columns moving over the distant plain.

Saturday, November 11. I rode out to Cedar Springs to get some more of Barney Norton and, spending Sunday there, returned on the good horse Yellowstone that Edwards let me have whenever I wanted him. When I told them that I must go on Wednesday, they protested kindly, and Mrs. Arnold wished me at least to stay till the encampment was over; but my time draws short, and I was not doing as much work as I ought. So I came away, the last being more invitations and good wishes.

FORT GRANT, ARIZONA

Tuesday, November 14

Dearest Mother:

I'm going to San Francisco tomorrow, which brings me there on Friday the 17th. I had originally intended to see something of Southern California—San Diego, Los Angeles—but there's no time. When at the Palace Hotel, my days will be rigidly systematized, though subjected to high temptation from my various friends there. But the looming Editor of *Harper's* wants a story by December 20, and I must sit down in my room each morning and write it till it's done and mailed, for I propose having it ready by December first. When I return, it must be with a second under way or I shall know no repose.

Since I last wrote, the days have gone much in the same way, except that Saturday I rode out some twenty miles to spend that and Sunday night with an old rascal who had seen early days in Arizona and was very clever about them. We sat and drank whiskey together, and certainly this United States is an irrepressible country. I have heard many things, all of them in some superlative degree [so] funny or horrible that my terms of thought and standard of measure are entirely changed. Take for instance meeting a Mormon Bishop who has been in hiding for polygamy in his day, on account of nine wives; he has forty-seven children and can't read or write but signs contracts and letters with an X. He is seventy-four and the other day had twins. Now don't you see that it's quite impossible to preserve any proportion? Nothing can henceforth move my surprise.

Your loving son,

D.

Sunday, November 19, San Francisco. Frank Michael was at the ferry to meet me on Friday night, and we went to the Palace Hotel and had a little supper, I brewing some "Nile Water" in honor of the auspicious reunion. Then we went to the Club, and there I brewed "Sitana Cocktail" in honor the auspicious reunion, which lasted until two for me and five for others. I found I was known to some as the author of "Em'ly," and several men to whom I was introduced said pleasant things about the story.

Next day I read a large mail which had no bad news and was full of congratulations upon the *Atlantic* and *Harper's* articles. Many friends had taken the trouble to sit down and give me their good word, and I know no higher pleasure than the appreciation and encouragement that have been showered on me in the last year.

Mrs. Whitman's words made my eyes moist, and Frederic Remington wrote more than heartily about "A Kinsman of Red Cloud" that he is illustrating now. Ah, Muse, don't give out, nor become vain! As a matter of fact, all this praise makes me feel quite humble and soft and haunts me with a burning to do better. Then there was a slip from the N.Y. *Tribune*, saying Owen Wister's was a new name in current literature but one they would "fain become better acquainted with," and they spoke well of "Em'ly."

UNIVERSITY CLUB, SAN FRANCISCO

December 6

Dearest Mother:

Only a few stingy lines to say I'm well and that I hope you and my father are and also the cook, the man servant, the maid servant, and all that in them is. My story is finished and traveling eastward to Mr. Alden. I wish I could have had the benefit of your criticism or Harry Mercer's or John Stewardson's as to one thing, but it's too late. I undertook the difficult task of following the development of a state of mind and feeling by the objective method

entirely and prohibited myself from any analysis. And I
wanted to know if the invisible had been made visible at
all or not. For a few discreet explanations and comments by
the author inserted in the text might help. Ted Cabot's death
I was expecting, too.

Your loving son,
D.

UNIVERSITY CLUB, SAN FRANCISCO

December 9

Dearest Mother:

Just a line to thank you for your letter that came
today. We must endure the *Nation.* Its tone about the
hunting book was not friendly as it should have been for
an enterprise that is so purely disinterested and rational
and which makes no pretense of being in anyway belonging
to art.[5] And as for the *Nation's* passing over my stories, you
wait! One of these days I shall be visited with a northeasterly
drizzle from them. There'll be a brief estimate in which I
shall be described as aiming for Bret Harte and Kipling
and achieving a mild species of dime novels, "which is
apparently a welcome form of fiction to many readers at
present." Those are the words I prophesy they'll use. You
see. I would rather have their approval, of course, but a
plebiscite from the *Tribune* and papers in Wyoming, and
McLarvin, and Edith Wister, and army officers, and cowboys, are good enough to keep one going.

Your loving son,
D.

En route to Portland. December 12. I left San Francisco
last night, Frank Michael coming to the ferry, where I parted
with him as I had met him. Our farewell was not forever, as
there is some likelihood I must return in the winter. I have got

5 [*Boone and Crockett Club Book*].

194

enough from Wells and Fargo to make perhaps one good story for the adventure stories, but there are such mines of wealth waiting that I did not have time to touch, that it seems a pity to leave them so, when the company is so well disposed towards my project. In fact, I see that one should really tell the history of Wells and Fargo from the beginning, not as a short story, but a long book.

They began in 1852 and were at once a vital organ of California. To tell their growth and experiences would be to tell of the mines, the mails, the pony express, the stagecoaches, and a world of courage and skill not much like anything else in the world. Such a book might be called "The Romance of a Corporation." It would need a long study and the meeting and knowing well many people, "old-timers" who don't as a rule talk to order and, however friendly in intention, must be lured into unconsciousness over a cigar late at night. I should like to write such a book.

It would be a real contribution to our literature and a new thing too, I think. No one has yet made a corporation his hero. But then, it's a long way to come from home and the two lonely people there.

Monday, December 18, Portland. My stay here is over, and I go tonight. The morning of my arrival, Major Jackson, to whom Edwards had written, called upon me, and in the afternoon Captain Boutelle came over from Vancouver Barracks. I talked all morning with Jackson in his office, and he showed me maps of Tule Lake and the lava beds, also many photographs taken during the Modoc campaign.

Thursday, December 15. I spent [the day] at Vancouver Barracks with Captain Boutelle. This Post lies on the Columbia, among green levels and huge fir trees, which has

snow on Mount St. Helena shining over the purple hills to the
east, up the wide river—a very beautiful Post. In the evening
called on Bishop Morris. I pursued my talks with Major
Jackson on Friday and got at some of the personality of the
Modoc War. We had previously gone over maps, and I had
read his articles. Thus I knew the outside, but there was much
inside, and this I in part had from him. He lunched with me.

Granger, Wyoming, Wednesday, December 20. By evening we shall have passed Rawlins, and all this is mine own
country with nothing to note save that it looks as it should,
and the days are beautiful. We had a sift of snow lying on the
mountains through Oregon and Idaho, and this morning in
Utah there was some. But here the plains are gray with the
sagebrush. Some of us kill time with card games.

*Between Harrisburg and Philadelphia, Saturday, Decem-
ber 23.* At Harrisburg I bought the January *Harper's*, which
has "Balaam and Pedro" in it. I am curious to have a verdict
on this story. I know that I have never done anything so
good, or that contains so big a swallow of Wyoming, but the
event related is cruel; and "artistic" motives led me to ex-
clude all sunshine. This is not the kind of thing the general
public likes.

Later. My first verdict on "Balaam and Pedro" was given
me with miraculous promptness. A youth whose name I know
not, and with whom I have been playing whist through the
uninteresting states of Indiana and Ohio, came about an hour
ago and sat down by me. "Did you say you had *Scribner* for
January?" said he. I told him to get it from my valise at his
side. He got out *Harper's*. "It's the same," said he, and began
looking at the illustrations. When he came to Remington's of
the horse deal, he stopped and looked at it three times as long

196

as at the others. Then he read a few sentences in the text opposite and, turning some more leaves, finished all the illustrations the number contains. Then he returned and looked at Remington again. After that he found the beginning of the story and began to read it. When he had read about three pages, he turned to me and said, "Don't it make you hot to read about cruelty and horses being abused?" to which I said "Yes, is that story about such things?" "Yes it is. The way those cowboys treat dumb animals makes me mad. I've seen it." After which he continued the story till it was about half finished. Then took to skipping and at length read the end.

My author's pride was chastened by his not reading every word I had written, of course. But he read nothing else in the number, looked at the pictures in the advertisements, and then put the volume back in my valise. "You can take *Scribner*," said I. "It's in there." "No, much obliged. It's all the same, *Scribner* and *Harper* both generally have one good story, and that's all I wanted."

This youth is a matter-of-fact youth, not showing in talk at least any literary interests; and his business is banking, real estate, and fire insurance, West Superior, Wisconsin. If such as this will read me, I am secure. But I think I owe it to Remington's picture; otherwise he might not have been arrested.

Butler Place, December 31, Midnight. Good night, 1893! I shall not see you again. You brought me the beginnings of a success that I pray the power be granted me to make more worthy. My father has just wished me Happy New Year. I trust it may be so to him.

SOME DIALECT AND GLOSSARY

To uncork a horse (Arizona cowboy) to ride a bucking horse till he bucks himself quiet.

To hunt leather to hold on by the horn of the saddle, or any strap or string.

To hunt dirt to fall off

To hobble stirrups to fasten them under a horse's belly

Gringo Mexican for "outsider" (in bad sense), stranger

Cheva, Caberon two of the most opprobrious terms a Mexican can apply.

Peeler cowpuncher

Lick, Larrup syrup, molasses

Sleeper a cow with earmark and no brand

Dog-robber (military) striker

Doughboy (military) what cavalry calls infantry

Hot in the collar angry

May–August, 1894

BOWIE, BAYARD, GRANT, BISBIE, TOMBSTONE, TUCSON, SAN FRANCISCO, CHEYENNE

THE 1894 Journal, in which Owen Wister scorns legal practice as a "detested occupation," records his search for material on which to base stories for *Harper's*. He traveled great distances in the spring and summer of '94, but undoubtedly he was most interested in Tombstone, Arizona, where he hoped to gather background for a story about the bloody Earp-Clanton feud.

What Wister heard and read about the feud is set down in a notebook labeled "Frontier Notes, 1894," separate from, but in many cases parallel to, the 1894 Journal. The "Frontier Notes" are condensed and unrelated facts about scattered events seen or heard about. There are bits of dialogue and scraps of stories Wister planned to write, as, for example, the following entry, which was surely the forerunner of the famous passage in *The Virginian:* "Fetterman Events, 1885–1886. Card game going on. Big money. Several desperadoes playing. One John Lawrence among others. A player calls him a son-of-a-b——. John Lawrence does not look as if he had heard it. Merely passes his fingers strokingly up and down his pile of chips. When hand is done, he looks across at the man and says, 'You smile when you call me that.' The man smiled and all was well."

Because it appears only in the "Notes," the account of the Earp-Clanton feud has been added to the 1894 Journal. It is impossible to tell which facts about the feud were told to Wister by Mr. Swain, whom he purposely questioned, and which facts were drawn from Arizona newspapers and other sources.

1894

April 29. This journey to the West is unlike any heretofore, but like many (I hope and suppose) to come. Until the last one, all the others were holidays from the law and my perfunctory days at the office—the forgetting for a moment a detested occupation. This made them delicious; and these Wind River days with George West had an enchantment that no doubt can never be wrought again. But the homecoming and prospect of the office and driveling legalities was a gloomy thing.

Last time came a change. That journey was made under the haunting doubt, Would it be a success? Would I be able to write successful stories, and would they satisfy the Harpers, my employers? How humiliating and damaging if I should fail as a declared and advertised writer of short fiction and go creeping back to the displeased law with my tail between my legs! But, thank heaven, no, it hasn't been that. Of eight stipulated manuscripts, five are safely complete and approved. The remaining three, short of a miracle, will be as readily done as the others. In fact, I know what they're going to be, for everything I need is to gather more of the original facts from the Army officers I'm going to see—who have been writing me the most delightful cordial letters to come and revisit them.

So far as the public goes, my readers, I have fallen into favor with an ease that suggests how easily I might fall out and be forgotten. Well, that shan't be, either, God willing. I'll deserve success anyhow by that capacity for taking infinite pains which some uninspired ass—Southey(?)—said was genius! Yes, I'm popular enough to have moved that purveyor of mere popularity *The Youth's Companion* to write me unsolicited for a story. That speaks more to the essence than even a good notice in a paper, one that's a genuine notice and not a publisher's "ad."

The only people who, as a class, find fault with what I write are my acquaintances who live in the same town. This I suppose must always be so. The herd, who sees one of themselves eat his soup just like all the rest, can't conceive his doing some trick that perhaps all the rest cannot quite do. Then as for these acquaintances, there are a number of honorable exceptions who console and cheer me on, with discrimination, putting useful critical fingers on weak places and by so doing helping me often and exceedingly.

FORT BOWIE

May 14

Dearest Mother:

It has not rained here since my visit last October— but it has blown the roofs off twice instead. Then the usual spring went dry, and they had to haul water. They could haul enough for cooking and drinking purposes generally, and for washing sometimes, but there were days when there wasn't enough to make the coffee for breakfast. So the Major telegraphed Gen. McCook, Department Commander, that the Post would have to be abandoned unless water could be found. But the politicians of Arizona don't want the Post abandoned, because they could no longer sell hay to it at $100 a ton. McCook said "try to find water." So, as a last chance, the Major took giant powder to the spring that had gone dry and blew the bottom out of a mountain, finding water quite as surprisingly as Moses did—and that's how your Augustus George is able to have a bath. I go from here to Fort Bayard in New Mexico, from thence to Fort Grant, Arizona again.

Your loving son,

D.

May 23, Deming.   It's three weeks since I wrote in this record; but there has been not much to put down in it that has not already gone into my notes and memoranda. Major McGregor met me on his steps and mixed me a toddy. The Post was all in bed but the Major.

Next day I met Mrs. McGregor, of whom I had heard so much; and I am glad to say she approved of me, and we became friends. Thirty years of Indian campaigns, winter and summer in camp, danger, death of children, buffeting against nature and human nature too, have left her bold, cheerful, and pretty young.

My days at Bowie were one like another, and all the easy outdoor unruffled days that I like, spent in the company of people who feel as I do about things in life. Also, there was flattery, the real, delicious sort! I found that whenever the new *Harper's* came, they tore off the cover to see if I was inside anywhere.

And the quartermaster Sergeant, Tager, a steady old German said, "Mr. Wister, if I may take the liberty, I would like to express my appreciation of your very goot stories." Also, a private soldier in the telegraph office, who did some typewriting for me, looked at the title and said, "I read about him going East." So I told him I hadn't finished with Lin McLean yet. And when I paid him, he wanted to refuse, and said, "I'd typewrite for the pleasure of reading what you tell about." And young Fred Fowler, fifteen years old, wished to know if Wild Goose Jake was a real person. So I had quite as much incense as was wholesome. But incense is unluckily necessary for me; a lot of it scarcely counteracts a little of bad odor, and I'm always in danger of being more discouraged by adversity than prosperity encourages me. Unworthy, this!

One of the days we made an excursion to Bonita Canyon. Mrs. McGregor, Sergeant Poindexter, some of the children, and I went. We enjoyed ourselves, but how is one to love a land where no water is? Fifteen miles through Sulphur Springs

Valley over dry flat dust and then into the stony hills, Sergeant Poindexter and I set a cow on her legs. She had fallen from exhaustion and lay with her head tangled under her front legs in a curious and pitiful way. We thought her dead till we saw her tongue move. She had a little calf that was wandering round her, helpless, hungry, and bewildered. Up the cañon some water was running here and there, but it sank often and was altogether gone long before its course reached out into the open valley. The cattle come from Mexico thirty miles to drink this water and return to eat in Mexico, for there's nothing here.

We passed Mr. Stafford's cabin and saw that old retired Mormon and his young wife and bundle of children. She had not seen any visitor for five months, and this spring the frost has destroyed their orchard, their only livelihood. This southwest corner of our country is a forlorn wretched place, and we should be better off if we had never got it from Mexico. It's all right to write fire-and-smoke romances about, but there it ends. The lingering Spanish charm appeals strongly to my aesthetic sensibilities, to be sure! But as a citizen who believes in paying your debts and living within your income!

May 23. Some of my days at Bowie were spent in riding in company with Corporal Skirdin or, when he could not go, Private Pierce. Both have natures and histories that appeal to me strongly. Skirdin's family abandoned him when he was six, moving East from Arizona as soon as they could sell the father's property at his death. Since then Skirdin has shifted for himself, beginning when eight years old by pointing a gun at the old man with whom he lived and who beat him whenever he failed to find the horses in the morning. Skirdin left that house and the first night slept in the Pinal range, a boy of eight, possessing a pony, a gun, and a pair of trousers, in the middle of the Apache country. People were good to him. He got a mule team or burro pack and took supplies between the mines and Tempe.

His story, literally and faithfully recorded, would make a book as absorbing as Robinson Crusoe, and he's only twenty-seven now, but life has made him look thirty-five. His search and discovery of his family, a taking of many years for which he saved all his money, is deeply touching. Skirdin is uncouth, ugly, and knows only what he has taught himself. But his talk is as simple and strong as nature, and he has a most beautiful eye. The officers place a high value on him.

We grew very intimate, riding about the hot hills, and our views of life were precisely similar. His native wisdom is remarkable, and now and then he says something that many a celebrity would be glad to have phrased himself. E. G., "When I've said what I've got to say to a woman, she can have as many last words as she pleases." I parted with Skirdin with regret. I tried to make him take a gold piece, but it was no use. But he has promised to come and see me when he makes his younger sister the visit he has been planning for several years. She is younger than he, and the only member of his family he'll have anything to do with.

There's nothing makes this world seem so little evil as to meet good men in the humbler walks of life. It has been my luck to do so often; and their sensible comments have been tonics to my cynicism when they hadn't an idea of the secret poison they were providing with an antidote.

By the time I left Bowie, Major McGregor had come to call me "Old Man" at times, which was a better compliment than speaking well of my writing—much! Mrs. McGregor got up at five in the morning and drove the thirteen miles to Bowie Station and saw me off on the train. I hated my visit to be done. The friendly sameness of each day was a delightful thing, and I'll never forget the Major's punctual toddies—one before lunch, one before dinner. He would go into the dining room and mix them, and then I'd hear him making an awful attempt at whistling the "Water Call," upon which I rushed into the dining room myself.

May 19. I performed the crooked journey to Fort Bayard. Captain Markley met me at the station, and for the last three days I've been with him and Mrs. Markley enjoying myself very much.[1]

I must again and forever record my appreciation of any army welcome. No people on earth are more genuinely anxious to make their visitor's time pass brightly. I must record the barber at Deming. After shaving was finished, he atomized my face with some moderately objectionable perfume. "Dat peats England," said he. "Don't know," I said, "never was shaved there." "How long haf you been in dis country?" he inquired. "About two hundred years." "You are not English? No? I thought you were English vrom your dialect. Now I am very frequently taken by der pipple for a Frenchman."

Later, Willcox. At Bowie Station who should be on the platform but Major McGregor, bound for San Francisco. Also the naturalist D. Fisher and Fred Fowler going to hunt specimens in this neighborhood. I was delighted to see the Major once more. He told me of something at Bowie that I had certainly missed.

A man came there the day I left, stark naked. He had been caught at night camping five miles from San Simon

[1] [Here, as elsewhere in the Journals, Wister put an earlier date after a later one when he made his entries irregularly.]

station by the Apache Kid, taken by night to the Mexican line, shipped of horse and all, and set loose. He was one blister of sunburn. Two soldiers had found him by the drinking trough just about to plunge in and kill himself drinking water. They stopped this and saved his life, sending to the Post; the officer of the day came down with a pair of overalls and a stable coat and brought him in. He is now recovering at the hospital. On the platform here, a man met me sent with a team by Captain Edwards. So by tomorrow noon I shall be at Grant.

Fort Grant, June 20. Here I shall have been lingering four weeks tomorrow, possessed by an idleness almost complete. I don't think Arizona climate favorable to human energy and effort. It is certainly not so to mine. Instead of finishing and forwarding a MS for the November number of *Harper's,* I have lounged and of course loitered, eating, drinking, sleeping, card playing, riding a horse, and only on rare occasions mustering vigor to make a note or two.

The steady living at an army post, however, has made me day by day familiar with the atmosphere of garrison life, and I think it will be easy for me hereafter to be truthful in whatever writing of garrisons I may do. To speak of our army except with kindness will forever be impossible. I may draw black sheep or ridicule somebody here and there, but these will only be daubs against a large landscape of heartiness and hospitality.

In the evening of the day I arrived, with a precipitate convention that is far more pleasant than the usual neglect one finds in civil life, the entire lot called, including Dr. Birmingham. So the porch was crowded with people, while in front of the gate the band gave me a serenade. Also a punctilious military custom done for all guests at a post, and pleasant also, I think. The bandmaster Erastus Walker is all music and enthusiasm and, I find, gives the Post programs which are a trifle taxing to the average military listener—the Andante from Beethoven's *Sonata Pathetique*, for instance, and Fugue in D Minor from the *Well Tempered Clavichord*. But Erastus Walker this evening played the "Minuet for Five Strings" by Boccherini, arranged for brass by himself, and with such delicate effect that the little piece took on a new beauty which I think would have amazed and pleased the old composer.

BENSON, ARIZONA

June 25

Dearest Mother:

Here I sit between the frying pan out of which I have stepped and the fire into which I shall be stepping in six hours or so. Just now it's only the oven, and quite tolerable. I'm in a very small garden. In front of me, shading the sun from this paper, is a clump of tall bamboos which are sweeping about and rustling in the hot wind. Some drinking water is cooling among them by evaporation, in an earthen olla, and outside the bamboos is a fence, a dusty litter of sheds and dwellings, and beyond those the hottest kind of desert and the starkest staringest mountains. But this is the first really hot day, and it's only in the sun that you notice it, or inside any building.

I have been down a copper mine near the Mexican border of Sonora, and then at the town of Tombstone, which has a past but nothing else. Today I came from there by stagecoach and rail here, and the train was the frying pan. It took two hours to go eighteen miles, with one stop. Tonight another train takes me two hours more to Tucson, and that I expect to be the fire. Tomorrow I visit an old Spanish mission, Tucson being the second oldest town in the country, and then I take my way direct to San Francisco, which I should reach on Thursday afternoon the 28th, this being Monday afternoon.

208

The hotels in this part of the world are so: You look
vaguely at the crowd that meets the stage or the train and
listen to what they say—choosing the name that appeals to
I suppose your literary sense or your historical association.
At the copper mine I chose the Arlington. That was association, I think. A sad man took me there, carrying my bag.

I was the only arrival, and he said that if he did not
also keep a store he would not get along. He showed me
up to a little room, big enough for a bed, a glass, a basin, but
not for a man and a slop jar in addition to the other
furniture. The walls were not thick. Feeling bored for the
moment, I stuck my toothpick through the party wall and
was entertained by watching what was going on in the next
house. I asked when dinner would be ready and found meals
were at all hours at the Can Can Saloon, meal tickets three
for a dollar. The hotel does not feed you.

The Can Can however was just across the street, and a
very calm and proper place where mild men came and whispered to you, "Roast beef, pork and beans, peach pie, iced
tea, will you eat soup?"

It was the same way at Tombstone. Only there, on
recommendation, I stopped at the Palace Hotel when my
literary sense would have taken me to the San Jose. But it
was the Can Can Oyster Parlors once more that the landlady sent me to for my meals. Here, also, there was no Can
Can whatever, but the same breed of mild whispering men,
and I think they must grow in the kitchen garden or be supplied by the company.

Tombstone's past is a past of wealth and murder—a
silver deluge of wealth; walk a few steps and you see a hole
from which two hundred thousand dollars was taken, and
the surrounding hills are full of such holes. Murder was
done in the streets, mostly in the day time, people at night
being too busy over cards and billiards to do any shooting.
Very few assassinations occurred for a long while. It was

chiefly standup battles, and nobody dared to arrest anybody. But now all is done, and most of the people are, not unnaturally, dead.

The frontier has yielded to a merely commonplace society which lacks at once picturesqueness and civilization. When I heard that the Apache squaws now give their babies condensed milk, my sympathy for them chilled. The survivors of Tombstone sit there and dwell on how things used to be. In 1882 there were from six to eight thousand people; there are now six hundred, and all over the adjacent hills stand silent silver mines—the machinery rusty, falling to pieces, and a good deal of it burned.

Of course no river flows by Tombstone. The nearest running water is eight miles off. A stream of about the size of the Wingohocking but called the San Pedro River. It runs dry at times, is dry now in places. Then after a rain it rips the railroad to pieces and is twenty feet deep. So Tombstone gets its water from some mountains thirty miles away. This is expensive, but as the town burned to ashes twice, it was thought best to have water there in quantity. Each human is paying two dollars a month for water. A barrel of water costs twenty-five cents. If you have a bathroom, that costs you two dollars a month more. My landlady has a tree in front of her house. To water that costs her a dollar a month. This brings it about that many trees (of the few) in Tombstone are either dead or dying. The bank is closed. There is no bank there at all. The building is rented by the express company, which shares it with the stage company to save rent. For the same reason —to save rent—the surviving candy shop has moved into the telegraph office.

Many blocks of buildings stand entirely deserted. Houses, saloons, hotels, large shops—their doors nailed up and the panes cracked out of the windows. Some were two

210

and three stories high, but when the town last burned up, they built no more; so where one story was left standing, there it stands, sometimes repaired and inhabited, sometimes crumbling and empty; but I did not see a two-story private house in the town, and only a few other buildings of the hundreds there used to be have more than the ground floor. But the people manage to be merry.

The man to whom I brought a letter, formerly a judge, and now one of the leading lawyers, was very civil and in the evening took me to the Parlor Saloon and introduced me to the barkeeper, the mayor, the probate judge, a deputy sheriff, the county clerk, the agent of the express company and about thirty others, private citizens, during the coming evening. We all treated each other to drinks and the barkeeper treated everybody quite often too. I don't see how he makes anything. I confined myself to claret and appollinarie strictly, and consequently at two in the morning was still playing a perfectly clear-headed game of whist in the back of the saloon with the express agent, a freight-wagon driver, and a young Englishman who had come from Natal and was visiting the doctor. But in the front of the saloon they drank stronger things and found some firecrackers of a new and large make. The probate judge blew up the deputy sheriff's chair, and in the morning the barkeeper found himself with a headache and unable to attend to his duties, which were performed by a Chinaman. My friend the lawyer took me out driving in the morning and showed me the deserted mines and the neighborhood generally.

In the evening I met him again (a German settler) at the Parlor Saloon, but he excused himself, saying he was going over to his office to sing. During the next hour we heard him across the way. Then he came out, and the express agent, the freight-wagon driver, he, and myself

went to see the doctor and his visitor the Englishman from
Natal. The doctor had a piano and Teuton a violin. He
played some waltzes exceedingly well, and then without
accompaniment played Schumann, "Traümerai," from
memory with much expression and feeling. The doctor sang
to the guitar. The Englishman and the express agent sang,
and I played Wagner and Offenbach, also singing. Finally
we all danced. Today I bade them good bye, and they hoped
I would visit Tombstone again. But I shall never do that.

Your loving son,
D.

Fort Grant, Tuesday, June 25.   I went a third time to
the Hooker Ranch with Roach, and, oh, the bad luck! Just
as I was getting saddled to return home, appeared the man of
all others I could have wished to see, one of the Earps of
Tombstone fame. With a few informal hours in his company,
I could have gathered golden facts, and as I was departing I
said: "Sorry not to have met you sooner, Mr. Earp, for I
should have asked you to tell me some of the stories you
know." That's what I wanted to hear. He grinned heavily,
but at any rate I saw him and understood the type of man
they must have been.

Benson, June 25.   My stay at Tombstone was pro-
longed a day through the persuasion of Mr. Swain, to whom I
had a letter.[2] I reached the town by the stage from Fairbanks
about noon. Tombstone is quite the most depressing town I
have ever seen. "The glory is departed" is written on every
street and building. On Saturday evening Mr. Swain, who had

[2] ["Mr. Earp" was Wyatt, the only brother still alive. "Mr.
Swain," according to the Arizona Pioneers' Historical Society, was
probably George W. Swaim, who moved to Tombstone with his wife
and child in 1880 and died there in 1911.]

showed me the places of interest during the afternoon, especially the sites of the various Earp and Clanton murders, took
me to the Parlor Saloon, and there I was introduced to some
thirty people. I went to bed at two, after an entertaining
evening. The last three days, Friday, Saturday, and Sunday,
what between the copper mine and Tombstone, have added
to my experience.

But though we made merry at night, it was sad to see these
stranded people in their lonely dead town. I think, though I
have not heard many slight details of the Earp-Clanton feud,
I have heard enough to make something interesting out of
that business. I am puzzled how best to tell it. Whether im-
personally as in "Specimen Jones," in good English, or else to
put it in the mouth of a local narrator. In this way I could gain
humor, and in the other I suppose the tragic parts would go
better. Well, we shall see.

There's no hurry about that. I had expected to make the
story one of my eight for the Harpers, but there is too much
of it to be told in a single number. I think it will require at
least two. And now I must scurry along with something for the
November number, if I'm not too late already. Arizona has
made me shockingly lazy. I'll do it in San Francisco and have
Frank Michael criticize it. Tonight I sleep in Tucson and
spend tomorrow there. I read somewhere it's the second oldest
town in our country.

Feud began November 26, 1881, when Billy Clanton and
Frank and Thomas McLowrey lost their lives. Feud's origin
in the unlawful relations existing between the persons interested. Earp Brothers 5: James, Virgil, Wyatt, Morgan, and
Warren. James, smallest and eldest—and so in order down to
Warren. James a saloon man. Served in war and is the most
agreeable one of the family. No active hand in feud. About
thirty-six. Virgil—rawboned, six-foot. Sinister expression.
Deputy U.S. Marshal for years. Earned position by leading

sheriff and posse out of Prescott to arrest two rowdies who had been firing their pistols within city limits—killed both himself while the posse was dodging about in the brush. On the day of the triple homicides he was City Marshal of the town—a place he had been seeking for months and got not by election (for he had tried that) but by appointment from the City Council, it being left vacant by the departure of the regularly elected officer.

Wyatt, another six-footer. More refined than the rest. Dresses in excellent taste—handsome man. Gambler, cold, etc., brains of the outfit. Consulted on all occasions. Does not know the taste of liquor and only occasionally smokes a cigar. Morgan, handsomest and most reckless—at times all the others had to combine to hold him down—six feet, 160 pounds. Gambler for living although for a short time employed by Wells and Fargo as a messenger before robberies began on the Benson road. Warren, youngest—twenty—but an Earp. Was at Colton but left as soon as trouble began. Dark. All other blond, with blue eyes and closely shaven except for long sandy mustaches. Doc Holliday—consumptive looking, thirty, gray hair—said that Wyatt Earp owes him his life, which he saved in a row when Wyatt was Marshal of Dodge City, Kansas.

Three Clantons—Ike, Phineas (Phinn), and Billy. Lived at a cattle ranch on the San Pedro, twelve miles from Tombstone. Old man Clanton murdered in August by Mexicans with five others. His heirs well fixed in cattle. Fine specimens. Billy, only seventeen, was over six feet and built in proportion, while Isaac and Phineas are wiry determined-looking men without a pound of surplus flesh.

Trouble between them grew out of robbery of Benson stage, March 15, 1881. It left Tombstone for Benson with large treasure—"Bud" Philfit driving, and Bob Paul as messenger. Coach left at 6 p.m. At 7:30, not two hundred yards out from first station, order to halt. Two shots. Driver killed.

214

Cushion perforated under Paul. Driver fell off carrying lines—
horses ran. Paul fired—running fight. One passenger on top
killed. Paul stopped team, got lines, drove to Benson, telegraphed news to Tombstone. Agent Williams (N.B. I learned
at Tombstone this man was in league of Wells and Fargo)
and the Earp brothers rousing about to hunt robbers.

At 8:30 the same evening Doc Holliday had ridden up to
a saloon in Charleston ten miles below scene of robbery and
inquired for Billy Clanton. Hearing not there, started in direction of Tombstone and about ten rode up to saloon back of
Tombstone and called for a big drink of whiskey—gulped
without dismounting. Horse all foam. At night after news of
robbery, Earp brothers with Holliday left town to meet Paul.
Too dark to trail. Camped. Found three masks made of hay
rope—and twenty large-size rifle cartridges. Took trail and
followed it for three weeks without catching anyone but a
supposed accomplice, and he was assisted by some unknown
person to escape from the custody of the sheriff while consulting with his lawyer.

Holliday's ride got known. Early that afternoon (of the
robbery) he had been seen mounted and armed, ostensibly
going to Mexico.

Before the return of the agent's posse it became known
that Billy Leonard, Tim Crane, and Harry Head were interested in the murder, and it was their trail that Paul was
following. Wells Fargo offered big reward—no use. So matters
rested for some time until, as Ike Clanton swears, Wyatt Earp
called him aside and told him that he would guarantee him all
of Wells and Fargo's reward and $1,000 more on top of it if
he would induce Leonard and Head to come to some ranch in
the neighborhood of Tombstone so that he (Wyatt) could
surprise and kill them. He gave as his reasons that they had
failed to realize anything out of the attempted robbery and
that Leonard and Head might "squeal" sometime. Crane had

been killed with old man Clanton. To satisfy Ike that he meant business, Earp had Wells and Fargo's agent telegraph to San Francisco asking whether the reward would be paid dead. Answer, yes. But during negotiations Leonard and Head both killed in New Mexico for cattle stealing. Clanton told of proposition, and Earp heard so. This made bad blood. All this time Doc Holliday under bond for attempting to kill a saloonkeeper who objected to his presence in the house, and Holliday was awaiting action of grand jury.

Meanwhile, also, Holliday had a quarrel with a woman he had been living with, and she swore that Doc had a rope mask in his trunk for a month before the killing of Philfit and that she knew he was implicated in the murder. He was arrested and discharged for lack of evidence. Finally Ike Clanton came into Tombstone with Tom McLowrey from the Clanton ranch, expecting to meet Billy Clanton and Frank McLowrey from the Clanton ranch, who were to come and all proceed together to New Mexico where they were to buy a band of sheep. McLowreys had a ranch about twenty miles from Tombstone. Well educated, especially Tom. He was sober and industrious. Not finding their respective brothers, they concluded to spend the night in town, and so they both got into a poker game in which Virgil Earp the City Marshal was playing.

During game, Holliday walked into room and, addressing Clanton, said, "You cow-thieving —— you have been talking about myself and my friends, and you must fight me." Clanton replied that he was just at that time unarmed but would accommodate him at any time. To which Holliday replied: "Heel yourself and stay that way." Ike and Tom then left the house. In the morning Ike appeared on the street with a pistol in his hat and a rifle in his hand, for which offense Virgil Earp struck him over the head with a six-shooter and disarmed him. He arrested him and brought him before the

judge and had him fined $30. While this was going on, Wyatt
Earp met Tom McLowrey and struck him over the head with
a six-shooter, saying at the same time: "You are another of
those cow thieves that wants to fight the Earp brothers." In
the Public Court Clanton stood with his head tied up and, in
response to a remark made by one of the Earps, replied:
"Fight is my racket, and I only want four feet of ground to
fight on."

Just at this time Frank McLowrey and Billy Clanton rode
into town, both armed, and met their brothers near the stable.
They dismounted to hold a consultation and, to be out of the
way of passers-by, stepped into a vacant space between two
buildings. Frank and Billy were holding their horses when the
sheriff came up and said: "Boys I will have to disarm you."
Ike and Tom had no arms, but Billy and Frank had, so Frank
said he would not submit to be disarmed unless the Earp
brothers were also disarmed. At this moment Wyatt, Morgan,
and Virgil and Doc came down the street. Holliday had shotgun and pistol, rest pistols. As they approached, they headed
for the Clanton party. The sheriff threw up his hands and
said, "For God's sake, Earp, don't go down there, those men
are unarmed." They paid no attention, but pushed on.
Virgil had deputized his brother and Holliday as special
policemen to assist in disarming the Clanton party. As the
Marshal approached he said, "You ——, you wanted a fight—
now you can have it. Throw up your hands." Almost immediately the shooting began which ended in the death of
Tom and Frank McLowrey and Billy Clanton. Ike ran, being
unarmed. Virgil hit in leg. Morgan in the shoulder.

Ike had Earps arrested. Three weeks examination. Several
thousand dollars. Prisoners discharged on ground they were
officers doing their duty, though three witnesses swore that
Billy and Tom were shot with their hands in the air and that
Holliday fired the first shot with a shotgun into Tom Mc-

Lowrey. Then the victims' friends began vengeance. Virgil shot at eleven-thirty one night when leaving Oriental Saloon. Hit in arm and back. Got well about when Morgan was killed and Wyatt shot at. Earps all married except Warren.

On Saturday, March 18, after the theatre Morgan Earp and D. G. Tiphon, a friend, passed up Fremont Street to Fifth and then into the Oriental Saloon. Remaining there about fifteen minutes, they went to Campbell and Hatch's Saloon. They had been there only a few minutes when Bob Hatch, one of the proprietors, came in and entered into a game of pool with the deceased. The first game was quickly ended. Another was commenced, and Wyatt, Morgan's brother asked to join them in the game but was refused. When the game was nearly finished, just as Hatch had [taken his] shot [at pool] and Earp was a few feet to his right, the fatal bullet was fired quickly followed by another which struck the wall some twelve feet high, just above the seats. Immediately after the shot before Morgan fell, Wyatt and Warren Earp, McMaster, and D. G. Tiphon were at his side and removed him to the card room where he died in less than forty minutes. When being moved to card room: "Don't, I can't stand it." As death was about to claim him, Howard Lee bending over him said, "Do you know me, Morg?" He opened his eyes and shook his head. His brother Wyatt then spoke to him and said, "Morg, it's Howard. Don't you know him?" He muttered, "Yes, I know him. Howard, old boy, I've played my last game of pool." A few minutes later he spoke again to his brother Wyatt. "Oh, give me something to put me to sleep." In these words there is a singular coincidence, as almost the last words of Billy Clanton when writhing in the agonies of death in a little frame house on the corner of Fremont and Third Streets after being shot by the same parties: "Oh, boys, give me something to put me to sleep." A few minutes after the request, something to deaden pain was administered, and soon after he died.

218

Body to Colton, with James and Virgil, who was recovering from attempted assassination of December 28 (1881).

Excitement in Tombstone this evening, March 21, [1882]. Earp party (Wyatt, Doc, McMaster, and man Johnson) came into town about noon. About one Sheriff Bekan receives telegram from Tucson to arrest them for murder of Stillwell. Party refused to be arrested and, heavily armed, left the Cosmopolitan Hotel, walked down Allen Street, mounted their horses, and left town. Sheriff trailed horses, going on trail at 5 A.M. Nothing has been heard of the Earp party, who it is generally believed did the bloody work on Monday night. They left Tombstone ten or twelve strongly armed last night. Sheriff Paul left here this morning (Tucson) and was met at Contention by Sheriff Bekan of Cochise County with a posse of six men. They at once started in search of the Earps. The entire police force of Tucson and several extras were at the depot on the arrival of the passenger train tonight, armed with shotguns, expecting that the Earps would pass through on it. But they were not on board.[3]

June 22. Bisbie.   Well, my man Reed is a drifter. We had much conversation at dinner, helped by some champagne. He told me two things a propos of Earps and Chambers. John Ringgold was tried once for something, with two six-shooters in his belt and horses at the door. If he had not been acquitted,

[3] [For an account favorable to the Earps, in which the Clantons are described as rustlers and gunfighters, see Stuart N. Lake, *Wyatt Earp* (Boston: Houghton Mifflin Co., 1931). After he had killed Frank Stillwell, who he thought had murdered Morgan, Wyatt fled to Colorado accompanied by Doc Holliday. Both died a peaceful death, Doc in a Colorado sanitorium and Wyatt at the age of eighty-one in California. The John Ringgold mentioned in the June 22 entry was the gunfighter known as John Ringo, who reportedly worked for the Clantons and who was finally shot through the head while sleeping off a drunk.]

the judge would have been shot first. Doc Holliday if any
stranger entered Tombstone wearing a post hat would follow
him round the street ringing a dinner bell. The Wells and
Fargo agent at Tombstone stood in with the Earps.

Tombstone, June 23. Two good expressions: "If a
man drinks that, he's liable to go home and steal his own
pants." "I never drink 'cept when I'm alone or with somebody." Eastern people have an idea people in the West are
barbarians, know nothing about such things as gas. Why in
the East they think nothing socially of a saloonkeeper.

En route June 27. Reaching Tucson at 11:30. I am
glad to have stopped there, for I don't like to write about
places that I have not been, and Tucson is likely to come into
one or two stories. Moreover added to my general knowledge
of Arizona matters, and in particular about the Wham
robbery. After they were acquitted, the prisoners and their
counsel were photographed in a group! I don't think I ever
have heard any performance so discreditable throughout to
all concerned as was this robbery. I saw the photograph, a set
of average Western unscrupulous faces. The face of Mark
Smith, member for Congress (territorial representative) and
defender of thieves against the government he was elected to
serve, being not distinguishable in quality from those of the
Cunninghams or Follets, the robbers.[4] For the ordinary
traveler Tucson is not worth a visit.

San Francisco, Sunday, July 8. I found a note from
Frank Michael at the hotel. He was out of town as I expected,

[4] [For Wister's later remarks about the Wham robbery, see
p. 244.]

and I had a long leisurely bath and everything clean. At the club some mail, but not any from the office. Good and bad news, like life! The news from John Ingham, who also enclosed me a slip from the *New York Tribune*, the most flattering notice yet conferred upon me. They say I've already "won my spurs," and if not "spoiled by undue literary petting" I shall probably etc., etc. I don't think I've won my spurs, though I propose to. But I'm glad they think so, and as many other friendly critics as possible. As for the spoiling, there's less and less chance of it. My success has but one inward effect, to increase the desire to do better.

Then I've been reading Henry James and Kipling, in both cases to my great, very great, delight. I think nothing better of the sort has ever been done by anybody than "Kaa's Hunting," "Mowglis Brother," "The Real Thing," and "The Wheel of Time." I caught a miserable cold and stayed one day in my room and the next in bed, which has wrought my cure. And in those rather doleful hours I greedily devoured James and Kipling almost simultaneously in Room 705 of this large hotel. Which gave me the more pleasure? I can't say. Several times I laughed not from amusement but admiration during the jungle stories, and though James didn't produce laughter, he produced audible exclamations at his masterly skill. I don't think "Toomlai of the Elephants" as high an achievement as "Kaa's Hunting" for one little reason; it's a marvelous description of a scene, but not more.

In Kaa you have a description nearly if not quite as marvelous and besides that an idea very much more original than the idea that elephants meet and dance, namely, the contempt of the other animals of the jungle for the monkeys as being not serious people. There's a depth of humor in that as universal and allegoric as any I know. One thing I noticed, each distinguished author has a "word." Kipling uses "very" till it amounts to a mannerism, and James uses "vague."

221

These little immaterialities are interesting in their way. I wonder how many such tricks I have? One I'll confess to; on occasions when I wish to be sonorous and all that, I imitate the Homeric method of simile: "And as . . ." (such and such well known things will happen), "so did . . ." (the particular things I'm telling about). I don't do it often, but if I become distinguished enough to be analyzed, some critic will probably smell this out and be duly and virtuously indignant.

My other news from home was not so good. Butler Place seemed (June 1 my mother was writing) on the verge of domestic troubles below stairs, which means I know very well that the ill-starred mistress of the house had been at home long enough to harass the servants to the striking point. Our life these last years has resolved itself into cycles of absence and peace, presence and war, varied by intervals when the house was totally closed and ourselves in some neighboring hotel. But this is petty misery after all. We haven't lost our fortune, we haven't died, we've done nothing disgraceful. I think we have our share of the world's good things. I think I have more.

August 2. Through Nebraska. To resume. My last morning of getting ready to go away from San Francisco was made pleasant by my visit to Captain Bradford and Hume of Wells and Fargo. Both have been very kind and interested in my behest. Hume told me many technical things about treasure-stealing and stage-robbing, but I shall not try to write any story from this material at present. I feel not sufficiently familiar with the details and should commit inaccuracies. Hume listened while I told him the outline of such a story. It was one I had hoped to make quite interesting, and I expected to have written it soon. "Well," said Hume, "that'll please Eastern people, but nobody here would care for it. You see, holding up stages is too well known about here. Folks know all about how it's done. It's, well I might call it our chief industry." So I abandoned my story on the spot. I value accuracy more than any other quality in such stories as I write. I don't care how effective they are, if they're false, they're spoiled for me. I noticed a good instance of this in John Heard's story in the current *Cosmopolitan*, made from two real incidents of the army in Arizona both familiar to me previously. Heard makes his captain (who is meant for Crawford) use the sign language to the Indians. Those southern Indians do not have the sign language.

Sunday we reached Cheyenne three hours late. Barber was on platform to meet me, and there also was an ambulance to take me to the Post. But I could not go to stay at the Post. Barber expected me at his house, and so I made out my apologies to Captain Green (who was there to meet me and steer me to the ambulance) and went to Barber's.

My visit to Cheyenne ends with this Western journey. Tomorrow at this time, unless we get eight hours late instead of four, I shall be in the Limited with Chicago behind me.

May—August, 1895

═══════════════

NEW MEXICO, ARIZONA, CALIFORNIA,
COLORADO, CHEYENNE, FORT MEADE

IN the 1895 Journal Owen Wister describes with enthusiasm Dean Duke, a relatively young ranch foreman who got on Wister's westbound train at El Paso. Later, with undiminished enthusiasm, Wister wrote in the Preface to the Collected Edition that Duke "did and said many things which reminded me of the Virginian." Apparently he first heard of Duke through William Kellogg of San Francisco, a wealthy cattleman who was employing Duke in 1894. When Wister endured the Apache scare of 1895, Duke was employed by Haggin, Hearst, and Tevis of Arizona.

The Wham robbery, referred to in the Journal as an incident and as the subject of a story by Wister, took place on May 11, 1889. Wham and his armed escort, carrying government money, were attacked by a body of men in ambush between Fort Grant and Thomas, Arizona. After wounding eight of the eleven men forming the escort—one fatally—the murderers and robbers made off with $29,000, mostly in gold coins. By June 5 the authorities had arrested eleven men suspected of the crime, including M. E. Cunningham and the Follett brothers. Although, according to the *Weekly Phoenix Herald*, the government presented much evidence against the suspects in a trial held at Tucson, the jury returned a verdict of not guilty on December 14, 1889.

Near the end of the Journal Wister speaks familiarly of Rudyard Kipling, with whom he had dined at Theodore Roosevelt's house in Washington on April 5, 1895, and whom he had probably met earlier.

1895

May 16.　On train between Deming and Willcox. A week ago, almost to this hour, I bade them good-bye at home more unwilling to leave them than ever before in my life. And at night when the train started, it took me away without giving me any feeling of satisfaction in going West. I should not have gone if I had not believed it very important to my store of frontier experience and information, and during the next two days I was sunk in homesickness.

Quite a pleasant coincidence happened on the train between New Orleans and El Paso—although an unknown compliment fell to my lot earlier still and diverted me secretly. A party of evidently Eastern people sat near me—four of them—and as the train ran through the first really desolate scenery, which was in the afternoon between San Antonio and Del Rio, we crossed a dry river on a high bridge. The lady looked out at the hot sand and dry stones and said to one of the men, "How do you think that compares with the Allegheny?" "Too deep," said he. "It's like a story I've just read in *Harper's*," said she—and then recommended my story. "Oh, you mean about the teamster. I've read it," the man said. "Isn't it pretty?" said she. And my vanity was caressed, though to have the word pretty applied to the "Tinaja Bonita" seemed to me a trifle wide of exactitude.

But these accidents are sweeter than the most deliberate praises, surely. Then in the evening I noticed that a foreigner, with whom I had talked a little, was interested in literary matters; and just afterwards a Captain Phillips of our Navy, who was on his way to San Diego, told me this foreigner was a Russian, had left Russia after the murder of the Czar in 1881, and lived in Los Angeles. I concluded he must be the Mr. Demens who has been writing to me from Los Angeles about translating my stories for a St. Petersburg magazine and also inquiring about my life!—which I wrote him some time ago was most humble in its commonplace lack of events and its average respectability and good fortune. So I set to work to approach him in a circuitous manner. I was reading Max Nordan's *Degeneration*, about which reading people have been lately somewhat overexcited, it seems to me, and I handed the book to the Russian with a remark about something I had just read. This of course precipitated a conversation.

Then he inquired where I came from and, on my telling him, looked at me curiously and said, "I know an author from Philadelphia. Owen Wister. Do you know him?" "Je dois vous apprendre, monsieur," said I, for we spoke a species of polyglot together, "que je suis cet homme." He rushed to get out his card, but I said "Et je vous connais depuis quelque minutes." So I told him his name, and he grasped my hand and became more voluble than ever. "But your last story—do you know?—it is very bad," said he, earnestly. "Will you pardon me?" Of course I told him that after his cordial praise of other things he must say anything that he thought and I should be most obliged and interested. So we sat up late that evening.

On Monday our Pullman company of travelers had become most friendly, and again came the compliments, only this time after we all knew our respective names. I can see how very easily one can become intolerable with conceit— but I am determined to be above such bosh if I can. At El Paso my lost Duke was waiting on the platform for me. He did not know me at once, having been told by Kellogg that I had a beard. I had expected him at Deming, his address, but he had come here with Colonel Bliss, now, I'm glad to say,

Brigadier General Bliss, on his way to his command at San Antonio.

Some years ago in this country when U.S. judges rode on circuit, Judge Egan—whom I met and traveled with yesterday, and a very quiet pleasant man he is—could not find enough unprejudiced people to have for jury. People were scarce anyhow. So he boarded a South Pacific train at Nordsburg and subpoenaed the passengers! "I don't live here," said one. "That's all right—you'll get out." So he got his twelve. Eleven were for conviction. One stood out for acquittal. "You tell him," said Judge Egan, "that I'll give him five minutes and then I'll come and talk to him myself." Unanimous verdict in one minute.

May 17.   On train between Deming and Nordsburg. At El Paso our company of travelers in the Pullman and Duke got into a horsecar drawn by a single mule and crossed the Rio Grande to Ciudad El Paso del Norte, Mexican but uninteresting. One very typical sight: on the Custom House, which is the most important and largest building of the town, is a clock painted! I think this expresses the Republic of Mexico with un seul trait. During our sightseeing I rapidly discovered Duke my host to be a man of superlative humor, and when we were in the train again, he kept the smoking compartment in a steady roar of laughter with his reminiscences of his not very long life. The Russian said to me, "That young man should give you many points. How old is he?" So I told Duke we were guessing his age. "At times I think you are twenty-two," said the Russian. From the Duke's exceedingly varied experience and obvious capability (of which I had heard much from Kellogg last year in San Francisco), I guessed thirty-five—but he is twenty-seven and does not work [for Kellogg] any more. At Deming our party separated.

What a familiar spot on this broad surface of the Earth Deming is growing to be to me! At best 3,000 miles from home, and a forlorn wind-parched hole, I turn upon it and return upon it. Ever since my first journey in search of material, now already eighteen months ago, I've pivoted upon this junction. This time I spent the night there and found out several things. Another great disappointment, the First Cavalry is being transferred from Grant to Riley, and I shall see none of them.

I telegraphed Edwards there, and my message was returned. He had already gone. Captain Markley telegraphed me from Bayard that my room was waiting me and that Captain Pitcher had left that (Monday) morning on a scout for Indians in Arizona. Then reports began to come that forty Apaches had left the reservation at San Carlos. Duke and I concluded this was because they had taken advantage of the transfer of the First and Seventh Cavalry.

The next afternoon (Tuesday 14th) Duke and I went to Separ. Separ is about an hour beyond Deming westward; it will be our next station as I now write and is where Duke and many other cattlemen ship their stock. Forlorn spot like all the others. Some sidings, off the long straight endless main line that merely goes out of sight over a hill; a section house, rather snug with a double roof and clustering fruit trees—the only green anywhere—the tank, the pumphouse, the station, a boarding house, a store, corral, and cattle chute; and enveloping all these buildings the empty desert. We had a frontier meal at the boarding house, I throwing my bag on my bed to retain it at Duke's instruction, he throwing his pistol on his. After tea we visited the young lady express agent at Separ.

Then, as we were to get up at two-thirty in the morning to drive thirty miles before it should grow hot, we sought our beds. I was amused to find Duke's pistol had been laid on my bed and a stranger peacefully sleeping in possession of Duke's bed. We concluded to go outside and sleep on the ground in his blankets and bedding, which he told me were in his wagon. As we crossed the space between the buildings, cowboys were sleeping everywhere on the ground—for Duke's bed was not in his wagon, and some cowboys in bed near the wagon knew nothing of it. We looked in the store where a man was sleeping, but the bed was not there. On coming out and going round the corner, there was the bed sprawling in the wagon with every sign of haste, and on the ground one bed less, and in the nearest bed a pile of breathless bodies under the blankets, snickering convulsively—inquiries were useless. After we had got in our bed, two rueful figures in their drawers crawled out of the adjacent pile and began explaining how they had been told this bed was not going to be used.

At two-thirty we were aroused and soon got away. The moon was beautiful, but I grew a little chilly in my thin clothes and was glad to see the approach of sunrise. When we came among some mountains, very bleak and stony, Duke got out the two rifles, and we filled their magazines with cartridges and held them in our laps. In the last four years fourteen of Duke's cowboys have been killed by either Mexicans or Indians. Just beyond this pass as you come out in the Playas Valley is a cabin where we stopped for news of Duke's expected cattle. But the man there (it is called Davenshort's and has the typical dreary wood cabin and windmill and cattle post) knew nothing of this herd.

Two men were murdered at this cabin last year, nobody knows by whose hand. These things made me decidedly watchful and uneasy, and I was very glad my parents could have no notion of what sort of place I have come to. By and by we met the cattle and by eight o'clock came to a ruinous adobe cabin on the borders of a dry dead lake. But a spring trickles out of the hill behind the cabin. A dead cow was lying in its mud. She had evidently gone to drink and been unable to extricate herself. I did my best in my story of the Tinaja Bonita to represent the lonely horror of this sunshine desert, but the real thing outdoes anything my words can convey. At this cabin we unharnessed and lay down to rest through the hot hours, planning to drive the fifteen miles farther in the afternoon. We had come thirty.

At noon a cowboy came with a message sent from the foreman of the herd we had passed. He ate some lunch and then continued his way to another herd that was approaching from the Animas Valley across the hills to our southwest. About two minutes after he had gone, as we lay on our bed in the cabin, we heard two shots fired. Duke sprang up and seized his rifle, and I took mine and at his advice got away from the window. Then we went outside, Duke running up the hill cautiously to see what he could, and I, highly cautious, walking after him more slowly. Duke peered about for some time and came back to me and our cowboy driver. He did not like the shots, because he said the cowboy was not a squanderer of ammunition and he had never known of his shooting idly at passing objects. I said that if there was anything wrong the rider would have come back to tell us. "If he could get back," said Duke. We went back to our cabin and continued our not very restful siesta, and I found I was saying to myself, "Que diable allais-je faire dans cette galere?" with a good deal of zest.

But there was nothing to do now but stay it out cheerfully, and so I ate some crackers and various sorts of canned lunch and sucked lemons. Duke said that if any more shots like those came, he would start across country for Deming at a high rate of speed. But no more did come. I have never been so frightened as that before and am glad to know the sensation, though I hope it will not be repeated. In the afternoon Duke pondered whether we had better drive the fifteen miles to Chase's ranch or five to the cattle herd approaching, which would camp this side of the mountain.

I remarked I thought our next steps were a serious matter of study. He decided at length to go to Chase's because of hay for our mules and asked me what I thought. I much preferred going the five and sleeping in the cowboy camp but said that his opinion was mine, for I had no means of judging. But a wagon came down the hill, which proved the main wagon for water, and we found they were camping only about three miles [away]. We drove there by four and decided to stay. I was glad to see the bedding down at night and the throwing of the bed ground in the morning of so many cattle, and furthermore my personal satisfaction at sleeping with a company of twenty cowboys instead of at a lonely cabin in the country for which the Indians might be making was deep. The business of supper behind and the main wagon, and the jokes, and the breakfast and troublesome horses was all interesting. I slept well, and getting up at three-thirty did not seem so bad after going to bed at nine.

The splendor of the moon and of the sunrise was surpassing. And the apparitions of the horses and riders dashing among their own dust in a blur of gold from the sun as it came up from behind the hills is something worth the journey of itself. We bade them good-bye, and Duke, having superintended and given his orders, took me back to Separ—carrying our rifles across our knees. On the train we took for Deming we heard Pitcher and his command were to camp at Lordsburg, beyond Separ; so at Deming (from where I had been going to Captain Markley at Bayard) Duke telegraphed to Pitcher—for it seemed a capital chance for me to go on the scout if the Captain would take me. Pitcher wired he was going to Willcox for the night, returning next day—today that is—and so once again Duke and I trundled westward on the Southern Pacific. Pitcher got in at Lordsburg. Duke had not

mentioned me in his telegram, purposely, and I was introduced as Mr. Challis of California for the sake of the joke of
seeing how soon Pitcher would recognize me.

We sat in the smoking compartment, and presently I
began to ask him questions. He looked at me puzzled, and in
about half a minute it dawned on him. We supped at Bowie
and at Willcox (how familiar are all these remote holes growing
to be!), talked, and slept after Pitcher had inquired about the
Indian reports for which Willcox citizens had been responsible.
They are sensational, vague, and contradictory.

Pitcher asked me at once to accompany him on his scout,
and I am going. He told me that Captain Edwards had left
Grant some time ago on sick leave. I am very sorry to hear
this. This morning we all came back. Duke and Pitcher got off
at Lordsburg, and I once more went to Deming, got some
clothes, and took a much needed bath. So now here I am, for
the third time in one week, on this westbound train, bound for
Lordsburg and the military. The conductors and brakemen
all know me now and imagine, I think, that I'm a cattleman
doing some large stroke of business.

Apache Tejo, June 9. My travels seem already like
ancient history, and if I don't overcome my laziness in recording them, they will be irrevocably lost in my memory.

May 17. Is where I return to. I got out of the train at
Lordsburg, where Duke and Lieutenant Jenks met me on the
platform—Jenks I remembered pleasantly from November,
1893, when I first stayed at Grant with Captain Edwards, and
the regimental drill was had for two weeks. After a preliminary
visit to the saloon we went down to where J Troop was
camped. Pitcher came out of his tent and warned me he was

messing with the troop and that I must be prepared for the worst. But in spite of this formidable news I ate the dinner we had at once with composure, drinking a tin pint of coffee. After a cigar we went up into the "town" of Lordsburg and passed the evening at the house of a hospitable gentleman, a cattleman, named Hart, who had a piano, an aeolian, and other musical instruments. Jenks sang, and I played, and about ten I returned with Pitcher to camp. He made me extremely comfortable in a cot, and the quite sharp dust storm we had failed to keep me awake.

May 18. Reveille at five, and at seven we started. Duke's business detained him between Deming and Separ, so that he could not go. The railroad's failure to be in time with cars for shipping the cattle caused Separ, the shipping point, to be congested with incoming herds for which there was very little food or water—and Duke's responsibility as superintendent for Messrs. Haggin, Hearst, and Tevis compelled him to be on hand. So I, his guest, bade him good-bye after but three days and deserted him for this cavalry scout—with a light conscience, if with regret, for as my journey is fundamentally for information, I turn to whatever source is most likely to give it to me and especially lose no chance of seeing and hearing as much military life as possible. So I marched away from Duke my host with cheerful fickleness. My horse Kelton, a sorrel, belonged to Sergeant Abel, guidon bearer, and was a very delightful and playful animal. One thing I notice about the enlisted man, and that is that he is nearly always kind to his horse, making a pet of him. Our road from Lordsburg lay north or nearly north, over forlorn plains.

We halted about eleven for lunch, and it rained quite hard during twenty minutes—a new thing to me in this country, or almost new. We saw two rattlesnakes. By degrees, toward

one o'clock we came to the edge of the plain and the land began to sink in broken gullies toward the Gila River. Long
before we reached it, we saw the trees on its banks—a pleasant
sight—and about three we came to "24 Ranch," belonging to
Hart of Lordsburg, crossed the stream, and camped on sand
among cottonwoods. It had been only twenty-seven miles;
but seven hours in the saddle was a big pull for me.

I had not been upon a horse since the preceding June, or
taken any considerable exercise, and my whole body was most
abominably tired. I lay on the sand, and after Pitcher's and
Jenks' tents were pitched, I lay on my cot and from prudence
ate no dinner. Past experience has warned me to eat nothing
when tired from exercise like this. I told Pitcher that a truly
great man can ignore his weary clay and be as lively in spirit
as ever and that I sorrowfully realized I was not a truly great
man. And I manufactured some faint cheerfulness during the
afternoon, but as a matter of fact was most dolefully afraid
the next day might find me with one of my bilious attacks and
hence a ludicrous burden. But my fever and fatigue were
nearly gone by seven. I drank a pint of coffee, somewhat less
whiskey, and slept a long good sleep.

May 19. Next day, our march being short, we had
reveille at five-thirty and started at leisure. There was a
Mexican ranch here, well irrigated and charming with green
fields, and also a little queer chapel. The place is called Richmond, and I suppose twenty people may live nearby. I notice
always how civil and courteous the humblest Mexican is in
his manners. One came to our camp and sat on his horse and
held a conversation with us consisting of four words and five
minutes, during which he smiled with continual gaiety. He
was a patch of rags but perfectly happy—and when he bade us
good-bye and rode away, we all commented upon the pleasant

manner he had. It is certainly something we of the north cannot achieve, and it renders genial the unimportant—which
are the most numerous—moments of life. Our march this day
was but twelve miles down the Gila River to the town of
Duncan, opposite which we camped at an early hour, soon
after twelve.

A narrow railroad rises through Duncan between Lordsburg and Clifton, and I was able to send a postal home, which
is something I have tried to be more regular about than ever
before. At the store in Duncan, where I refurnished our lunch
basket with some delicacies that later proved almost inedible,
we found a curious character, an old prospector. A frayed but
respectable tail coat and trousers—low shoes and no stockings.
He had silver hair which flowed nearly to his collar with a
benevolent silken undulation, and he was slightly touched as
to his brain. I cannot reproduce his conversation, but he
spoke with mild tones and the speed of lightning—running
one sentence into another.

"My name is Henry Murphy," said he, "and I've been up
and down, rich and poor, Earl Marquis, walking the track and
again come out with a jackass load of money. I've been from
Hell to Cape Horn. I've made the best map of the United
States extant, and finally my adventures don't fall much
short of yours!"

As he announced this, he rose nimbly from his chair and
advanced on Pitcher amicably. By this time the storekeeper
had crowded my lunch purchases in a box, I got on Kelton,
and Pitcher, Jenks, and I returned across the river to camp,
leaving the silver-haired gentleman bowing and smiling at us.
Pitcher was for my sake sorry he had not encouraged him to
visit us in camp; and perhaps he could have told us interesting
adventures, but he was almost too incoherent. As it stands,
his character is a good suggestion and not like any I have met
before.

The short march we made on this day was the right thing for me, and I felt none of my former fatigue but ate with excellent appetite and during the afternoon in this quiet valley was altogether at ease. The men took advantage of the river to wash themselves and their clothes, and some of them fished, with no great results. I took a number of photographs and made acquaintances with the soldiers—familiarizing myself with what a troop does on the march. I think that now with this second experience of marching it will come easy to me to write of such matters with fair accuracy. I wish we could have stayed longer at Duncan or in such country as Duncan lies in, for one comes to prize running water and trees as blessings and boons in this country. We went to bed by nine o'clock, and no pint of coffee could keep me awake—I fell asleep at once breathing cool air.

May 20.   Our march this day had to be pretty long— forty-two miles over to Solomonville in the San Simon Valley, and away from the river and all water. So we made an early start, rising at four-thirty. At this hour I noticed the mountains to be as they always are utterly beautiful—more beautiful in light and color than I have ever seen elsewhere, though in broad day they become seared and horrible in the hot sunlight.

We left the Gila, taking a road that makes the string to the bow of the river, and going up through intolerably rough region of hills and gullies fourteen miles to Ash Springs. This is a hole in rocks where there is a little water, enough to drink for a few men, but not enough to water a troop. We halted here for a little while, and I took more photographs. We went on still always uphill over a sort of divide and during this day had three sorts of weather—hot sun, violent rain, and a heavy sand storm after that. But I enjoyed the journey completely, joking and gossiping along with Pitcher and Jenks at the head of the column.

When we had made thirty-six miles and had been in the saddle from six until five, Solomonville being in sight six miles in front of us in the new valley we came down into, Pitcher persuaded me to get into his wagon and drive the rest of the way. I wanted (from reasons of pride that will not bear the test of common sense) to ride the whole distance, but sense conquered pride and I exchanged places with Sergeant Abel, he getting upon Kelton and I into the Captain's wagon. He sent me ahead to order the forage. So here I was once more at Solomonville!

I had been writing a story about being there for so many weeks before leaving home that the fiction was still somehow in my mind and made a comical jumble with the fact. I had certainly never expected to see the place again. Its name is from the one white man of enterprise who lives there and has lived there for twenty years. There are a few other white people, and the rest are Mexicans. The irrigation from the Gila has made the immediate neighborhood charming with growing crops and trees—but I was mistaken in representing Solomonville as a Mormon settlement. The Mormons begin a few miles down the valley, and this must be corrected in the proof of my story. It is curious to hear the two classes of people spoken of as Mormons and Americans. I drove up to the new store that Solomon built since my visit in 1893, ordered the forage of his son, and was very hospitably asked to supper but declined, thinking it better to wait for my captain and lieutenant to arrive. I was about an hour in advance of them and had time to shave and wash a little.

Soon after the troop came into town and I met them with two bottles of beer, we went to camp behind Solomon's corrals, and Pitcher, Jenks, and I took supper with the family.

The leading citizens of Solomonville, an attorney, an

editor, and a judge, gathered at Pitcher's tent to bid him welcome. The judge was speechless with inebriation, the others quite sober. The editor talked about Indians. It was his policy, he said, to be frank and report Indian raids candidly. Some blamed him for publishing news—calculated to discourage newcomers from settling in the territory—but he believed in being above board. On this occasion, we told him, it was our impression the raid was but little likely to discourage anybody. The fact is, every report of Indians that we traced faded into ungrounded myth. But of course it is greatly to the interest of forage agents and all possible contractors to keep the soldiers busy. And it's good for the men, too, this occasional scouting. It teaches them field duty and keeps them contented. So Pitcher was very far from regretting that he had been sent on a wild goose chase.

Solomonville, May 21. The men wandered down the corral through the fields and swam, and so did I. There has never been a time when I was not fond of being among grain and the smell of hay, but in this country I revelled in it and could not look too much at the waving tops of the grass. The place that I found to bathe delighted me so that after dinner I took Jenks there, and we spent a pastoral afternoon lounging among the farms.

That evening we had music. Jenks sang, and in accompanying him in the "Toreador's Song" I broke two notes on the very good piano. But our evening was certainly jovial, and the Solomons most kind. We drank beer and sat up late for camping hours.

May 22. From Solomonville to Williamson's ranch in Stockton Pass. I think we went about thirty miles, but do not remember. We left the Gila Valley and the farms finally and rode up and along a barren mesa with Graham Mountain to our right the whole forenoon. A young fellow caught up and rode with us for an hour, and I am sorry not to have seen him longer. He was born or certainly brought up hereabouts—and looked it. He lived at Dos Caberas and was returning from a visit to friends in the Gila. From his talk I could see he knew much of the happenings in the country.

What first interested me in him was that he corresponded in appearance almost precisely with my imaginary portrait of Black Curly in the Wham robbery story. His hair was not curly, but with that exception he was identical, and I wish I could have photographed him. It happens very seldom that I see anyone who comes near my own mental image of any character, and I often wonder just how this image is formed. Whether it is a "composite" memory or whether an unconscious reminiscence of some one face seen at some time in passing. Anyhow I discover that I always have a very clear notion of the face and figure of any character upon which I have dwelt at all—and it comes without any act of will.

This youthful rider of Dos Caberas talked about Point of Mountain on the old stage line in Sulphur Springs Valley. He told us how the men that established the road ranch there made their fortune. They dug a well—water was supposed to be many hundred feet underground—and the well they dug was in fact a deep one. But it was hardly done before they found water about twelve feet under surface—or even less. This second hole they promptly filled in and for years charged twenty-five cents for watering every animal—no traveler finding the cheat. The young fellow had a couple of roses stuck in his hatband, and that item I shall add to Black Curly's appearance when I correct the proof in San Francisco.

When half the day was over, our road took us in among the hills of Graham Mountain, and the whole latter part of the march was very picturesque. Only running water was lacking—endless dry courses all day ready and gaping for the stream, but not a single drop. We camped at Williamson's ranch, where there is every beauty except a brook, and the well is all the supply, good and sparkling certainly. But I cannot forgive a place like this one—a sheltered mountain nook, with trees and verdure, yet lacking the spirit of mountains. For a stream is surely the moving life that holds the essence of mountain charm. I am so homesick for Fort Washakie and my beloved Wind River that if I possibly can, I'll go there on my way eastward and get a taste of those lakes and streams.

May 23.   We had a very short march of eight miles to Fort Grant. As we came near, Lieutenant Osborn rode out to meet us. Pitcher and I had speculated a good deal upon what officers of the First Cavalry we should find remaining with the two troops not transferred to Riley—Osborn was a most agreeable surprise. He and the Quartermaster McDonald (I had not known him before) were left. We found the ladies of the Seventh Cavalry already arrived—being entertained by the Osborns, who had also entertained the entire First after it had become dismantled and packed up.

The First had departed the very day before—I was sorry to have missed them so narrowly—and the Seventh was even now in sight among its dust, toiling along the Willcox Road. The ladies of the Seventh were aghast at Arizona. And they begged me to pity them, which I did. Their packing boxes strewed the line and front yards and more arrived continually, while people carried basins and mirrors distractedly about.

The troops of the Seventh arrived with Colonel Sumner, who made himself very pleasant to me. There was really something diverting in the disgusted humor of the Seventh as a body over Arizona. In the earlier part of the day the ladies had told me their woes, and now the officers began. I saw one lieutenant stand and stare across the valley at Hooker's ranch in silence. "Good God," he finally muttered, turned on his heel and went into the club.

Willcox, Arizona, May 26, 6:30 A.M.   This morning I have regretfully said good-bye to the cavalry, my time drawing short. I have been marching and camping with them for ten days. Yesterday we reached the railroad again; and while they now proceed along its line and then to their post, Fort Bayard, I take the train to Fort Bayard. This takes me one day only. I don't know precisely what day I'll finally go to Los Angeles, but in five or six at the most. My hands and face are burned, and my riding muscles all limber and in excellent order. I get up at five and at five-thirty drink a tin pint of coffee without milk and eat fat bacon. The fact is, this climate makes me feel about twice as well as any other.

Remember that during those long scouts in Bannock Campaign transportation was much more ample. The troop (then numbering a hundred) would sometimes have about 1 mule to a man. Each day 1 troop took its turn (herding the pack train). Lately when I was with Pitcher, he had 47 men and 7 mules—or 8 if you count the one ridden by the packer. Not enough. Bad economy on part of Quartermaster General. He has reduced doubly upon an equipment that had itself been a recent reduction. Should we have any real trouble, it would cost thousands and much delay to get adequate transportation out to the army.

May 24.   Fine band at guard mount—coming from Riley the Colonel had not allowed the instruments to be packed, so they had had music all the way, and at important stops a concert. This was an excellent device for preserving discipline. The music brought each way town in force to the railroad platform, including all the saloonkeepers. Thus the soldiers could find nobody to sell them whiskey. There were no deserters. When the First and Seventh met at Willcox, the First's band had all its instruments packed and was unable to return the Seventh's complimentary serenade. Over this the ladies and officers of the Seventh made a jubilant crowing, most naturally.

At Bowie I greeted Mr. Bugbee once more, breakfasted as usual, and saw that old rascal Tevis. As he does not know me, he will never know what a villainous base use I've put him to in building Mr. Mowry from him in my story of the Wham robbery. At Deming Duke was on the platform, and I spent the rest of the day with him.

After reception, to the club—always, at every post and from every officer of our army the same friendliness and hearty welcome and hospitality. I found Cartwright had been the man who worked up all the evidence for the Government in the Wham case. Would I had met him before! And would that before I had met Sheriff Breckinridge of Tombstone and Tucson, to whom Duke introduced me at Deming and who made the first arrest in this same case—arrested Cunningham! But here is an odd thing: I have connected Bishop Leighton, the Mormon, with the affair entirely from my own imagining, really thinking he had nothing to do with it—and I find he played a part not wholly unlike the one I've invented for him.

May 28. In the evening the Colonel sent his compliments and would Mr. Wister dine with him at seven? When the ladies left the table, General Schofield and Colonel Kent spoke of Indian matters, and I was able to enjoy an interesting talk. The General bade me tell him about the Modoc War and its cause. I drew back and remarked that he was the person who should tell me. But he definitely asked me, and I did in some confusion—inward confusion. But when it was finished, Schofield said, "That's all quite true," and later he asked me to come and see him in the East.

We had a shooting match at clay pigeons. Duke is truly an admirable shot—hitting clay pigeons with a rifle bullet 4 in 5, and with a shotgun 28 in 30. His life compels him to be. Have never met any man so young—he's but twenty-seven—who has passed through so many desperate chances.

June 5

Dearest Mother: ·

Nothing new to tell you since yesterday except that I haven't gone to California yet but instead am shortly to start once more for Apache Tejo and then to another place named Cow Springs. I trust this frequent if brief news of me is not amiss as it trickles in through the week. I wish I could eat strawberries—or rather had some to eat. And I wish I were like Charles Dickens. For then I should write a whole long book about Deming.

Your loving son,
D.

June 8.   Before starting again for Apache Tejo, Duke startled his cowboy foreman Henry Brock in a diverting manner. Brock had been sent to town for both business and pleasure the day before, and had during the evening seen us several times at the saloon and gambling place, "The White House," and exchanged greetings. But he had not been aware of our presence behind him at a notoriously sordid place of entertainment, where we had had a glimpse of him playing cards with one of the most ungainly females I have ever looked upon. He was enthusiastically absorbed in his game, a bottle of beer by his feet and another by the lady's. "Hullo, Henry!" said Duke [later], hailing him in the street among many by-standers. "Have a good time?" "Fair," replied the innocent Brock. "I was sure you were enjoying yourself. Fellows, you ought to have heard Henry slap down a card and shout "How's a 4-spot for low?" Brock was utterly caught and blushed to the roots of his hair—which made me like him. I have liked several of Duke's cowboys. They are of the manly, simple, humorous, American type which I hold to be the best and bravest we possess and our hope in the future. They work hard, they play hard, and they don't go on strikes.

[Once] the saloon element hired for $50 a month [a cowboy] to hire [himself out] to Duke [as a ranch hand], to slap his face, and kill him. Duke's predecessor paid cowboys in town. Hence they spent their wages there—got drunk—trouble. Duke changed this plan of pay. Paid by cheques out on ranches. Cowboys now spent money no longer in town in saloons but bought things from Montgomery Ward (for they always must spend somehow). Saloons angry—conspired—sent cowboy as stated above. He came and got himself hired. Ugly eye, Duke noticed. Duke suspected something was wrong, so one night after supper in camp he began: "You're a good cowboy ain't you?" friendly as possible. "Yes." "Rope anything?" "Yes." "Ride anything?" "Yes." "I thought so." "Yu did think so? Yu didn't doubt it? For any son-of-a-b——that said I couldn't," etc, etc. (work up). Thus Duke traps him through his desire to pick a fight into "making a talk" and bragging in a manner that antagonizes the cowboys who gather round to listen. Next morning Duke puts him on a bad horse which bucks him off. He complains. Cowboys derisive. He says nothing and nobody could ride that horse. Duke calls Henry Brock. Brock rides horse—whips him all round. Cowboys down on this braggart—his quarrel is with

246

them now and not with Duke, and they practically run him out of camp.

Cowboys despise soldiers. They say: "A poor lot! Why they daren't get on their horse or off him till a man tells 'em to." But Duke tells me that whenever cowboys are thrown with soldiers (as they have been on his Deer Creek ranch, where Indians were so bad he had soldiers, guarding his men as they built a fence), they soon grow to great friendship and comradery together.

June 11. Deming to Tucson. My New Mexico visit is over at last, and over with a good rich crop of material. Sheriff Breckinridge traveled with us and told me about Tombstone—the Earps—and especially about Ringgold, who was a singular and interesting character. Unluckily time and place were unfavorable for notes, and I must trust to my memory.

San Francisco, June 24. I spent Friday in calling on various friends, Major Bates, Colonel Lee, and others upon whom I could call in traveling clothes—for my black coat was creased like the torn wrapper of a cigar. Friday I went with Duke to be measured for a pair of *chaparajos* he proposed to give me. I have always been shy of wearing or owning these garments, as being not enough of a frontiersman to be entitled to them. But Duke says that I am, so I yield gracefully! Saturday and Sunday I was engaged to go to the Berry's at Ross Valley. In the afternoon "by special request" I read them the proofs of my Wham robbery story. Naglee punch and lying in the grass gave me an indulgent audience composed of Frank, Griffith, Professor Bacon,

Ells, and Berry. It is scarcely a story at all—much more like a narrative of travel. But they seemed to find it entertaining. I think the picture it gives of Arizona is faithful.

In my mail, all sorts of things. News good from home. Critics favorable to "Tinaja," but the New Orleans one says I should learn to condense. That is bosh. The story is extremely condensed and would not bear any shortening. My Chicago critic says that it's one of my best and he (or she) forgives me for repeating myself on past occasions. I dread that accusation, but so help me I'm not aware of being guilty so far, unless in the matter of poker games. A note from Kipling suggesting an admirable notion for the motive of a story I told him in the train about Bourke and an Indian he trained to speak in jad dialect. Also Kipling says he is a thief and has stolen a word I told him—"Tootl-ke-ay." He's more than welcome! A note from the editor of the *Chautauquan* offering $25 for 3,000 words on Western progress. Refused his terms. Faut se faire valoir. And as the Messrs. Harper pay me $25 and $35 for 1,000 words, I think I am right. A note from *Munsey's* magazine proposing interviews regarding my writing for them. Think not. Wrote an "evasive answer."

San Francisco, July 2. One thing—a surprisingly pleasant one—I have nearly forgotten. Wednesday morning I stepped into the elevator. "Good morning, sir," said the man with a heartiness that struck me, so I returned him the same. As we went down he suddenly burst out: "Well, sure I'd like to live as you do, sir, and look so smiling and happy every morning. It's a pleasure to see your face." This embarrassed me so completely that all I could say was to exclaim as he reached the bottom, "Is that true? Why that's delightful."

Curiously enough, only the evening before at our dinner

Frank had been quoting Stevenson's lines about, "If I have faltered more or less in my great task of happiness," and we had all admired their beauty and their ethics. Well, I do not always feel happy; I do hope I generally seem so; and certainly in San Francisco the cup was full this time.

July 10. This is Fort Logan ink with which the record has been resumed. Captain Fowler joined me in the noon suburban train and brought me here. He told me his very alluring plan for camping a month in the mountains, and I shall accept his invitation to make one of the party. Yet I miss Bowie! This well-kept suburb of Denver is utterly commonplace.

Fort Logan, July 17. I have been glad to see Corporal Skirdin again. And he most faithfully traced my lost trunks, carrying one on his shoulders from the station on Monday, when it came at length. Fowler tells me I won the Corporal's loyalty last winter when he came on furlough to see his sister. Well! What is better than the regard of a good man? Woman's? Ah—I've never won that; yet I believe one who does not know both is partially starved. Yesterday, I went riding with Skirdin, and should have gone all today, but it rains, rains, rains.

Skirdin, telling us in camp the other day how he had silenced a bragging civilian who had been talking of the Texas Rangers and comparing the soldiers unfavorably to them, said that he gave it to him pretty strong and straight "and good grammar, too." This set Fowler and me laughing, whereupon Skirdin added, "Some I didn't understand myself."

As I finish this volume of notes, we are drawing near

Cheyenne—and how I wish the next weeks could be on Wind River! I shall not die of nostalgia for the region, but no one will ever know how unreasonably much it is to me, and how I long for it through the year. If the gods are propitious, I shall treat myself to a summer of loafing among those streams and mountains next year. Damn material-hunting! I'm filled and sick with it! But the hand is on the plough and must remain faithful.

Epilogue

LOOKING back at the Journals and letters, we see that Owen Wister freed himself from what to him was a deadly life; he rose beyond his regimented childhood and detested law practice to become both historian of the West and maker of the cowboy legend. The very first Journal shows him struck with wonder by the landscape and at the same time meticulously listing the number of buildings in the town of Medicine Bow. His response to the beauty of the West led him into making a hero of the cowboy, but his ability to observe made him a historian.

In writing his Western stories for *Harper's Magazine*, Wister strove from the beginning to be accurate. From the Journals he transcribed dialogue using words and phrases new to him but in use at that time in the West. He also used in his stories many real happenings that he had seen and true tales of violence told by the men who had participated in them. But "the plain talk in my Western tales published in *Harper's* (1893) . . . never 'got by' the blue pencil of . . . Henry Millys Alden liberal as he was for those genteel times."[1] That same year when Wister showed a story he had just written for *Harper's,* Alden said, "Your story is very bloody," and Wister answered that you could not get much Western adventure without blood. He had been engaged by *Harper's* to go West and recount and report what was taking place there, but the magazine could not print what Wister saw and heard without diluting it. He gave in

[1] Wister, *Roosevelt, The Story of a Friendship* (New York: Macmillan Co., 1930).

to Theodore Roosevelt and omitted the gouging of the horse's eye from the story of Balaam and Pedro when it became a chapter in *The Virginian.*

The fiction prevailing in America at that time now sounds to us as if it had been written by a long-winded eunuch. A good sixty years before Wister published Western stories, Fanny Kemble wrote, "In America I can not say I put my leg over the pummel of my side saddle as American women do not have legs,"[2] but the pussyfooting vocabulary acceptable in conversation and the pasteurized prose in print were still the rule. Wister found this hard to endure, and he was as realistic as his publisher would allow him to be.

In the raw state of Texas the disparity between life as lived and the language permitted before women had reached an absurd extreme encompassing "male cow" as one of many ridiculous euphemisms. Exasperated and amused, Wister wrote the following poem at the end of the Texas Journal (1893):

There are some things we say but must not hear;
There are some things we do yet cannot know;
Our clean starched image prinked up thus and so
Utters "Mama! Papa!" and walks so near
The life, 'twere monstrous not to hold it dear;
No vandal shall intrude to aim a blow
And mar our mannikin, and overthrow
The pious clock-work we have toiled to rear.

Immortal ostrich! Anglosaxon bird!
Bury your head in print so none shall see
Your large wise body looming through the sham.
Let not reality be ever heard;
It is unfit and shocking; but let me
Meanwhile sit in some corner and say damn! (O sugar!)

Yes, I'm aware your daughter cannot read it;
I don't forget your piano stands on limbs.

[2] Frances Ann Kemble, *Records of a Girlhood* (New York: Henry Holt & Co., 1879).

253

Life's so indelicate, we have agreed it
Must be concealed by fig leaves and by hymns.
Sculpture's so bare, and painting so illicit,
And poets unconventional at best;
Give Art a chance and Art will never miss it;
Art has a craving to parade undressed.

In the Journal called "Frontier Notes—May to August, 1894"
Wister says this about writing stories about the West:

> Our wide country has been until lately so very wide as to
> resemble a man whose east hand knows not what his west
> hand doeth. Americans in New York, or Massachusetts, or
> Virginia, have lived one sort of life in almost complete igno-
> rance of Americans in Texas, or Idaho, or Oregon; and it may
> be said that during the past thirty years more kinds of life
> have been going on at once in the United States unaware of
> each other than in any other single country in the world.
> Therefore, it has happened that many of these stories, which
> deal exclusively with out shifting and now well-nigh vanished
> Frontier, have been called improbable by Eastern critics,
> while to Western readers they have had the good fortune to
> seem accurate pictures of men and events in that region.
>   In my own case I am writing from special knowledge, and
> I keep as wary an eye as I can on my general sense of propor-
> tion. On more than one occasion before deciding to write a
> certain story, I have asked other people if they thought such
> and such things would be interesting.

In the Preface to "When West was West" Wister wrote: "In
February, 1893, I grew familiar with many of the doings and most of
the conventions of a wide, wild farm and ranch community, spotted
with remote towns, and veined with infrequent railroads, in the
central part of Texas. In February, 1893, I hadn't begun to as yet
hunt material deliberately, but in consequence of "Hank's Woman"
and "How Lin McLean Went East," which *Harper's* had already

254

published, every second or third person that I met, promptly said, 'I'll tell you a thing you ought to write up.' It became a familiar spectacle—me, passive in the clutches of a determined narrator; so that my companions used to poke each other's ribs and say, 'Look at Wister. So-and-so has got him now!' And I became a brilliant listener. Yet oftener than not, it wasn't what they told me, it was something else that drifted accidentally into sight or hearing, and which seemed worthless to them, but flashed on me as the true nugget in the tailings." He says later in the same Preface that he "detailed the raw material (of a Texas story) to a discreet and shocked friend, who said, 'Don't try such a thing, It can't be told.'—'But it belongs to the whole picture.'—'Leave it out.' " Owen Wister waited thirty-one years before using that material in a short story.

Whatever the pressures on his fiction, Wister's judgment of people was essentially uncompromising. Though he says several times in the Journals that he enjoys being with the cowboys and hearing them banter, only two of the men he knew in the West seem to have won his heartfelt admiration—Corporal Skirdin and Dean Duke. There is no account in the Journals of anyone truly resembling the Virginian, despite the fact that several chapters of the novel stem directly from the Journals. The cowboys of Wister's short stories often appear in brave and delightful roles, but none of them measures up to the Virginian. In the Preface to *The Virginian* (Collected Edition) he writes:

At Fort Bowie, Arizona, during October of that year, 1893, I rode many miles of desert and mountain with Corporal Skirdin, born in Arizona, cowpuncher, scout, everything, and just then in the Second Cavalry, detailed to companion me in my wanderings. He seemed to me a sort of incarnation of my imaginary Virginian; he ratified my imagination. Two Kansas boys at Las Playas in New Mexico the next year, again, were a ratification; and in the same year at Apache Tejo, the foreman of that ranch did and said things which reminded me of the Virginian. By 1902, I had seen a great deal of cowpunchers, and had become an intimate friend of Skirdin.

. . . Into the Virginian I wove one of Skirdin's actual practical jokes—narrated faithfully in the third chapter. He, more definitely than any frontier character I had met, continually realized and ratified my imaginary portrait, made me sure of my ground, confident that I was keeping well inside the actualities of frontier characters; so that, within six months after the book's appearance, letters—half a dozen at least—had come to me, in which each writer was quite sure he knew who the "original" of the Virginian was—and it was never the same original, nor were any of them known to me.

The foreman of the ranch at Apache Tejo was Dean Duke who is spoken of so much in the 1895 Journal. Wister knew these men well. He was fond of Skirdin and Duke; he admired and perhaps envied them. Skirdin had grown up with no family, no church teaching, and in his trial for murder it came out that he had lived for several years with the Indians when he was roaming by himself as a young boy. He joined the Army to learn to read and write. Wister does not say anything about Duke's past but speaks about his courage and how much his employers trusted him. These men without what in those days was referred to as "advantages," Skirdin particularly, had grown to be capable and honorable men and led lives of responsibility.

When Skirdin was a boy alone with a gun and a pair of pants in the Apache country, fending for himself, Wister, who since birth had been hedged around by decorum and Victorian restraints, was singing in the choir at school, holding a hymn book, wearing a white starched collar and white surplice. When Dean Duke at twenty-two with nerve and skill was mastering drunken cowboys and keeping his employers' herd intact, Wister in Bayreuth was playing his own composition to Franz Liszt. Yet these men's histories and personalities appealed to Wister so strongly that he felt they were like his imagined Virginian.

He wrote in his last Journal, "It is imagination that takes the load of fact, supplied by experience, and lifts it into universal truth." Wister had fifteen long journeys with endless experience in the West, and he gathered many facts which he used. But we must look to an article entitled "The Evolution of the Cowpuncher" rather than to the Journals for a real foretaste of the romantic hero he was to create in *The Virginian.*

In that article (published by *Harper's Magazine* in 1895) he explains that to him the Knight of the Round Table is the ancestor of the cowpuncher:

From the tournament to the round-up! Deprive the Saxon of his horse, and put him to forest-clearing or in a counting-house for a couple of generations and you may pass him by without ever seeing that his legs are designed for the gripping of saddles. . . . So upon land has the horse been his foster-brother, his ally, his playfellow, from the tournament of Camelot to the roundup at Abilene, where he learned quickly what the Mexican vaquero had to teach him.

The cowpuncher's play-ground in those first glorious days of his prosperity included battle and murder and sudden death as every-day matters. From 1865 to 1878 in Texas he fought his way with knife and gun, and any hour of the twenty-four might see him flattened behind the rocks among the whizz of bullets and the flight of arrows, or dragged bloody and folded together from some adobe hovel. Seventy-five dollars a month and absolute health and strength were his wages; and when the news of all this excellence drifted from Texas eastward, they came in shoals—Saxon boys of picked courage (none but plucky ones could survive) from South and North, from town and country. Every sort and degree of home tradition came with them from their far birthplaces. Some had knelt in the family prayers at one time, others could remember no parent or teacher except the street; some spoke with the gentle accent of Virginia, others in the dialect of baked beans and codfish; here and there was the bacca-laureate, already beginning to forget his Greek Alphabet.

With speech and dress of his own, then, the cowpuncher drove his herds to Abilene or Westport Landing in the Texas times, and the easy abundant dollars came, and left him for spurs and bridles of barbaric decoration. Let it be remembered that the Mexican was the original cowboy, that the American improved on him. Those were the days in which he was long in advance of settlers, and when he literally fought his right of way. Along the waste hundreds of miles that he had to journey, three sorts of inveterate enemies infested the road—the cattle and the horse thief who were as daring as himself; the supplanted Mexican, who hated the new encroaching Northern race; and the Indian, whose hand was against all races but his own immediate tribe, and who flayed the feet of his captives and made them walk so through the mountain passes to the fires in which he slowly burned them. Among these perils the cowpuncher took wild pleasure in existing. No soldier of fortune ever adventured with bolder carelessness, no fiercer blood ever stained a border. War they made in plenty, but not love; for the woman they saw was not the woman a man can take into his heart.

To Wister, the ponderous knight on his snorting charger was the ancestor of the lithe cowboy with his six-shooter and his sinuous, knowing pony. The nineteenth-century conception of valor bred in Wister cast a glow for him over the cowboy. If Wister had not felt that the cowboy was the romantic descendant of the knight, he could not have written *The Virginian*. In having his hero win the hand of a pure woman in combat and become her lord and master after triumphing over evil, he identified the cowboy with the knight and gave their adventures the same ending.

As well as making the cowboy a hero, Wister proved to be an articulate observer during the years of his far-flung journeys. His Journals and stories are history written by the man with education and talent to grasp and write about what was taking place in the West. It would not have been possible except for the astonishing way he was accepted by the men he wanted to hear talk about the frontier.

This is the most difficult of Wister's traits to account for—his capacity to be at ease and to make the most of the circumstances in which he found himself. His clothes and his manner of speech did not come between him and the unlettered adventurers he met. Something in his bearing made them enjoy talking as much as he enjoyed listening. Obviously he was liked wherever he went.

How was he able at twenty-two to converse in French with Franz Liszt and play the piano to him and at twenty-five ride on a stage-coach in Wyoming, at once recognizing a glorious new world? How could he play whist with the probate judge in Tombstone, Arizona, and become the valued friend of Corporal Skirdin and many cowpunchers? He was congenial with Lizst, the probate judge, and Skirdin. He was at home wherever his interests were engaged. His provenience was no barrier when his imagination was aroused, nor was his horizon limited by what he was used to or knew. He had a gift for observation, which was matched by his ability to fit into his surroundings. These traits combined with a sympathy in listening to others made him at ease in the several worlds he loved.

What did Wister say about the West he first saw? "It is a vanished world. No journeys, save those which memory can take, will bring you to it now." How did he feel about the character to whom he gave so limitless a future? "What is become of the horseman, the cow-puncher, the last romantic figure upon our soil?" "He will never come again. He rides in his historic yesterday." But, Wister added: "His wild kind has been among us always, since the beginning; a young man with his temptations, a hero without wings."

A WISTER BIBLIOGRAPHY

ACKNOWLEDGMENTS

INDEX

To compile a bibliography that listed Wister's magazine pieces and the reprints of his books, to say nothing of references to him and to his works, would be an undertaking in itself. Therefore—except to suggest that Wister's family background can be seen in Frances Ann Kemble's *Records of a Girlhood* (New York: Henry Holt & Co., 1879) and *Records of Later Life* (New York: Henry Holt & Co., 1882)—this bibliography is restricted to listing first editions of Wister's books in the order in which they appeared.

The New Swiss Family Robinson. *Cambridge, Mass.: C. W. Sever, 1882. A burlesque of* Swiss Family Robinson.

The Dragon of Wantley. *Philadelphia: J. B. Lippincott Co., 1892. A fairy story.*

Red Men and White. *New York: Harper & Bros., 1896. The first volume of Western stories.*

Lin McLean. *New York and London: Harper & Bros., 1898. Western stories.*

The Jimmyjohn Boss and Other Stories. *New York and London: Harper & Bros., 1900. Western stories.*

Ulysses S. Grant. *Boston: Small, Maynard & Co., 1900. A biography.*

The Virginian. *New York: Macmillan Co., 1902. A Western novel that has been reissued many times as well as dramatized. The origin of several of its chapters may be traced in the Journals. Chapter 1, 1885 Journal. Chapter 2, Frontier Notes, 1894. Chapter 3,*

1894 Journal, as told to Wister by Corporal Skirdin. Chapter 10, 1893 (Spring) Journal. Chapter 26, 1891 Journal.

Philosophy 4. *New York: Macmillan Co., 1903. A humorous tale about Harvard students.*

A Journey in Search of Christmas. *New York and London: Harper & Bros. 1904. Five Lin McLean stories, with illustrations by Frederic Remington.*

Lady Baltimore. *New York and London: Macmillan Co., 1906. A novel set in Charleston, South Carolina between the close of the Civil War and 1900.*

How Doth the Simple Spelling Bee. *New York and London: Macmillan Co., 1907. An English story not set in the West.*

Mother. *New York: Dodd, Mead & Co., 1907. A story—in which Wister imitated the style of Frank Stockton—entered in anonymous competition.*

The Seven Ages of Washington. *New York: Macmillan Co., 1907. A biography.*

Members of the Family. *New York: Macmillan Co., 1911. Western stories.*

Padre Ignacio. *New York: Harper & Bros., 1911. A story of a Catholic priest in the Southwest.*

The Pentecost of Calamity. *New York and London: Macmillan Co., 1915. An essay urging the United States to join England and France against Germany in World War I.*

A Straight Deal; or, the Ancient Grudge. *New York and London: Macmillan Co., 1920. An essay on America's inherited dislike for England and the prospects of future Anglo-American understanding.*

Indispensable Information for Infants. *New York: Macmillan Co., 1921. A book of comic short verses.*

Neighbors Henceforth. *New York: Macmillan Co., 1922. An essay on the plight of France after World War I and the hope for American aid.*

Watch Your Thirst; A Dry Opera in Three Acts. *Limited Edition. New York: Macmillan Co., 1923. A comic opera in verse with an anti-prohibition theme.*

When West Was West. *New York: Macmillan Co., 1928. Western stories.*

Roosevelt, The Story of a Friendship. *New York: Macmillan Co., 1930. An account of Wister's long friendship with Theodore Roosevelt.*

An edition of Wister's collected works was published by the Macmillan Company in 1928.

ACKNOWLEDGMENTS

I wish to thank:

Mr. and Mrs. Sydney L. Wright, who urged me into beginning this book and without whose vigorous encouragement it would not have been finished.

Mr. N. Orwin Rush, former Director of the University of Wyoming Library, who in 1951 instigated my search for the Journals.

Mr. Edwin T. P. Boone, Jr., the first person to suggest that I combine the letters and Journals into a book.

Mr. David C. Mearns, Chief of the Manuscript Division of the Library of Congress, whose courtesy and consideration made my work in the Library delightful.

Mr. Robert H. Land, Assistant Chief of the Manuscript Division of the Library of Congress, whose interest and prompt response to all my many requests were of such great help to me.

Mr. Edward N. Waters, Assistant Chief of the Music Division of the Library of Congress, who found the letter of July 5, 1902, after I had overlooked it.

Mr. George Freedley, Curator of the Theatre Collection of the New York Public Library, who made available to me the material on *The Virginian* as a play and as a movie.

Mr. Mark A. DeWolfe Howe, who gave me his history of the Tavern Club and lent Wister letters.

Professor Mark DeWolfe Howe, who lent Wister letters.

Mr. Robert Cutler and Mr. William Stanley Parker, who gave me information about the Tavern Club.

265

Mr. Copley Amory, who gave me the photograph of Wister's 1887 hunting party.

Mrs. Richmond Viall, who was constructive and helpful on my behalf.

Mrs. George V. Strong, who helped me with the Epilogue.

Mrs. T. Evans Dunn, Mrs. Joseph Harrison, Jr., Mrs. Horace B. Hare, Mrs. Franshaw Lindsley, Mrs. Edmund R. Purves, and Mrs. Owen B. Rhoads for their moral support.

Mr. Max de Schauensee, music critic for the *Philadelphia Evening Bulletin*, who gave me musical data.

My husband, Walter Stokes, who was patient and helpful through the years of my work on this book.

INDEX

Alden, Henry Millys, 12, 165–69, 179, 183–85, 252
Amory, Copely, 43, 49 ff., 126, 266

Balaam and Pedro," 96, 168, 181, 196–97
Bannock Campaign, 243
"Bear Creek Barbecue, The," 165–66, 168
Biddle, Louis, 89
Boone and Crockett Club, 164, 182, 194
Brock, Henry, 245–46
Brooks, Lawrence, 100, 120, 123 ff.
Brown, Ace, 153, 156
Brownwood, Texas, 150
Butler, Peirce, xii, 3–4
Butler Place, xi–xiii, 5–6

Campo, Frank, 19
Canton, Frank B., 115, 174
Casper, Wyoming, 102
Cheyenne, Wyoming, 223
Clanton brothers, 213–19
Conover, Frank, 150, 157
Coulee City, Washington, 135–37, 145
Custer, George, 177

Demens, Mr., 227–28
Deming, New Mexico, 206, 230, 245
Douglas, Wyoming, 100–102
Dragon of Wantley, The, 114, 164
Duke, Dean, 226, 228–35, 244–47, 255–56

Earp brothers, 213–19, 247
Earp, Wyatt, 212, 214
Edwards, Captain F. A., 184 ff., 207, 230
Egan, Judge, 229
"Em'ly," 15, 184, 193

Farnum, Dustin, 19–20
First Cavalry Regiment, 242–44
Fort Bayard, New Mexico, 206
Fort Bowie, Arizona, 186–87, 202–6
Fort Grant, Arizona, 189–92, 207–8, 242
Fort McKinney, Wyoming, 115–16
Fort Washakie, Wyoming, 47–48, 67, 120–21, 175, 242
Fox, Mary, 42, 89
"Frontier Notes, 1894," 28, 200
Furness, Walter, 11–12

Gila Valley, 188 ff., 237–38
Grand Coulee, 137, 144–45
Grijaloa, Merijildo, 189–90
Groome, Harry, 150, 157

Hank's Woman," 12, 106, 185, 254
Harper's Magazine, 13, 96, 164–65, 193, 200, 254, 257
Heard, John, 223
Hemingway, Ernest, 23
Higginson, Major Henry Lee, 7, 10, 12
Holliday, Doc, 214–20
Holmes, Oliver Wendell, Jr., 15–16, 96, 136

Howells, William Dean, 7, 10–11
"How Lin McLean Went East," 12, 146–47, 254

Irwin, Masie, 29
Irwin, Sophy, 29, 40

Jackson Hole, Wyoming, xiv–xix, 24
James, Henry, 4, 13, 25, 221
Jenks, Lieutenant, 234 ff.
JY Ranch, xv–xvii

Kemble, Frances Ann, xii, 3–5, 7, 14, 96, 253
"Kinsman of Red Cloud, A," 180–81, 183, 193
Kipling, Rudyard, 13, 221, 226, 248

LaShell, Kirk, 19
Leighton, Bishop, 188
LeRose, Paul, 64, 67 ff.
Library of Congress, 25
Liszt, Franz, 8–10, 256
Longhouse, 25

McGregor, Major, 186, 203 ff.
McLowrey brothers, 213 ff.
Markley, Captain, 206, 230
Mason, George, 47 ff., 64, 67 ff.
Medicine Bow, Wyoming, 29, 35–36
Michael, Frank, 185, 192, 194, 213, 220
Mitchell, John K., 21, 29
Moss, Molly, 169

Nation, The, 194
New Swiss Family Robinson, The, 8
Norman, George, 43, 49 ff., 64 ff., 126
Neil, Jim, 156–57

Partners, The," 168
Pentecost of Calamity, The, 21–22
Penrose, Charles, 100, 120, 124
Pitcher, Captain, 230, 233 ff.
Porcellian Club, 7, 113–14, 140
"Promised Land, The," 183, 185

Ralston, Robert, 11, 88, 91, 100, 120–22, 124
Rawle, Francis, 11, 20, 88
Ray, Captain, 121, 175, 177–78
Red Men and White, 13
Remington, Frederic, 12–14, 164, 168, 179, 181–83, 196–97
Ringgold, John, 219–20, 247
Roosevelt, Theodore, xiii–xiv, 7, 11–12, 16, 21, 96, 129, 164, 226, 253
Rush, N. Orwin, 24–26, 265

St. Paul's School, 6
Savage, Fitzhugh, 150 ff.
Schofield, General, 244–45
Seventh Cavalry Regiment, 242–44
Sheridan Trail, 51, 181
Simes, Bob, 64 ff.
Skirdin, Corporal, 20, 164, 187, 205–6, 249, 255–56
Smith, Henry, 106, 117–18
Snake River, xvi, 57, 69–70, 133
Solomonville, Arizona, 187, 239–40
"Specimen Jones," 213
Stewardson, John, 164, 167, 172 ff.
Superstition Trail, 16
Swaim, George W., 200, 211–13

Tavern Club, 10, 23–24
"Ten Thousand Cattle," 19, 24
Teton Mountains, xvi, 125
Thomas, Theodore, 170–71
Tibbits, Ned, 89
Tigie, 43, 47 ff., 85–86, 175
"Tinaja Bonita," 227, 232, 248
Tisdale, 103 ff.
Tombstone, Arizona, 200, 208 ff.

University of Wyoming Library, 24–26

Virginian, The, xiii–xiv, 2–3, 14–20, 96, 200, 253, 255–56, 262–63

Wagner, Richard, 8–9
Walla Walla, Washington, 132
Waln, Maurice, 88, 96

Waring, George, 89, 132, 140–41
Washakie, Chief, 175–76
Washakie, Dick, 64, 67 ff.
Watch Your Thirst, 24
Wells, Fargo Company, 195
West, George, 47 ff., 64, 67 ff., 121 ff., 132, 167, 175 ff., 201
Wham robbery, 220, 226
Wind River, 50–51, 68, 124, 130, 201, 242, 250
"Winning of the Biscuit Shooter, The," 170, 179

Wister, Dr. Owen Jones, 3–5
Wister, Mary Channing, 13–14, 20–21, 169
Wister, Sarah Butler, xi–xii, 3–5, 17, 25
Wolcott, Major Frank, 28, 31 ff., 112, 115, 174
World's Fair, 142–43, 171
Wyoming, xviii, 113, 137

Yellowstone Park, 58–60, 126–29
Youth's Companion, The, 201–2

PRINTED IN U.S.A.